TURKEY CREEK

Published by Seacoast Press, an imprint of MindStir Media, LLC
1931 Woodbury Ave. #182 | Portsmouth, New Hampshire 03801 | USA
1.800.767.0531 | www.seacoastpress.com

Printed in the United States of America
ISBN-13: 978-1-7344892-9-3

TURKEY CREEK

W.S. HENDRICHOVSKY

July 2019, North Mississippi

FATHER BYRNE IS ATTEMPTING AN EXORCISM
ON TYLER MATOSKE.

A faint drum beat started off in the distance as Father Byrne battled the terrible beast. The experienced exorcist's clothes were saturated in sweat as his heart pumped blood full of adrenaline throughout his body. He stood looking down over the powerful demon inhabiting the innocent boy's body. Following the textbook procedure he had memorized decades earlier, Father Byrne began sternly yelling down at the beast to reveal its name. Calmness had escaped the normally cool-headed priest due to the demon digging its long, sharp fingernails deep into the skin that covered the boy's palms. Thick, red blood dripped onto the floor from the chair's arm the demon was tied to.

Again, Father Byrne yelled at the beast, "Give me your name, demon! In the name of God the Father, God the Son, and God the Holy Ghost, I demand you relinquish your name!"

Greenish, foamy goo that circled the demon's mouth splattered the priest with each deep breath as the demon panted and fought the straps holding it to the chair.

"Why you keep bother me priest? Do you not know God sends

5

me to collect the souls?" the demon growled in its African accent, but from the boy's mouth!

"Leave this boy's body and return to the pits of hell," the priest commanded. Still struggling to free itself, the demon broke the wooden arm away from the chair, instantly swinging it as a weapon towards the priest's head. The twenty plus years of Taekwondo training paid off as Father Byrne, hearing the wood break, anticipated the unsuccessful swat of the chair's arm toward his head. The well-trained priest quickly grabbed the possessed boy's wrist, twisting it before positioning the arm behind his back. Father Byrne's quick reflex helped overcome the abnormal strength the boy's body received from its inhabitant. Grabbing a zip tie from the supply bag attached to his belt, the priest tied the boy's wrist to the back of the chair in the same manner a cop restrains a suspect.

"Why you keep bother me priest?" the demon again grunted, splattering green goo as it spoke. "Your power will not stop God's will." The demon continued to fight the strap, and now the zip tie holding it to the back of the chair.

Ignoring the demon's foolish babble, Father Byrne placed his knees against the boy's chest to help hold the demon-controlled body steady. Reaching again for his supply bag, Father Byrne removed the crimson tin container of holy oil and white plastic bottle full of holy water. He rubbed holy oil across the boy's forehead while mumbling the Our Father before he sprinkled holy water over the boy's head. He began the Glory Be in Latin, "GLORIA Patri, et Filio, et Spiritui Sancto. Sicut erat in principio, et nunc, et semper, et in saecula saeculorum. Amen."

The demon laughed out loud as its black silhouette engulfed the boy's body, revealing its deep blue eyes. "You have no power over me," the demon again laughed before leaving the boy's body.

The boy's exhausted body went limp, temporarily released from the demon's control. The boy opened his eyes, confused, not remembering the fierce battle between Father Byrne and the demon. A rush of unexpected emotion overcame the boy struggling against the restraints that held the demon. Looking down at the exhausted boy unloading raw emotions with torn flesh leaking dark red blood from his palms, Father Byrne realized he needed help fighting this powerful demon.

THE FOLLOWING WEEK

Driving south from Memphis, through the green pine tree barrier planted by the highway department to keep noise away from the hiding neighborhoods along Interstate 55, Father Byrne began explaining his current exorcism of Tyler Matoske to Father Cashin. Father Cashin was assigned by the Archbishop to observe and assist Father Byrne, the senior exorcist in the southeast. Father Cashin had recently returned from Rome, where he received training to become an exorcist, and was eager to witness an exorcism in person.

Father Byrne explained the situation: "Six weeks earlier, the Matoske family: Henry, Sharon, their sons Tyler and Will, moved into their dream house built on two hundred acres in Skuna Valley Mississippi, a small farming community an hour and a half south of Memphis. Sharon was hired as the head volleyball coach at the University of North Mississippi in Coffeeville, just twenty miles up highway 330. A couple of days after moving into their newly built modern house, the family noticed strange shadows crossing rooms, they became aware of the feeling of being watched, and occasionally the rooms had awful odors. Being in a newly built house, the family dismissed the abnormalities. Henry started to notice Tyler was uncharacteristically keeping to himself. He was not engaging in family activities. Henry first suspected the cause was Sharon being gone so much for her job of recruiting athletes and coaching volleyball matches. Over Sharon's career, she was away so much that Henry and the boys laughed about how they could not keep up from week to week, not knowing where she was or where she had been. Being a Division 1 head volleyball coach is demanding, but it was part of the job. Henry and the boys enjoyed being involved with the University and the athletes. When Tyler withdrew from his friends, spending most of his time in his room playing video games, Henry decided it was time to talk to his son. The concerned parents sat Tyler down to talk, hoping to figure out his issues. At first, Tyler tried to fend off the questions by saying nothing was wrong before he reluctantly revealed his relationship with the entity. Disguising their uneasiness, Henry and Sharon inquired about this entity in the same manner they would with a new school friend.

Tyler described the entity as black as night, a head full of long blonde hair to its waist, long blonde hair around its neck, long blonde hair from waist to knees, and woven blonde hair around wrist and ankles. It has deep blue eyes, is about the same height as Tyler, and it goes by the name Shak. Tyler went on to tell his parents that they talk, discussing video games and other stuff. Henry and Sharon assumed Shak was an imaginary friend and this was just a phase. They decided to leave Tyler's imaginary friend alone for now. They asked Tyler to work on spending more time with family and friends. Tyler assured his parents he would.

Tyler did not make much of an attempt to reconnect with his family or friends. Concerned for Tyler's mental health, Sharon spoke with some of her colleagues at the University, which confirmed that Tyler was much too old for an imaginary friend. Henry and Sharon decided to take Tyler to see a pediatric psychologist. After a few sessions with Dr. Capps, the only pediatric psychologist in the Coffeeville area, Tyler became angry. He started cutting and biting himself. His posture changed a bit, sitting with his head tilted a little to the left and eyebrows bowed up. He developed a slight gargle with a deep pitch when he talked, although at times he was completely normal. Will became an easy target for hitting and hateful comments. After a couple of sessions, Dr. Capps realized he was not qualified to handle this type of situation. He suggested Tyler needed spiritual help from the Catholic Church. So, Henry contacted their local Catholic Church, Saint Paul the Apostle in Coffeeville. The

Archbishop reviewed the case before deciding to send me to investigate," Father Byrne continued.

"The first meeting, Henry and Sharon familiarized me with their situation and gave a quick background. I decided to sit Tyler down to pray, not sure if we were dealing with a psychological issue, medical issue, or a candidate for actual exorcism. As we began the Our Father, I placed my hand on his head, making the sign of the cross with blessed oil on his forehead. Tyler became agitated, jittery, and nervous. His body began trembling. His eyes rolled back into his head! Then he completely shut down as his body became limp. Tyler's eyes opened, staring at me with disgust as he began uttering an unrecognized language. Realizing the situation, I began the Athanasian Creed in Latin.

> "'Whosoever will be saved, before all things it is necessary that he hold the Catholic faith. Which faith unless everyone do keep whole and undefiled, without doubt he shall perish everlastingly. And the Catholic faith is this: that we worship one God in Trinity, and Trinity in Unity; neither confounding the Persons, nor dividing the Essence. For there is one Person of the Father, another of the Son, and another of the Holy Ghost. But the Godhead of the Father, of the Son, and of the Holy Ghost, is all one; the Glory equal, the Majesty coeternal. Such as the Father is; such is the Son; and such is the Holy Ghost. The Father uncreated; the Son uncreated; and the Holy Ghost uncreated. The Father unlimited; the Son unlimited; and the Holy Ghost unlimited. The Father eternal;'

"The demon spat greenish goo in my face, stopping the creed for a moment. After cleaning the foul liquid off my face, I continued the creed until completion. Henry and Sharon both stood off to the side in horrified, stricken disbelief, watching the demon speak through their son's body. Standing up, I shouted with force, demanded the demon's name.

"With an African accent, the demon spoke in broken English,

'You are not welcome here. You are not welcome here, priest. This is my land. You not welcome here.'

"I then yelled for the demon leave this boy's body in the name of the Father, the Son, and the Holy Spirit! I splashed holy water down on Tyler's head. 'I am not a demon, priest,' the demon yelled. As I was making the sign of the cross, the demon let out a loud, boisterous laugh before Tyler's body went limp. I continued to pray for God to remove the demon from Tyler's body.

"Soon Tyler woke up feeling tired, relieved, confused, and ashamed. We decided to just tell him that he passed out since he had no memory of what just occurred. Tyler's parents were completely freaked out after witnessing the demon speaking through Tyler. I sat Henry and Sharon down to explain the next step and what to expect."

Father Byrne slammed on his brakes before swerving to miss a blown-out truck tire lying in the lane he was traveling.

"Boy, my butt puckered a little," Father Cashin laughed.

Regathering his thoughts after the near miss, Father Byrne continued explaining the Matoske case to Father Cashin. "I explained the exorcism steps to the uneasy parents. First, we must determine how the evil spirit entered into Tyler's body. There are only two ways in which a person can be possessed: the permission of God for the demon to enter the body, or a witch's incantations inducing the demons to take possession. Second, we must learn the demon's name to design a specific plan to expel it. Third, we need to know how many demons have entered and how long they plan to stay. Fourth, in an intense battle, I will bring the demon to a breaking point while insisting to learn more information. Demons want to inhabit a body to stay out of hell. Last, victory will be won. In the name of Jesus, the demon will leave the body. Having finished explaining, I asked the couple if they had any questions. They sat quietly in disbelief, trying to process the information. I asked them to go about their normal routine, not treating Tyler any different.

"The following week I returned for the second attempt to remove the demon. I sat Tyler down in an antique cedar chair in the middle of Sharon's home office to begin. We began praying the Our Father, Tyler's body beginning to quiver and convulse as perspiration formed on the bridge of his nose and forehead. I quickly restrained his wrist to the chair. Starting the Athanasian Creed, Tyler's eyes rolled back before protruding out, then sinking back into his skull.

"The entity then spoke. 'Why you here, priest, this is my land.'

"I continued to pray, holding the crucifix in one hand and the prayer book in the other. 'What is your name, demon?' I yelled. The demon laughed at my question. I again yelled my command for its name. Forcefully shoving the crucifix onto its chest, I exclaimed, 'I expel you, demon, in the name of God the almighty.'

"The entity laughed from deep within his belly. Slimy, vile saliva saturated its face. Its hands rolled back, bending in an unnatural direction. The demon's morbid breath caused a nauseous feeling in my throat.

"He laughed, 'Priest, you have no power over me, this is my land.' Laughing as I continued to pray. 'I am not a demon, priest.'

"I placed the prayer book down and sprinkled holy water on Tyler, making the sign of the cross. Once again, the demon let out a loud boisterous laugh saying, 'You have no power over me, God send me to collect his souls. My God protects me, priest.' A dark silhouette overtook Tyler's body, revealing its dark blue eyes and yellow hair before returning to back into his body.

"I stepped back in disbelief, witnessing a demon revealing itself for the first time in my career. Tyler's body went limp as I finished my prayer. Tyler woke, still restrained to the chair, tired and confused. We told Tyler about the darkness living inside him.

"After two sessions, Tyler seemed to be getting worse. Late at night, Tyler could be heard laughing out loud, weeping uncontrollably, and talking in a foreign language. The entity began attacking the family. Henry woke up feeling a hand around his neck trying to choke him. One night, both Henry and Sharon were thrown off their bed. Will kept getting pinched and poked. Their cat was thrown up against a wall. Pictures were thrown onto the floor. They all witnessed a silhouette standing around the house."

The two priests arrived at the Matoskes' house. The newly built contemporary ranch style had clean lines, with large windows devoid of decorative trim. The exterior was a mixture of siding, stone, brick, and wood. The roof was shallow pitched with great overhangs. Sharon greeted them at the frosted glass front door. Father Byrne and Father Cashin followed Sharon to join Henry in the living area. Stepping down from the front foyer, the two priests could see out back through the large ceiling-to-floor windows overlooking a cedar wood patio that sat above the dark green grassy field down towards the creek. The living area had whisper white walls trimmed with dark grey molding. Four dark grey beams held up the white ceiling. A black top-grain leather sectional sat against the wall facing a 65" flat screen TV above the red, whitewashed brick fireplace. The fireplace hid wooden stairs leading to the second level. The walls were decorated with modern paintings and pictures. The new house scent was mixed with honey spice scented candles Sharon had burning around the house. Taking a seat in the leather roll-arm chair to the side of the sectional, Father Byrne introduce Father Cashin to the Matoskes.

After introductions, Father Byrne asked Henry and Sharon how the past week had gone and how they were holding up. The emotionally exhausted parents shared that there were no improvements with Tyler. Henry had taken a leave of absence from his work to be with Tyler.

"We were trying to keep Tyler away from Will, but still include him in day-to-day family activity. Yesterday, Tyler locked Will in his closet while trying to set the closet on fire. Hearing Will yelling, Henry rushed up to the room finding Tyler in the act of lighting the fire. We have been discussing if we need to commit him to the state insane asylum to protect our family. We just can't trust Tyler anymore," Sharon sadly shared as tears filled around her eyes.

"Oh no, you can't send him to the state insane asylum!" Father Byrne firmly blurted. "They do not have the resources or experience to treat a possession. I can assure you Tyler is possessed and needs the help of the church. We would like to take Tyler to St. Treasea's hospital psych ward to continue the exorcism process," Father Byrne suggested. "The asylum will not get rid of the demon, they will only keep him drugged up and locked away. Tyler will spend the rest of his life fighting the demon alone," Father Byrne finished. Henry and Sharon, both emotional, agreed that St. Treasea's sounded much better than the state's asylum.

Father Cashin began asking questions as Father Byrne excused himself to go upstairs to see Tyler. Heading up the wooden stairs, he noticed most of the pictures were off-centered or broken. The air temperature dropped as he moved up the stairs with an unfamiliar stench scorching his nose. Standing outside Tyler's door, Father Byrne could hear a faint chant, "Uba uba uba yah yah, uba uba uba yah yah!" He could sense the demon was in the room. Taking a moment before knocking, the priest said a quick prayer for strength.

"As I go to work, be with me Lord. Be the patience when I'm frustrated. Be the endurance when I am tired. Be the wisdom when I am uncertain. Be the inspiration when I'm out of ideas. Be the peacemaker when I feel hurt. Be the comforter when I feel overwhelmed. Be the energy when I am weary. Be the guide when I am confused. Be the forgiver when I get it wrong. Be with me Lord, today. Amen."

Knocking on Tyler's door before he announced himself, the priest opened the door to enter. A flash of red and black preceded the sound of crushing bone that echoed in Father Byrne's head as his cheek bones and nose were shattered by Tyler's Louisville Slugger. Father Byrne's blood splattered the wall and the door, as his eyes rolled back into his head from the unbearable pain of what felt like a thousand needles being shoved into his face at once. Blood began soaking the tan carpet dark red as he lay on the bedroom floor. Tyler stood over the unconscious priest holding the Louisville Slugger chanting, "Uba uba uba yah yah, uba uba uba yah yah!"

THE SHIPMENT
March 6, 1860, Alabama

Captain Michael Craig carefully navigated across the Mobile Bay into the Spanish River as blinding fog blanketed the unusually warm night. Cautiously, he weaved his ship in and out of broken stumps, trying to avoid underwater islands. The captain's navigational skill would be tested as he piloted the dangerous river, not being able to see more than a few yards ahead of his ship. The copper sheathed protected the hull from not only salt water, but the occasional impact of logs and other debris. Captain Craig, a seasoned sailor, was tired and quite irritated. The voyage from West Africa was long and stressful. The *Polievka*, originally built for battle, was converted for the illegal cargo. In West Africa, Captain Craig toured an old musky warehouse selecting groups of cargo for purchase. After carefully inspecting the cargo, they were washed and fed before being transported to the dock for loading. Not wanting to be caught, Captain Craig had his crew load the illegal cargo in the dead of night during an intense rainstorm with on shore winds. One by one, the cargo was taken below to be shackled as the crew tried to keep their balance from the waves crashing into the hull of the ship. As the schooner was almost loaded, the nervous Captain spotted an old patrol steamer off the port. He ordered the crew to leave immediately, although only ninety-percent of the cargo was loaded. Luckily, they were able reach the open waters before the old patrol steamer was close enough to become suspicious.

The lengthy trip was brutal, dodging squalls and other ships. Captain Craig knew if he were caught, he would surely be prosecuted for violating the Act of 1807, which prohibited the very cargo he was hauling. The ship sailed south of Cuba into the Gulf of Mexico. Once across the Gulf of Mexico, the ship made its way to the Alabama coast. The *Polievka* was anchored just off the coast of Bayou La Batre. Due to the nature of the illegal cargo, Captain Craig was escorted for protection by horseback to Mobile to meet with the sponsors. Returning with the secret rendezvous location, he prepared his ship to enter the dangerous Mobile Bay. Captain Craig maneuvered the schooner quietly into Mobile Bay, then up the Spanish River into the Alabama River, dodging obstacles and nervously scouring the shoreline for the rendezvous. The moisture from the thick fog drenched the ship ,making it hard for the crewmen to stay on their feet while performing their duties. A chorus of frogs chirping filled the air, while an occasional set of gator eyes flashed as the crew scanned the bank. Finally, a deckhand spotted the wooden dock just visible in the dark night. Captain Craig quietly prayed that the transitions would go smoothly. He wanted the stressful night to be over. He eased the schooner alongside the makeshift dock barely protruding out above the river's current, not concerned about damaging the side of the *Polievka* for her end was near. The deckhands secured the schooner as Captain Craig went below for a final inspection of the cargo that survived the painful journey. He gasped, covering his mouth and nose from the smell of throw-up and body waste that had collected since the last cleaning. One hundred twenty of the one hundred twenty-three were still alive. Not bad for the poor conditions below. At $1100.00 a head, he would profit $120,000, making the grueling voyage well worth his effort. The full expenses of ship and crew were prepaid by his sponsors. This was Captain

Craig's last voyage before settling down on the land he purchased in Colorado, where he hoped to raise cattle. Captain Craig went back up on deck to instruct the exhausted crew to start sorting the cargo for each order. He would have to adjust the quantity due to the quick departure and the deaths during transit, but this was common for this business. Captain Craig ordered the remains of the dead to be tossed into the river for the gators and sharks to enjoy. Captain Craig went ashore to settle up with his eager sponsors. Soon he returned, ordering his crew to unload the schooner. Once everyone was satisfied, he sailed the schooner a couple of miles up the river before running it aground. Captain Craig had the crew fill the schooner with brush before setting her on fire. He paid his crew their remaining payment before he headed out to Colorado.

***

CASSIUS LOU SHANNON

Cassius Lou Shannon, a plantation owner, made the long journey to the Mobile Bay by wagons with his oldest two boys from Skuna Valley, Mississippi, where he owned over 2000 acres of prime cotton fields. Cassius, in his late 50s, was a blue-eyed, tall man at 6'4, with wide shoulders and off-centered posture. A rugged man, he had a swagger when he walked that most women loved. His solid, greyish white hair was slicked straight back when he was not wearing his black gambler hat. The good dresser wore a black vest with matching boots. Most men hated the fearsome Cassius. He was not afraid to steal, cheat, or kill to get his way.

Cassius grew up in the small river town of Savannah, Tennessee, where he had a difficult upbringing. His father, Lucian Shannon, was a good, God-fearing man who worked honestly and hard on the Tennessee River to provide for his family. He was gone for long periods of time, but was always sending money home for the family. Cassius's mother Tilda was blue-eyed, petite, and a quite stunning, loose woman. She enjoyed staying out drinking, dancing, and some-times sleeping with anyone willing to have her. Late one evening, Lucian returned home early and caught Tilda with Mr. Lovejoy, their crooked landlord. The furious Lucian tried to walk away, but anger got the best of him. The next day, Lucian went to town to confront Mr. Lovejoy. He waited across the street from the general store until Mr. Lovejoy came out and returned to his buggy. Lucian yelled at Mr. Lovejoy from across the street. The two men exchanged threats before Mr. Lovejoy pulled out his revolver. The quick-react-ing Lucian was able to out-draw the older Mr. Lovejoy, shooting him in the chest. Mr. Lovejoy was able to get one shot off before dying, which grazed Lucian's left shoulder. During the lengthy trial, many witnesses confirmed Mr. Lovejoy drew his gun first. Due to a lack of money, Lucian was found guilty, and spent the next seven years in jail. The town folks enjoyed saying how Lucian was never sure if all five of Tilda's children were actually his kids. Cassius grew up an angry child, often taking his anger out on others and fighting anyone who pointed out his mother was a whore and father a mur-derer. Cassius dreamed about the day he could move from Savannah. He longed for a fresh start where no one knew his family past.

At age 15, Cassius bounced around doing odd jobs to help sup-port his struggling mom and younger siblings while his father was in jail. His older sister Beverly married before moving to Arkansas to live on the Smith plantation with her husband, leaving Cassius to fend for the family alone. Cassius was hired by Silas Grover, a crook-ed plantation owner just north of Savannah. Cassius was taught how to oversee the slaves and run day-to-day operations of the planta-tion. He quickly impressed Silas with his ability to follow orders and control the slaves. The harsh punishments Cassius dealt out to un-derperforming and disobedient slaves proved he would do whatever it took to get the job done. As production increased on the planta-tion, Silas increased Cassius's authority. Silas began sending Cassius out to collect old debts and settle personal disputes. Collecting debt became easy once word circulated around town about the raw, medieval torture Cassius inflicted on problem debtors. By the time his father returned from jail, Cassius had saved enough money to buy a small stretch of unused land from Silas Grover in Skuna Valley, Mississippi. Finally, he would be able to escape his troubled childhood for a fresh start, far away from his dysfunctional family's past.

With the help of Boo, a trusted young slave he bought from Silas along with twenty acres, Cassius began building his own plantation. Half of his newly purchased land was mature hardwood covering rolling hills, the other was open, flat fields with a spring-fed pond loaded with fish on the edge of the hardwood section. Little by little, he began buying troubled farms and plantations around his property.

Cassius's plantation was split in half by a neighboring plantation, causing Cassius to lose work hours shuffling slaves back and forth, costing him money. The land running between the two most productive fields of Cassius's plantation was owned by the area's only black plantation owner, Zebulon Whitten. Zeb was a hard-working, arrogant man who treated his slaves harshly. He moved down from Maine with his wife Jena after purchasing the land. They did not have any kids, only using slave labor and hired hands to work their land. The couple was non-social in the little community, only going to town for supplies or to gamble. Wanting to connect his land, Cassius offered top dollar to purchase the plantation from Zeb. Not interested in selling, Zeb continued to turn down Cassius's offers.

Cassius began bullying and harassing Zeb, causing a strong dislike between the two neighbors. One evening after picking up supplies in town, Cassius stopped at the local drinking establishment to have a few drinks. Cassius enjoyed sitting at the bar listening to the grapevine for town gossip. He also enjoyed watching people socialize. A loud commotion turned his attention outside of the smoke-filled bar. Zeb and another black man were intensely arguing over a game of dice along the outside wall of the bar. After a rough shoving match, threats were made between the two drunk men. Cassius watched carefully as Zeb stumbled over to his horse. Realizing Zeb was wallpapered, Cassius knew this was the opportunity.

Cassius waited a few minutes before slipping out the side door. He quickly rode a back trail to get ahead of Zeb. As Zeb's horse slowly approached, Cassius, hiding down in a ditch, grasped a ridged river stone tightly. Once in range, Cassius threw the river stone, hitting Zeb in the back of the head and knocking him off his horse. Cassius ran up, slamming another river rock into Zeb's head before slapping the horse on the rear end, encouraging it to ride off, and dragged the unconscious Zeb down into the ditch. Waiting a moment to make sure no one witnessed the ambush, Cassius held the unconscious Zeb underwater while he shoved his Bowie knife into Zeb's throat, slicing around then up, almost decapitating his head from his body. He held the body underwater until it stopped flopping. After cleaning his knife, Cassius followed the ditch back to his horse and rode off. Cassius stayed on his plantation until he heard Zeb's body was found and the man from outside the bar was arrested for murder. Cassius knew even if he was caught, he would only spend a little time in jail, if any, for killing the black man.

After a few weeks, Cassius began talking to Zeb's widow Jena, wanting her to sell the plantation. Not having any luck convincing her to sell, Cassius began letting Jena's livestock out late at night, then helped her gather them all up the next day. After a few months of running the plantation herself, Jena realized the job was too big for her to handle. She finally approached Cassius about buying the plantation. Cassius offered much less than he had offered Zeb. The naïve widow took the offer, leaving Cassius with the land, slaves, and the beautiful plantation mansion. Jena moved back to Maine, leaving the plantation life behind.

Cassius's first wife Trisha died after giving birth to their only child. Having no use for a girl, he coldly shipped the baby off to an orphanage in north Alabama. His second wife, Tanyia Lorren Talley, was almost a decade younger, a full-figured, pretty-faced, brown-eyed blonde. She had a skin tag on the left side of her chin that people sometimes mistook for a booger. She was known around town as a nice, gentle lady willing to help the less fortunate. She was well respected in the community and at church, where she regularly attended Sunday service. Tanyia met the handsome Cassius at the annual watermelon festival when she was 16. She was drawn in by his charm, not aware of his past. Cassius, being experienced with ladies, knew how to spoil the shy Tanyia, and gave her the attention she so longed for. She was the middle child of 11, mostly spending her time taking care of her younger siblings and milking cows, along with house duties. Tanyia's family owned a small plantation just outside the town of Coffeeville, the county seat of Yalobusha County, Mississippi. Her father Wesley Talley owned the small general store on the edge of town, where he spent most of his time. He left the plantation operation to his boys. The few slaves he owned were treated like family. Beatings were not allowed on the Talley Plantation. The threat of selling the slave was enough to keep control. The slaves knew about the harsh treatment of slaves on other plantations, and worked hard to please Wesley. At his store, he was able to hear the town gossip while being social, which he enjoyed. Wesley also enjoyed helping the less fortunate. He was known for erasing debt owed from the less fortunate customers. Hearing that Tanyia had caught the eye of Cassius Shannon deeply concerned Wesley. By doing business with Cassius over the years, Wesley knew Cassius to be dishonest and mean. He had seen firsthand how Cassius treated not only slaves, but people in general. Wesley nicely asked Cassius to stay away from his daughter, which Cassius did at first. Not being able to forget Tanyia's beauty, Cassius took every opportunity to speak to her. For once in his life, he attended Sunday service, although only pretending to be a good, God-fearing Christian. Tanyia liked the attention from Cassius, especially knowing her family did not like him. Wesley finally demanded for Cassius to stay away from Tanyia. They heard the rumors and feared for her wellbeing. One night, Tanyia snuck off to town to visit him. Cassius took her back to his plantation to woo her. Before she knew what was happening, Cassius took advantage of her inexperience, having his way with her.

Before she could come to her senses to stop him, he had finished. Scared to return home to her family, she decided to run off and marry Cassius. The relationship was abusive at times, and she knew he was regularly unfaithful, but she could not resist his charm and good looks. Deep down, she enjoyed their occasional fights. All the women around town talked about how handsome he was, and she liked the attention she received for being his wife. Most importantly, she lived comfortably and had everything she needed. She had given him five strong boys. The oldest, William, was 30, followed by Thaddeus. The two boys were only 10 months apart. Both boys had sharp, blue, evil eyes like Cassius and blonde hair like their mom. Both were hotheaded, always looking to fight. They were very close and always together. Buckner came 4 years later. He was a redheaded, freckle-faced, goofy looking kid, tall like his dad with his mom's good heart. Laid back and well liked. The identical twins Clifton and Malley were a surprise when Tanyia was almost 40. They were a handful, and she loved them dearly.

Cassius and his older two boys had arrived two weeks early to Mobile, Alabama. The March air was warm and humid, much more humid than their North Mississippi plantation. The musky smell from the swamp was enough to make a man sick. The oak trees were different from the trees back home, short with low hanging branches reaching out in different directions and covered with moss. The mosquitos were as big as birds, attacking every evening on schedule. Cassius encouraged the boys to have fun in town, but insisted they keep a low profile and avoid trouble. The Shannons camped just outside of the city. They spent most of the time gambling, drinking, and laying up with the local whores. While in town, Cassius wandered in and out of the local saloons where he learned about the arsenal raid in Virginia. Violent abolitionists kept trying to start an uprising. The failed raid had heightened fears of a slave revolt. Mississippi and other slave states were pledging support to resist antislavery aggression. Cassius did not want the war, but he also did not want to lose all his slaves, not to mention his way of life. He sat around listening, but kept his mouth closed and his opinions to himself. Cassius learned at an early age that most people did not like him, his opinion, or his sarcasm. Plus, he enjoyed listening for information. Cassius learned about the illegal shipment of African slaves from a cotton buyer he did business with in Coffeeville. Most of Cassius's cotton was sold and shipped to Europe through the Mobile port. Cassius met with a Mobile purchaser, wanting to cut out the buyer from Coffeeville. Transporting the cotton could double his profit. Although he could increase his profit, the risk of war and bandits kept him from making the deal. Getting word that the shipment was anchored off the coast, the Shannons loaded up their camp before heading to the rendezvous area. Cassius had expected 25 slaves but settled for 23. He paid the Captain, divided his newly purchased property between the three covered wagons, chaining them together, then began the five-day trip back to Skuna Valley. There was no need to hurry. The illegal cargo from West Africa was legal once loaded and moved away from the river. The proof of sale document was fake, but clearly stated the cargo was legally purchased from the Sloan tobacco farm just outside of Way, Georgia.

***

1860, WEST AFRICA

As a boy, Dred learned to read, write, and speak English from the Catholic Church Mission Society. The Missionaries lived in his village for a few years teaching the tribe about Christianity and building churches. He attended the study sessions daily. Dred was fascinated with the English. He enjoyed sitting for hours, listening to stories about England and the New World and asking thousands of questions. Dred dreamed of leaving his village one day to explore this New World. His Ewe tribe was located in the coastal region of West Africa, southeast of the Volta River. The tribe sat in the middle of a group of scattered whistling thorn trees, surrounded by tall grassy fields. Dred grew up as most tribal boys, pretending to fight and hunt like his father. He worked hard to become a powerful warrior along with an reliable hunter. His 6'3" frame and chiseled body made him a force. He excelled at all the warrior skills passed down to him from his father. Dred enjoyed woodcarving, dancing, and racing against his friends. At age seventeen, Dred was taken by his father blindfolded up the river to the sacred cave. He would survive there alone for two moon cycles. This was the traditional path to manhood, and Dred was excited for his turn at the tribal challenge. He had been practicing for this day since he was little. Unknown to Dred, his father would check in on him from a distance every few days. Dred was able to build his fire, make his weapons, and hunt for his food. He spent most of his time following the story of his tribe's history that the past generations had documented on the cave walls. Drinking from the spirit water allowed Dred to speak to past tribe elders. Meditation after drinking from the spirit water pushed Dred into a deep slumber. Dreams of childhood adventures with his friends ran through his head like a black and white picture movie. A loud crash from deep in the caves startled Dred from his slumber. Up on his feet, ready to protect himself, his heart raced looking back into the darkness. Tap tis, tap tis, tap tis, tap tis, the sound came up from the bottom of the cave. Dred followed the sound through the old ridged rock floor tunnel, trying to avoid spider webs and insects attempting to harm him during his search for the source of the sound. Tap tis, tap tis, tap tis, tap tis. He came to a tunnel just big enough around for him to squeeze through. Tap tis, tap tis, tap tis, tap tis. Dred inched his way through the tight tunnel while trying to avoid the razor sharp rocks protruding out from the tunnel's ceiling. He successfully made his way into the open cavity of the cave. Dred looked up into the white light reflecting off the water running down the algae covered cave walls. A heavy mist blew in from the back of the cave.

A deep voice called out to him, "Drrrreeeeed!"

"Yes," Dred answered. He looked up toward the voice through

the mist, seeing his fruitful land, his vibrant village, his safe world. A mighty lion stepped out into the land letting out a powerful roar, causing flocks of birds to fly off the surrounding trees in panic. The lion chased down a zebra for the kill, providing for his tribal family. Suddenly the lion was trapped, bonded down, struggling to free itself. Dred then saw a strange land of white fields, green meadows, a creek full of life, and beautiful green trees. Dred gasped at the beautiful land, smiling with happiness. The mighty lion stepped out onto the field, letting out another powerful roar before strutting across the field. The lion began trotting through the white field up onto the bank of the creek. Letting out another powerful roar, the lion looked down at the meadow. A lioness walked by with four beautiful cubs in tow. The proud lion watched as they walk past. Walking down the bank and across the creek, the lion saw a wounded cub curled up whimpering. The lion began to run, approaching the end of the meadow, stopping quickly to inspect a dead cub with a spear through its body, bubbling blood from the mouth. The lion looked up, letting out a sorrowful roar. Dred became emotional, with tears running down his face as he fell down to his knees. The lion began fighting a faceless white man as the mist blew out and the cave returned to darkness. Dred sat quietly, reflecting on the vision. Deep in his soul, Dred understood evil was to cross his path. He made his way back to his campsite. He sat by the fire wondering what evil he was to encounter. The moon cycles passed quickly, allowing Dred to be welcomed into manhood by his tribe. The elders had a cow killed for the celebration. The dancing and singing went late into the night.

His parents had arranged his marriage with the King's daughter, Arrah. Dred was good with the arrangement. Arrah was the most beautiful female in the tribe. He could not wait for her 14th birthday so they could marry. Their age difference was common in their tribe. Most couples had a 6-year gap. Dred fought his urge to leave his village, staying loyal to his tribe tradition, his rite of passage, and the promise of a beautiful bride.

Arrah was a light, milky brown-skinned girl with sharp green eyes. She had an athletic build with good birthing hips. She was raised with strong Christian beliefs, although her grandmother insisted she learn their Hoodoo magic that had been passed down through the generations. She did not mind since the Hoodoo was good magic. The Hoodoo spells were used for luck, wealth, love, and health. The Holy Bible is full of Hoodoo magic. Hoodoo is God's plan, helped along by the spirits. She spent her free time collecting the roots, leaves, and larva required for the spells. She enjoyed the time with her grandmother. Arrah often sat in while her grandmother performed the Hoodoo magic for tribe members. While practicing with her grandmother one afternoon, a tribal elder entered their shack. A rival tribe murdered two of their warriors. The elder insisted on a spell for revenge. Arrah's grandmother took blood from the dead warrior, smearing it across the seal of Solomon etched into the floor of the hut. She then sprinkled ingredients from her nation sack across the seal as she chanted a curse for revenge. Arrah sat back watching quietly. She had never witnessed a curse for revenge. She watched as her grandmother went into a trance, bouncing on her knees, praying to their Gods. Her grandmother called out, "SHANKPANA, SHANKPANA, SHANKPANA by the power of God and our ancestors, unleash your wrath against these evil men who have taken the lives of our brave warriors. SHANKPANA, SHANKPANA, SHANKPANA." Her grandmother continued to chant prayers and shout more commands. She then danced counterclockwise, continuing the prayer before collapsing onto the seal. Taking a blade, she slit her palm, squeezing out her blood onto the seal, looking up to the heavens. A black smoke rose out of the seal, exiting their hut. Once the spell was complete, she smeared the bloody mixture on the chest of the dead warriors before burying both bodies. Her grandmother continued to pray late into the night. The next morning, Arrah asked her grandmother about the curse. Her grandmother explained the curse was asking God to punish the murderers. Only God could decide their fate. Whatever happened would be God's plan. She went on explaining to Arrah the need for punishment, "We all have to be held accountable for our actions. In the end, everyone gets what they deserve."

Arrah was excited to be promised to Dred. He was a catch for any female. Beginning the courtship, Dred began spending time with Arrah. Helping each other with tasks and meeting with elder couples helped prepare them for their engagement. Completing their courtship, the young couple were married, then blessed with four kids, spacing the children two years apart.

The oldest Banjoe, 20, was a man, establishing himself as a future leader. He developed all the skills of his father. Next was Dayhoo, the silly son, who wanted to make everyone laugh, not concerned with tribal traditions. Then their son Cy, serious and smart, a rule follower and pleaser, always looking for his parents' approval. Lastly, their daughter Tinah was born four years after Cy. She was Dred's favorite, a feisty little girl that shared her mom's beautiful eyes. She kept everyone busy while exploring her world, thirsty for knowledge, pushing the boundaries of her parents' patience.

Two years before Tinah's birth, Arrah was pregnant with her fourth child. Five months into her pregnancy she began having severe back pain along with agonizing stomach cramps. After a couple days of milky white-pink mucus discharge, she began getting worried about her pregnancy. Speaking with a tribal elder, she was assured there was no reason to worry. A week later, Arrah collapsed while cooking food for her family. Dark red blood, along with two fetuses, discharges from her uterus. She bled out, and was non-responsive when she was found. A tribal elder sent for Dred, who was out hunting. Dred raced back to their hut after hearing the horrible news that his pregnant wife was dead. He raced across the hut's floor to his dead wife. In disbelief, he picked up her lifeless corpse and began to weep. Dred held her tight in his arms, not wanting to let her go. He gently carried her, placed her onto their bed, and began to clean her up. Once she was clean, Dred let his three little boys hug and kiss their dead mom.

Arrah's spirit rose up over her body, looking down at her lifelessness. She was greeted by her great-grandmother's spirit. Arrah was overcome by the love that encircled her, and she followed her great-grandmother's spirit onto a stained glass wing full of bright, beautiful colors she had never experienced. They rose up away from her world into the heavens. Arriving into their afterlife, she was greeted by spirits from past generations, all happy to welcome her home. At once, she knew this was not her first time in the afterlife. Glorious music filled her with tunes from magical horns. She felt the presence of her God although she could not see her God. Arrah moved through the crowd of spirits, soaking up warm greetings of love, until she came to a beautiful little girl. The beautiful little girl smiled before pointing for her to leave. Without saying a word, Arrah knew she was to return to earth to be this beautiful little girl's mom. Arrah was escorted back to the wing to be transported back to her earthly body. As she was returning to her body, a feeling of sadness overcame her having to leave the afterlife, until she saw her family deep in prayer around her corpse. Happiness again overwhelmed her as she took the deep breath of life. Arrah sat up, looking around a little confused but happy. Dred, unable to speak, fell back in disbelief. His wife was back from the dead! Her grandmother, who was leading the prayer ceremony, gasped with excitement, proclaiming their God had answered their prayers. The family celebrated Arrah's return from the dead. Arrah never spoke about her experience in the afterlife. Within a few days, she was back on her feet. Two years later, she was pregnant again with the beautiful little angel from heaven.

Life around the tribe was good. The men hunted and farmed while the women took care of the children and cooked. The lively, enthusiastic tribe enjoyed music and lavish parties. They were good weavers and pottery makers, good with leather and beads. Children ran around learning skills passed down from generation to generation. Dred, along with the other top warriors, heard stories of tribes being raided and captured for sale into slavery. They devised a plan to protect their tribe from invasion. Starting off with multiple night watch warriors, they slowly dropped to only one as the years went on with no invasions. Word spread that the slave trade was ending.

Trying to get a few more sales, the King of Dahomey, a tribe from across two rivers, ordered his warriors to raid the Ewe tribe. He had been raiding communities, taking the captured to Whydah and selling them at the slave market. The Dahomey worriers snuck in undetected, killing the night warrior guardian. Dred woke with a spear to his neck. The cool-headed Dred knew not to fight. The tribe was overtaken without resistance. He and the other tribe members were gathered and bonded together. The few that resisted were killed. Dred instructed his family to obey the warriors and stay together. They traveled by foot with their captors, now prisoners. Each Ewe member was connected by rope wrapped around their necks, with their hands tied in front. Dred kept telling his family to look forward and obey the commands. Once they arrived to Whydah, they were fed, then taken to a warehouse. The sweaty, bloody rope was unwrapped from their necks. The long walk had removed the skin, causing rope burns and bleeding. Salve and oil were applied to help the sores heal. The tribal members were then guided into an old livestock warehouse and sorted into stalls before being shackled. Dred made sure his family all made it into the same stall. One by one, the handlers came by, dousing them with water to knock off the dust and dirt from the long journey. Each prisoner was checked for any ailments that could drop their value for sale. The elderly, sick, and the weak were taken away to another warehouse to be discarded. The tribe waited in the warehouse to be selected. Once selected, they were escorted to the dock to be loaded. They were taken below the *Polievka* and shackled. The King of Dahomey had sold them into slavery. They soon would have to endure the harsh journey across the Atlantic Ocean to the New World. Dred continued to tell his family: obey and stay together, obey and stay together.

Dred was taken onto the ship where he stood on deck waiting his turn to be taken below. Amazed, Dred stared at the enormous gun on the front of the ship used for protection. Never in his life had he seen such a weapon. The deck was covered with crates full of food and supplies. The crew were yelling and whipping slaves who fought being taken under into the dark belly of the ship. The rain poured down, making the wait miserable as the ship rocked back and forth from the waves generated by the storm. Due to the low number of slaves loaded onto the ship, each slave had extra space for themselves, making the horrible voyage less horrible. The rough waters caused most the slaves to get sick before the ship made open water.

Once everything settled and the ship had left port, Dred spoke to his family. "Do everything they ask, do not fight. We will come up with a better plan later," Dred explained. He had listened to the exchange and realized they were headed to the New World to be slaves. Dred had to prepare his scared family for what was to come. The crew took extra good care of their slaves because it was the last shipment for Captain Craig. The slaves were taken up on deck twice a day for exercise. They were made to jump, hop, and sometimes dance to keep their muscles from deteriorating. Women and kids were able to walk around freely, while the men were kept chained since they were more likely to cause problems. Slaves that resisted exercise or food were flogged until they complied. Captain Craig did not let crew members take advantage of the female slaves. He needed as many healthy slaves to survive the voyage as possible. The conditions below deteriorated day by day. Blood, sweat, and mucus covered the floor along with feces and urine. The smell caused slaves to throw up, making conditions worse. Captain Craig had deck hands clean underneath with sand and citrus, trying to help keep down the smell.

During the afternoon, bread, a pipe of tobacco, and a drink of brandy would be offered to the slaves. Before dark, the slaves would be fed a meal of beans and peas with salted meat or fish, before being taken down for the long night. Due to bad weather, the slaves could be locked below in their chains for days at a time. The air was noxious. The constant rubbing of their chains raised sores on wrists and ankles. Around two weeks out, deck hands would begin rubbing various healing oils and creams on sores to prepare the slaves for sale.

Trying to keep his family mentally stable, Dred told them stories from his childhood, along with some stories he had heard from the elders. He tried to keep a positive attitude while remaining strong for his stressed family. After a few days, they adjusted to their new miserable routine. As bad as the conditions were on the ship, Dred knew that what was to come could be worse. Keeping his family together and safe was his top priority. The crew's excitement from above indicated that land was in sight. Although Dred would be happy to leave the poor conditions of the boat, he also was afraid for the future.

***

SHANNON PLANTATION, MISSISSIPPI

The Shannon Plantation had a 3-story Greek Revival mansion with Italianate and Gothic influences. Surrounding the house were twelve columns of molded brick and plaster which stood 32 feet high, set on paneled stiles. Large, white granite Corinthian capitals were placed atop each column, with different tiger gargoyles protruding from each. Five chimneys rose from the roof, fed from ten fireplaces with marble mantels. Rainwater was stored in large tanks in the attic and supplied three bathrooms. Central halls divided rooms that included two sixteen by eighteen-foot rooms on each side of the hallways of the main floors. The full basement contained storage rooms and dairy. The residential floor had a parlor, a library, the master suite, and many bedrooms. The two-story wings provided a kitchen, a pantry, and a dining room. Some house slaves' living quarters were just off the west wing. On top of the house was an observatory room. From this, Cassius could see his entire plantation. The area around the mansion was planted with beautiful plants highlighted with colorful flowers. The large oak trees provided shade during the summer, as they provided protection from the winds kicked up by intense storms. Down the hill was the blacksmith's hut, where trained slaves, mended broken ploughs, made and repaired farm and garden tools, and shod horses. There was also a furniture hut to make and repair furniture for the mansion and slave shacks. The plantation garden grew vegetables including peas, beans, corn, carrots, and pumpkins. The plantation kept cows, sheep, and chickens to provide fresh meat, milk, and eggs. The slave community had fifteen dogtrot houses not far from Turkey Creek. Each was raised off the ground, and had a wide front porch spanning the entire length of the house. There was only one room off each side of the breezeway: a kitchen with a fireplace on one side, and a bedroom with a living space on the other. The cracks in the floor and windows helped cool the rooms in the summer, and chickens helped keep the bugs away. Seven to ten slaves lived in each house. There was a central cookhouse for lunch, dinner, and special occasions. Tanyia Shannon made sure the slaves had a nicer than normal slave community, although she turned a blind eye to the harsh punishments Cassius dealt out to problem slaves. The work hours began an hour after dawn, with an hour lunch break, and ended an hour before dusk with Sundays off. They even had a small church for Sunday worship. The Shannons, unlike most owners, encouraged slaves to have a vibrant social and cultural life, allowing gatherings, celebrations, and marriages. They realized years earlier how a social slave community produced better workers. The slave community had their own livestock and a vegetable garden. They also had access to Turkey Creek for fishing, bathing, and swimming. Five slave drivers, older slaves promoted by Cassius, had responsibilities to govern the village. They directed the daily work and reported to Cassius. The drivers made sure there were no uprisings. Most punishments handed down by Cassius were through the drivers, which helped keep the peace. Most punishments were given out on rainy days in order not to interrupt production. The drivers watched the slaves throughout the day, making sure they kept a good work pace. With 106 slaves, everything had to work smoothly. The few slaves that had escaped were usually caught and harshly punished by Cassius as an example. Cassius's punishments were horrible.

Skuna Valley was in sight! A brief excitement overcame Cassius at the sight of his fields. Long rows of freshly turned, dark brown dirt lay neatly, waiting to be planted, greeted their owner back from his long journey. Cassius and the boys were exhausted from their trip. They were pleased that the new slaves were low maintenance, not causing any problems. Usually there would be one or two beatings to get new slaves to behave. They had stopped a couple of times to rest, letting the slaves stretch their legs and eat while keeping them chained. They did not want any to die or escape on the trip home. Cassius insisted the boys unload, feed, and then shackle the slaves in the barn before visiting with the family. William's wife, Lilly Brittney, and Thaddeus's wife, Harriett Kristian, had brought their curious kids down to watch the new slaves being unloaded. The 27-year-old Lilly grew up on a plantation in Calhoun, Mississippi. She had three kids with William: Patty Lee, 10, Joe Jack, 8, and Wilma, 5. The 25-year-old Harriett was from Coldwater, Mississippi. She and Thaddeus had 3 kids: Billy, 6, Martha, 5, and Jouble, 3. Both Lilly and Harriett understood the slaves' value. Their kids were interested to watch their dads work. Joe Jack and Billy asked questions as Wilma, Martha, and Jouble lost interest and chased butterflies. Joe Jack asked where the slaves came from. Lilly explained that slaves came from Africa and Grandpa bought them over in Mobile. Billy asked if the slaves missed Africa. Lilly explained that slaves did not feel like whites, that they were like animals unable to feel emotions. Then he wanted to know where Africa was, and if he could go there, and what it was like in Africa. Losing interest in the slaves and focusing on Africa, Lilly patiently answered their questions while they waited to greet their husbands. Harriett kept watch over the other three, who were wandering around looking for something to get into. Jouble had turned his attention to an old bullfrog making its way to the creek. Lilly had found out after William left that she was pregnant, and could not wait to tell him. Buckner came up from the field where he was working on a fence to help. His wife Sarah did not come down to watch. Sarah, being from Chicago, did not care much for what went on down the hill. She was usually chasing their one-year-old Lorre around the house. Buckner had met Sarah while visiting his uncle in Chicago. He had to convince her to live in Mississippi. The upscale living was too much for her to resist.

Buckner, trying to be polite, asked Thaddeus, "How was the trip to Mobile?"

Thaddeus answered with a snarl, "Everything went ok."

Buckner could tell they were tired and irritated, and went on helping quietly. He did not much care for his two older brothers. He had never seen eye to eye with them. They had a tendency to push him around. He had learned at an early age to keep his distance. Tanyia had always kept him away from Cassius and the older boys when he was young. Buckner was always the good son with a good heart like his mom. His closeness with Tanyia kept him from leaving the plantation.

Once the slaves were fed and locked up, William and Thaddeus went over to greet their wives. Lilly ran up to William to share her news. "I am with child!" She exclaimed.

William smiled and shared in her excitement. Cassius and Thaddeus congratulated the couple as they made their way up to the house for some well deserved rest and a good cooked meal. Tanyia sent the butler to fetch the twins who were playing in the woods. Once everyone was washed up, they sat down for the meal. Tanyia asked about Mobile. She had always wanted to visit. The boys described the trees, heat, and local food. Much spicier than what they were used to on the plantation. They talked about the different fish than the catfish they pulled from Turkey Creek. The excited boys spoke about how the city celebrated Shrove Tuesday with a carnival-like parade, which marched down the road throwing food and trinkets to the revelers gathered to watch.

Once the women and kids had enough about the Mobile culture, they went on with dinner. After dinner, Cassius and his boys gathered in his library for drinks and conversation on how he wanted to break in the new slaves. He did not expect too much trouble since some of them could speak and understand English. This would cut the breaking-in process in half. William and Thaddeus agreed the training should go smoothly, but both boys hoped for trouble. Nothing excited them more than beating and torturing slaves. They both had killed slaves on many occasions. Cassius knew he would have to supervise.

***

SLAVES' NEW LIFE

Dred opened his eyes face down on the cold, dirt-covered hay. One hand was shackled to the chain. He sat up to look around, wiping off the dirt and hay sticking to his face. His head was spinning from the grueling journey. The past six weeks had taken a toll on not only his body, but also his mind. The barn was cool from the early morning air. The sunlight was starting to peek through the old oak plank wall. He looked down at his sleeping family. *At least we are together*, he thought to himself. Dred sat in silence, feeling helpless, wondering how much his family could endure before breaking. Arrah woke and sat up next to Dred.

"What is going to happen?" She asked.

Dred shook his head. He did not know. "Running and fighting will only get us killed. Keep calm, quiet, be obedient and submissive until we fully understand our situation." Arrah agreed. They woke their kids. Dred quietly explained their plan to stay calm, to stay quiet and obedient. Do not make eye contact, do not show emotion, and do not run. Stay alive, stay together.

Tinah said, "I am scared daddy."

Dred held her hand saying, "Me too."

The barn door burst open as Cassius appeared with his boys. William and Thaddeus began shouting at the slaves to get up. William snatched the chains binding the slaves together. They were taken to the blacksmith hut to be branded. One by one, the new slaves stepped up to get the hot iron pressed into their left shoulder, burning the flesh with "CLS." The slaves that resisted were beaten with a wooden axe handle across the back until they complied. Once branded, the slaves were then taken out to the whipping poles. The four oak poles stood eight feet tall, painted black. Each had a pulley at the top, and a rope with a hook that ran up and over the pulley, used to pull the slave up until their toes barely touched the ground.

Looking over his new property, Cassius asked with authority, "Do any of you understand English?" The slaves kept quiet with their heads down, not wanting to make eye contact. William and Thaddeus grinned knowing what was about to happen. Cassius already knew some of the slaves spoke English. He again demanded, "Do any of you understand the words coming out of my mouth?" With still no response, Cassius motioned to his boys. William and Thaddeus each grabbed a frightened male slave from the group, attaching their shackles to the hook before pulling the rope to correct position. The boys grabbed their leather whips, eagerly waiting for the command. One last time Cassius called out, "Do any of you all understand English?" With no response and a nod from Cassius, the boys started the beatings. The slaves cried with horrific pain, as their bodies began rocking and wobbling with no way to escape. Their piercing cries echoed throughout the pastures, with each twist of leather slicing their skin like razors. The slaves out working the nearby fields stopped to look up at the whipping poles, curious about the screams. Blood splattered with each painful blow.

Watching with uneasiness, Dred finally had enough. Stepping forward he proudly uttered with his African accent, "I understand your English." Cassius commanded the boys to stop the lashing. The two slaves hung limp, whimpering like beaten dogs with the shackles still hooked above their heads and blood running down their freshly torn skin.

Cassius asked, "What is your name, boy?"

"My name is Dred."

Cassius gazed at Dred before ordering him to translate for the group. Dred nodded yes, hoping the thrashings were finished. In his native tongue, Dred repeated Cassius's orders.

"Resist the laws on my plantation, you will be punished. Not working hard enough in the fields, you will be punished. Talking too much in your native language, you will be punished. Stealing from me, you will be punished. Trying to run away, you will be punished. Killing one of my slaves, you will be punished. Men must pick fifty pounds of cotton a day, or you will be punished. Women and kids must pick at least thirty pounds of cotton a day, or you will be punished."

The boys removed the two punished slaves and grabbed Dred, pulling him to the pole, then hooking his shackles before pulling the rope tight. With Dred's family watching in horror, Cassius walked over behind Dred, and picking up the whip, Cassius began Dred's punishment of five painful lashes, with only a slight flinch from Dred as the braids cut into his flesh. Not a sound as the blood ran down his back from his torn skin. When he was done, Cassius walked over to Dred, whispering, "Don't you try me boy." The driver, Boo, released Dred from the pole.

Once Cassius left the area, Arrah rushed over to Dred, still standing proudly next to the pole, and tended to the freshly torn wounds. Boo led the group of new slaves down to their living quarters. Ten slaves in each shack. Dred's family and four other slaves shared one shack. Boo gave each slave a set of clothes, a blanket, and job duties. Arrah was assigned to help the house slaves. Tinah would be cooking, cleaning, gardening, and mending cloth in the slave community. Dred and his three boys would be working in the hot fields.

Boo again went over the rules and reminded them of the punishment. He did not like beating other slaves, but he really did not like getting beaten himself. Boo went over the way of the community. "If ya cause trouble, there will be trouble. If ya do not wanna be beat, do what ya told."

Boo sent Arrah up to the house to get started learning what was expected of her. Dred, the boys, and the other new field slaves went with Boo to the fields. Tinah stayed behind to learn the community way. At the end of the day, they all found their way back to their little shack to begin their new life in the New World.

***

FEBRUARY 1862

Dred quickly became a leader around the community. Boo started to rely on Dred for help with projects and different chores around the plantation.

Being around Boo, Dred learned a war was brewing between the Northern and Southern states, with the possibility of all the slaves being freed. With this news, Dred instructed his family to continue to work hard and stay out of the way. The thought of being freed and experiencing the New World excited Dred. Everything he and his family had experienced over the past months could become a positive. Earning the trust of other slaves, Dred began having secret meetings to discuss what to do if slavery was abolished. He used the cover of the Sunday afternoon prayer song session to drown out their discussion. They left out Boo and the other overseers for fear they would tell Cassius. The group kept their meetings secret from all other slaves, afraid of getting caught. Each member of the group worked in different areas across the plantation. Each meeting, they would report back to Dred of any information they overheard. The trusted group consisted of Tommy the butler, Brandon the barn slave, Patrick the blacksmith, Joe Joe the garden slave, and Glen the kitchen slave. The group had the entire plantation covered, always listening for information.

Dred had overheard a conversation between Cassius and Boo. Cassius was explaining how slaves would be roaming around like wild animals looking for food, water, and shelter if they were free. "Do you like having food, water, clothes, and a place to live?" Cassius asked Boo. "Yes, yes sir, Boss," Boo happily answered while bouncing up and down on his toes due to his nervous tick. "I do like my stuff, Boss," Boo added.

"Here on my plantation, I allow you all to be free outside of work hours and provide you all with everything you need. So, why would any slave want to be free to fend for themselves?" Cassius asked.

"Ah, I do, I do not know, Boss," Boo answered. Dred knew, like any other slave talking to his master, that Boo would agree to anything Cassius said, more from fear than actual agreement. Any time anyone spoke of being free, Boo would quickly ask, "You wanna roam around like wild animals looking for food, water, and shelter? Be happy with what we got here. You all ain't got no sense wanting to be free." One of the overseer's jobs was to squash any talk of freedom. Cassius had given Boo enough information to complete the task.

Dred knew that Cassius was somewhat right about life after being freed. Where would they go? How would they survive? That was the very reason he had formed the group. Looking down the road and having a plan made Dred a great leader. Tommy the butler had heard about land out west where they could set up their own community in a free territory. Glen the kitchen slave had heard the same conversation. Brandon the barn slave was able to swipe a map from an old saddlebag to help plan their escape. The group decided to be prepared if they became free after the war. They would also be prepared to escape if the south won. Patrick the blacksmith began making tools and weapons in his spare time, keeping them hidden below the floor of the hut. Joe Joe the garden slave collected extra seeds to be planted once they arrived to their new land. Dred would lead the community out of slavery to set up a new community out west, far from Cassius. The plan of freedom brought Dred and the others much happiness. His dream of exploring the New World could come true. The group continued to listen for more information as they quietly prepared for their new beginning. As word of the war circulated, the group prayed for a northern victory. Glen reported to the group that Cassius was arguing with William and Thaddeus about joining the Confederate army. William and Thaddeus leaving could allow them to escape before the war ended, but Dred and the others knew Cassius had a strong grasp on the two boys that would keep them from going off to join the military.

***

DAVID RAY

Cassius drove his supply wagon to town every Saturday to get updates on the war and pick up supplies. One Saturday while in town, Cassius stumbled onto information about a slave auction. A flyer was hanging on the wall inside Talley's General Store, which Cassius thought was strange since the Talleys had only paid workers on their plantation. Once the war started, the Talleys freed their slaves, keeping only paid workers. Most of the slaves stayed due to the great living environment they were accustomed to on the Talley Plantation. The seven slaves up for auction were all caught trying to cross the Canadian border.

Cassius, always looking for a deal, strolled down to the auction. Inside the newly raised auction barn, Cassius looked over the livestock before turning his attention toward the slaves. After a careful inspection of the slaves, he decided to try his luck. Cassius sat by himself waiting for the auction to begin. Cassius started with the minimum bid and little increases, missing out on all of the first six slaves. For the last slave, Cassius kept going higher until he won. Higher than he wanted to go, but still a great deal. The slave's name was David Ray, and looked to be in his mid to late 20s. Cassius collected his newly purchased slave along with the paperwork. David Ray was loaded onto Cassius's wagon with the other supplies he had bought from Talley's General Store. After returning to the plantation, Cassius handed over the new slave to Boo. Without any instructions, Boo knew to take David Ray to the blacksmith shack to be branded, then down to the whipping pole. Cassius made his way down to the pole as well. After going over the rules of the plantation,

Cassius hit David Ray's lower back with a wooden axe handle, hoping to cease any thought of escaping. After the beating, Boo escorted David Ray down to the slave community for more instructions, clothes, and housing. Unknown to Cassius, the auction was set up by the Underground Railroad. The Talley Plantation had become a safe house station, and David Ray was an agent responsible for finding slaves able to make the dangerous journey to freedom in Canada.

David Ray worked the fields while scoping out the routine of the community. He looked for the strongest, hardworking slaves to consider. Only certain slaves would be selected for the harsh journey to freedom. Once selected, the group would make their way to the Talley Plantation under the cover of night. They would spend a few days in hiding to prepare for their grueling journey to the north. This allowed the plantation search party or hired slave hunters to either give up or get far enough away for a safe escape. A trained white guide would then escort the group from station to station on an indirect route until they reached their freedom. The dangers the runaways could endure were days without food, being attacked by wild animals, and being captured.

David Ray's plan was to send out two groups of twelve a few weeks apart. David Ray spent the first few weeks staying to himself, not wanting to attract any attention. Finally, David Ray approached Dred, introducing himself. In a deep tone, David Ray slowly pronounced each syllable of his words in his northern accent.

"My name is David Ray, I am from Cook, Illinois," David Ray said, looking into Dred's eyes for any sign of uneasiness. The confused Dred stared back, not sure what this guy wanted. "I was born a free man, and I belong to an organization that helps slaves escape to freedom in Canada," David Ray shared. I was sent here to assist two groups of slaves to freedom. Now having Dred's full attention, he asked, "Are you interested in escaping to your freedom in Canada?" Guarded, Dred nodded his head yes, not fully convinced the slow-talking man was sane. David Ray asked to meet with Dred in a secret meeting during the Sunday prayer song session. Dred agreed to the meeting. Dred decided to leave out his trusted group in case Cassius had sent David Ray to set them up.

The following Sunday, the two men met in Dred's shack. "I am a member of a group called the Underground Railroad. We smuggle slaves out of the south to freedom in Canada," David Ray started the meeting.

"Canada?" Dred asked.

"Yes, Canada is a country that allows blacks the freedom to live where they want, sit on juries, run for public office, and work for greenbacks. My group has safe houses and stations scattered out between here and Canada where you can eat and rest during the harsh journey," David Ray finished his opening.

"Why would you want to help us?" Dred asked, still skeptical. "Well, as a teen I had a vision from my God. I saw myself escorting the persecuted men to freedom. I was unsure of God's plan until I read the story about the Underground Railroad. God made his plan clear to me. Now, for the past eight years I have risked my life to help slaves escape their bondage," David Ray explained.

"We can meet again next Sunday?" Dred asked. David Ray agreed as the two exited the shack.

After Sunday dinner, Dred called his trusted group together. He went over the conversation he had with David Ray. After a long discussion, the group agreed to meet with David Ray together to find out more information. The next Sunday, Dred and his trusted group sat down with David Ray.

"My group would like to know how you plan to get us to your Canada." Dred started

"I will select the strong, then prepare a group of twelve. I will guide the group to the old dirt road leading to this plantation. The group will be loaded on two wagons, then taken to the safe house. Then I will return to the plantation before sun up. The group will stay at the safe house for a few days before starting the journey north. A conductor will guide the group from safe house to safe house along the way. The journey will be treacherous, days without food, sleeping in ditches, attacks by wild animals, and the threat of being captured. Some might die," David Ray finished. "How will you select the group?" Patrick the blacksmith asked.

"I will select twelve men who I feel will survive the journey."

"Only men?" Dred interrupted.

"Yes, men. The long journey is too harsh for women and children, they end up slowing the group down, increasing the chance of getting caught," David Ray answered. The group of trusted men began barking to each other about leaving their families, knowing how Cassius would punish or kill their family members left behind. "There is no other way to reach freedom," David Ray said defensively.

Dred, standing up, quieted the shack. "We all know Cassius will torture then kill our family if we leave them behind. We can only make the journey with our family intact. You do not understand the torture Cassius will put our families through," Dred finished.

David Ray sat in silence before standing up and removing his shirt, exposing the layers upon layers of scar tissue covering his chest and back. Turning around for the trusted group to observe, in his deep, slow speaking voice David Ray spoke carefully, "I was born a free man. I come from a family of wealth. I gave up my life of comfort to sacrifice my body, my blood, and my sanity for my God. Every scar on my body represents a slave that has become free, along with the ones who have died following my route to freedom. I have witnessed the evil of slavery. I have witnessed my friends strung up under the tall oak. I have witnessed the dignity of many black men and women wiped away in these crimes against humanity. You can sit here judging my intent and my way, but you cannot claim that I do not understand the torture these sinners inflict on our brothers and sisters," David Ray finished his emotional speech.

Dred stood speaking for the group. "We understand your sacrifice, but I, we, will not leave our families behind. We have to work out a way," Dred looked around the room, "a way to keep our families together." The room sat silent for a moment as they all took in what was at stake. Looking at the stressed men, David Ray asked, "How many? How many people would I be attempting to move?"

"About forty," Dred answered.

"That's too many. Exclude your elders," David Ray requested.

"Ah, thirty-four?" Dred recalculated.

"Okay, Saturday night this week I will meet with my people to see if it will work," David Ray decided.

"I will go with you to meet with your people," Dred offered.

"I have no problem with you accompanying me, but only you," David Ray agreed.

The following Saturday night, the two slaves snuck off the plantation shortly after dark. David Ray led Dred to the old dirt road where a covered wagon was waiting. Inside the wagon sat two men, The Reverend Absalom Cosson, a dark, big-boned black man dressed in a nice suit with a top hat and cane, and George Talley, a bald, short, skinny, pale man with a blondish red shaggy beard who was also Tanyia Shannon's younger brother. The two men helped finance the Underground Railroad in North Mississippi. The four were driven around while they met. Dred introduced himself before explaining the situation with leaving their families behind.

"Absolutely not," the Reverend quickly squashed the idea of women and children making the harsh journey. "We do not have the time or the resources to travel with women or children. Our guides already put their lives at risk guiding strong men to freedom," the Reverend angrily grunted.

Dred tried to plead his case, explaining the harsh torture Cassius inflicts on his slaves. Lucky for Dred, George had witnessed Cassius's treatment of slaves firsthand.

"Cassius's harsh treatment of slaves is one of the reasons my family became involved with the Underground Railroad," George shared. "When I was younger, I witnessed Cassius drive nails into a hogshead, as to leave the point of the nail just protruding in the inside of the cask. He would then pour salt and pepper covering the bottom of the hogshead two inches deep. Then Cassius stuffed a slave into the hogshead before rolling it down a steep hill for punishment, the nails stabbing the slave over and over with the salt and pepper burning the open flesh. This is just one example of the horrible things Cassius Shannon has done to punish his slaves. My family will sponsor three groups of twelve from the Shannon Plantation. Men, women, and children," George said, looking down at the Reverend. "We will expect the first group a week from tonight, March 10, the second group Saturday, April 14, then the last group Saturday, May 5."

The Reverend, not happy with the decision, made it clear that any woman or child not keeping pace would be left behind. He was not getting his guides caught due to slow-moving slaves. Dred and David Ray thanked the men as they were let out where they were picked up to make their way back to the slave community.

The next day, Dred's trusted group met again with David Ray to decide who would leave in which group. Tommy the butler and Brandon the barn slave would be in the first group, Patrick the blacksmith and Joe Joe the garden slave in the second group, with Glen the kitchen slave and Dred with the last group. David Ray insisted that all plans remain secret until the day of the group departure, and to only meet the Sunday before a group was to leave. "With the war inching closer to the area, I would not suspect too much retaliation from Cassius on the remaining slaves," David Ray suggested. Dred and his trusted group knew this to be false. Cassius would definitely punish someone. Dred left the meeting feeling good about his future. He spent the next few days dreaming about life in Canada. He actually did not know anything about Canada, but was excited to find out.

***

ESCAPE TO CANADA

On March 10, the first group met in Tommy the butler's shack and waited for instructions. A cold rain, mixed with sleet and snow, pounded on the shack's roof as night overtook the slave community. David Ray entered the warm shack, finding the group of twelve slaves bundled up and waiting for their frigid journey to freedom.

"The wintry weather has made the route to the wagon messy and slick. Be careful and everyone needs to stay together," David Ray commanded. With that, he led the group fifty yards into the tree line before ducking down into a cold muddy ditch. David Ray looked across the freezing slave community to make sure no one spotted them. The frozen weather had the community in hibernation for the night. The group followed David Ray on the fifty-five minute hike to the old dirt road toward their freedom. The cold, wet, icy conditions made the hike miserable. Waiting at the old dirt road were two covered wagons ready to carry the freezing slaves to the warmth of a safe house. Each slave was loaded onto a wagon, being careful of the slick conditions. David Ray confirmed the April 11 shipment before he returned to the slave community undetected.

The next morning, a blanket of fresh snow lay on top of the frozen ground, covering any evidence left by the escaped slaves. Sunday came and went without anyone noticing the missing slaves. David Ray and Dred stayed away from each other, not wanting to be linked together. Not long after work began on Monday, Boo was seen moving from shack to shack with the other drivers looking for the missing slaves. Working on the old oak bridge crossing Turkey Creek, Dred watched as Cassius sent Thaddeus, William, and Buckner, along with the dogs, out to search for the runaway slaves. The frozen weather had covered up any scent or track left behind, making the hunt almost impossible. Most slave owners hired slave hunters to find runaways, but Cassius knew better from past experience. Most hunters demanded money up front. The crooked hunters would find your slaves, then sell them to other plantations out of the area.

Later in the day, Cassius sent the drivers to round up all the slaves to the whipping poles. Cassius instructed Boo to attach each of the other four drivers to a pole. One by one, Cassius commanded Boo to give five lashes to each driver. The cold air made the brittle skin rip open with ease as the overseers cried out in unbearable pain.

Cassius's face turned red, with the big vein in his forehead bulging from his anger as he looked over the community of slaves before turning his attention back to the drivers. His eyes flashed hatred. With spit flying from his lips, he spoke to the five drivers.

"My boys are out tracking them sorry good for nothing slaves. If I find out you all had anything to do with those slaves escaping, I will kill you and your family." Looking back out over the slaves gathered watching, Cassius repeated his threat.

The slave community stood watching until Cassius walked away. Boo unhooked the four punished drivers, apologizing to each as he let them down off the pole. Dred felt pretty good about the punishment given out to the drivers. He was afraid the whole community would be punished.

William, Thaddeus, and Buckner were gone for almost a full week before returning, not finding any trace of the escaped slaves. The frozen weather was too much to overcome. Still working on the bridge, Dred witnessed Cassius punching William in the face for failing to find the escaped slaves before storming into the house.

On April 11, the second group waited in Joe Joe's shack. The nervous group wondered how they would escape the plantation now that the drivers were taking turns patrolling the community at night. David Ray eased out of his shack, hiding in the shadows while making his way to Joe Joe's shack undetected.

He entered announcing, "It is time to go. Once the driver turns the far corner, we will have only a few minutes to get into the woods and disappear. If we are discovered, you are on your own." David Ray peeked out the window of the dark shack, until the driver turned the corner heading away from Joe Joe's shack. The second group quietly scurried the fifty yards across the field into the dark woods before dropping down into the cold, dark ditch to hide. David Ray watched until the driver again turned the corner away from them. The escaping slaves followed David Ray for the fifty-five minute hike to the old dirt road where the two covered wagons again waited. David Ray confirmed with the driver he would be with the next group on May 5, and headed back to the slave community. Once again, the missing slaves were not noticed until Monday morning. Dred watched as Boo explained to Cassius that another group of slaves were missing. The hard backhand knocking Boo off his feet confirmed the news was taken poorly. Cassius yelled while pointing out toward the fields.

Boo scurried off as Cassius walked over to William and Thaddeus. "That is twenty-four slaves we have had run off in the past month. Someone is helping them escape," Cassius said to his boys. "You boys get with the drivers to snoop around the slave community to see what you all can find. I will check around town and see what I can hear from the grapevine. I am curious to know if anyone else has had slaves escape."

Cassius saddled up Old Bob then headed to town. His first stop was the Talley's general store. He knew Tanyia's family did not care for him but were too polite to express their feelings. Talley's General Store stood alone from other structures on the edge of town. The oak wood structure had a large front porch with an overhang. Tables and chairs were scattered around the porch for town folks to gather. A large glass window in the front displayed jewelry, lotions, tools, and boots for passing customers to view from the outside. The front of the store was decorated with tin sign advertising representing tobacco, cigars, soft drinks, and hardware. The entrance had double swinging doors, making it easy for customers to come and go. Shelves went up the walls with household supplies, as ropes, whips, and other items hung from the ceiling. Food, candy, medical supplies, and other expensive items were stored behind the long oak counter. Tanyia's brother Jesse Talley was putting up stock when he greeted Cassius with a smile as he walked into the store. "Hey Cassius, what can I do for you today?"

"I am looking for some information, Jesse. I have had a few slaves run off this past month. Have you heard of anyone else having the same problems?" Cassius asked.

"Yeah, there seem to be more and more slaves escaping since the battles have gotten closer," Jesse confirmed still smiling. "With most of our brave men off fighting in the war, it has been harder to keep the slaves put, I reckon," Jesse explained in his high-pitched voice.

"I guess that makes sense," Cassius replied. "Have you noticed anything odd around town?" Cassius asked.

"Other than the panic from the war moving closer, everything has been normal," Jessie answered, still smiling.

Hearing enough, Cassius excused himself to talk to more folks around town. "Tell my sister hello," Jesse said as Cassius exited the store.

Not having any luck around town, Cassius decided to check the drinking establishment before heading back to his plantation. The old wooden saloon cornered a row of shops on the east side of town across the street from the jail. The long, stained bar made from oak wood polished to shine stood surrounded with cigar smoke and drenched with spilled drinks. The bottom of the bar had a brass rail for a footrest mostly covered with dirt and mud. Spittoons were placed throughout the bar, encouraging customers not to spit on the wooden floor. Three large mirrors lined the wall behind the bar, reflecting the back of all the whiskey bottles and protecting the barkeep when his back was turned. Two large paintings of naked women in innocent poses hung between the mirrors. Tables and chairs were scattered around the bar, usually with some kind of gambling going on. Lanterns hung from the ceiling, giving the patrons light late into the night. In the front corner sat the hired pianist playing music to relax the sometimes tense crowd.

The old barkeep made his way down the crowded bar to pour Cassius a whiskey. The two talked for a bit before Cassius asked about the escaped slaves.

The barkeep looked around making sure no one was listening to the conversation before sharing. "I overheard a wallpapered Asian man say he belonged to a group placing some of them Black Yankees on plantations to help slaves escape. I do not know if he was telling the truth, but you are not the only plantation missing slaves."

"Black Yankee?" Cassius asked, never hearing the phrase before. Before answering, the old barkeep stepped away to pour a whiskey for a customer.

"What is a Black Yankee?" Cassius again asked.

"Black Yankees are free black men from up North who are paid to free slaves. They get sold to an unsuspecting slave owner so they can figure out the best way to help the slaves escape," the barkeep answered.

The big vein in Cassius forehead swelled. His face turned red as he realized he had one of those Black Yankees on his plantation. *I bet it is the slave I bought at the auction a few weeks back*, Cassius thought to himself.

He sat there for a few more drinks before riding Old Bob back to Talley's General Store. Cassius was suspicious his in-laws had something to do with the Black Yankee. Walking into the store, Jesse Talley again greeted him with a smile. "Hey Cassius, back again? What can I do for you?"

"What do you know about the flyer hanging in here a few weeks back with information about a slave auction?" Cassius asked while looking for guilt in Jesse's eyes.

"I saw that flyer and tore it down. Some people just think they can hang that stuff anywhere. You know we do not support slavery, but I believe the blacksmith across the way can tell you when the auction will happen," Jesse answered, still smiling.

"Ok, thanks Jesse," Cassius left the store. He could not tell if Jesse was telling the truth or not. He had never known if Jesse was really dumb or just acted dumb. Satisfied with the information he had gathered, Cassius headed back to the plantation. Cassius went up to his observation room to think about how he wanted to torture and kill this Black Yankee. He decided to wait until Saturday afternoon to settle up. Cassius went on with the week as usual, which surprised Dred and David Ray, making them both uneasy.

Returning from the field Saturday afternoon, Dred followed the slaves to the whipping poles as instructed. Once all the slaves were gathered, Boo grabbed David Ray from the crowd, shackling him to one of the whipping poles before ripping off his shirt. The crowd of slaves gasped at the layers upon layers of scar tissue across his body from past beatings. A cold sweat swept across Dred's body, not sure what was to become of his new friend.

Cassius stepped out, confronting the restrained Black Yankee. "Did you help my slaves escape?" Cassius grunted. David Ray stood proudly staring into Cassius's eyes with a smirk on his face, not answering the question. After a nod from Cassius, William let out his rebel yell as he took a step to punch David Ray in the side of his jaw. Shaking off the punch, David Ray spit out two teeth and some blood as he returned to his proud stance, looking back into Cassius's eyes. Turning to the slaves, Cassius explained, "This here is a Black Yankee sent down to cause problems on our plantation."

David Ray continued to stare into Cassius's eyes with his proud, bloody, arrogant smirk. With another nod, William sent another crushing blow, knocking out another tooth. Again, David Ray stood proudly, spitting the tooth and blood out of his mouth.

Cassius, suspicious someone in town was helping the Black Yankee, started to interrogate his prisoner. "Who sent you to my plantation?"

"God," replied the Black Yankee, still staring into Cassius's eyes. Another nod resulted with another punch to the jaw. Blood mixed with spit began oozing from his lips, running over his chin down his chest. David Ray continued to stand proudly.

"Who sent you to my plantation?" Cassius again demanded.

Looking out at Dred with excitement in his eyes, David Ray began his speech in the third person. In his deep, slow voice, David Ray pronounced every syllable in his northern accent.

"David Ray was sent to this evil plantation by our Lord, our God, the creator of the heavens and earth." With that answer, William began beating David Ray with the leather whip. "David Ray was sent by our one true God to release these humans from slavery." Ignoring the pain, only grunting with each blow of the whip, David Ray continued his speech between lashes. "As Moses led the Israelites out of Egypt, David Ray leads slaves off these evil plantations. David Ray stepped away from a life of comfort to sacrifice his body and his mind for the betterment of society for our black brothers held captive by the chains of slavery."

Cassius, becoming irritated by the foolish talk, yelled for William to stop after twenty painful lashes. Walking over to David Ray, Cassius shoved his five-inch dagger into the Black Yankee's left side, twisting the blade as he took it back out in hopes of silencing the man. Letting out a painful grunt, David Ray bit down, grinding his teeth, but still stood proudly with his shackles above his head fighting the excruciating pain from the dagger. Dred stood helpless, with eyes full of tears, as he watched his friend fight slavery from the pole.

Not ready to give up, the Black Yankee continued his speech. His slow deep voice began to break with every word, "This community of slaves must stand up with David Ray against these white devils holding us away from our freedom. We outnumber these evil men."

Having enough, Cassius signaled to William, who sliced David Ray's right Achilles tendon, interrupting David Ray in mid-sentence. The Black Yankee's body exploded with pain as he kicked and twisted, trying to escape the burning sensation running up the back of his leg. The Black Yankee yelled, followed by screams of agonizing pain. He hung there on the pole sobbing, unable to stop the pain. Cassius signaled again to William, who sliced the left Achilles tendon. David Ray, still sobbing, exploded in agony again as he kicked like a bronco being attacked by a panther, trying to escape the same pain all over again. He pulled both knees up to his chest trying to apply pressure to the sliced tendons.

William and Thaddeus both laughed at the slave flopping from the pain. The whole slave community stood in horror as they watched their fellow slave get tortured up on the pole. Cassius let the Black Yankee continue to hang while he spoke to the slave community.

"Who wants to be next? You? Or you?" Cassius pointed to random slaves, standing there watching. "Which one of you will be the next up here hanging from my pole?" Cassius asked. "Anyone of you caught escaping or helping slaves escape will find themselves up here on these poles." Again, Cassius's face turned deep red, "I will kill every last one of you before I let you escape my plantation!"

Cassius mumbled a command to William and Thaddeus before storming off. The boys released the Black Yankee before attaching his shackles to a chain. As commanded, Boo and two other drivers dragged David Ray to the bridge over Turkey Creek. Boo attached the chain to the center of the bridge before throwing the Black Yankee into the creek.

David Ray went under the water, not rising to the surface until Boo pulled the chain tight. The slow current caused his body to slant slightly down stream. The chain kept his arms extended toward the bridge, holding his shoulders just above the water. Exhausted from the events, David Ray hung from the bridge in silence as if he were sleeping. Boo began yelling for the slaves to move off, back to their community.

Dred watched David Ray from a distance, trying to decide how, or if, to rescue his broken friend. The rescue would be difficult with the drivers patrolling the community all night. Outside his shack, Dred paced back and forth, not coming up with a good plan. With no other options, Dred waited until a few hours before sun-up. He crept undetected to the creek, easing himself into the cold water. Quietly, he moved with only his face above water until he reached David Ray. Trying to remain unseen, Dred used a stick to poke his friend's side in order to wake him. To Dred's surprise, his body was stiff and lifeless. Dred returned from where he entered the creek, sad to have discovered his dead friend. He returned to his shack, warming up from his unsuccessful mission. Later in the morning, Dred and Glen the kitchen slave, along with most of the slave community, watched as Boo pulled the dead Black Yankee from Turkey Creek.

"What do we do now?" Glen asked.

"We go on as planned. They will be expecting us on May 5. David Ray gave his life for us to be free, so we will carry on as if he were still alive. When he was being tortured on that pole, he did not give up the fight, he did not break, he continued to fight for our freedom, so we will continue his fight," Dred insisted. "I know where the wagons will be on the old dirt road. I will lead us to the wagons. Keep everything quiet until the day we escape." The two slaves agreed as they both returned to their shacks. Dred spent the rest of the day dreaming about his freedom. Thursday night, May third, Dred had problems falling asleep. *Two more nights in the old shack before I am off to Canada, my first step of freedom.* Dred could not wait to share the plan with Arrah and the rest of his family. Keeping the secret was tough, but he knew it was for the best. He finally fell asleep with a big smile on his face.

***

MAY 4, 1862

Cassius sat sipping whiskey in his observatory room overlooking his plantation. He enjoyed watching the daily operations from above. Listening to the wonderful melodies sung by the slaves as they worked his fields, he thought about the Union forces battling up in Corinth. The war was forcing itself into his world. He had been successful keeping his family away, but the battles were getting much closer to his plantation than he liked. The thought of his boys and slaves leaving to fight aggravated him. Cassius was not as enthusiastic as his sons about the war. William and Thaddeus were talking non-stop about joining the Confederate Army. He had kept them away so far, but his boys wanted to take some of the loyal slaves and fight. Cassius was already mad over the other plantation owners coercing him into donating a chunk of money, not to mention already having 24 slaves escape. Now, they want soldiers? His sons? His slaves? How would he get the work done? Cassius's priority was money. *I already allow southern troops to take up camp on the outer parts of my land,* he thought to himself. *What else should I have to do?* Cassius was hoping to stay neutral in case the northern troops fought their way to his plantation. The thought of northern troops overtaking his land and freeing his slaves frightened Cassius. For once in his life, he felt things were out of his control. For the most part, all things on the plantation were working smoothly. The last thing he needed was the war to overtake his plantation.

Irritated and drunk, he strolled down the hill to the slave community. The housing area was empty except for a few community workers. He walked around, not looking for anything. Cassius gazed upon the young Tinah mending clothes on her porch. He slowly walked over to the porch, looking down at the young girl. Tinah looked up, surprised to see Cassius standing behind her. Before she could stand, Cassius grabbed her by the neck. He forced her into the shack. Cassius slammed her head against the table, busting her mouth open, spilling her blood onto the grimy table. Holding her down with one hand, he cut off her clothes with his knife, exposing her young body. Tinah softly cried as Cassius entered into her world, taking her twelve-year-old innocence away. Closing her eyes, she prayed to God for help.

It has been years since I have had a slave like this, Cassius thought as he finished. He shoved Tinah aside after he was done with her. Looking down at her, he arrogantly smiled before leaving the shack. Tinah continued to pray quietly as she lay soiled on the dirty floor. Dred and Banjoe, returning from the fields, spotted Cassius leaving their shack. Dred felt a knot form in his stomach as he ran toward the shack. Busting open the door, Dred found Tinah naked, weeping in the corner, curled up in a ball. Unfamiliar rage boiled in his blood from deep within, causing him to ignore the consequences of his fatherly action as he walked toward Cassius full of hate. Banjoe grabbed his father, trying to keep him from confronting Cassius.

Dred pushed Banjoe to the ground as he yelled for Cassius. "CASSIUS! CASSIUS!" Dred yelled for everyone to hear. The slave community all stopped to watch. Cassius fearlessly turned as Dred's fist shattered his nose. Cassius, sobering quickly, strained to keep his feet while fending off the rapid blows from the angry slave. Dred's mighty blows knocked Cassius to the ground. Not stopping, Dred continued his powerful blows to Cassius's face.

Banjoe stared in incredulity as his father unleashed his hatred on Cassius. He finally stepped in, trying to pull his father off as William tackled him to the ground. Thaddeus and Buckner wrestled Dred off Cassius. Cassius stumbled up, cussing as he ripped off his blood soaked shirt, throwing it at Dred, before falling back over a stump. Again, Cassius stood, "You will pay, boy!" Dred fought to break free, wanting to finish the beating Cassius deserved.

Dred yelled for everyone to hear, "Cassius forced himself on my baby girl. Cassius took her innocence away. You had your way with my Tinah."

Picking up a log, Cassius silenced Dred by hitting him across the face. Not wanting to be involved in the madness, Buckner left the uncomfortable scene to finish his work. Cassius instructed Boo to hogtie both slaves before attaching them to the buggy's hitch. Cassius kicked Dred in the face before ordering them up to the whipping poles.

William and Thaddeus drove the buggy, dragging Dred and Banjoe across the rough surface to the pole. The two boys yelled their rebel yell as they dragged the slaves behind the buggy, excited for what was to come. William kicked Dred in the stomach as he stepped down from the buggy. He tied Dred's neck, ankles, and hands behind the pole tightly. Thaddeus giggled as he ripped Banjoe's clothes off, exposing him to the watching community. He then tied a rope around one ankle, pulling it just enough to pull his left leg up in the air. Thaddeus kicked Banjoe repeatedly until Cassius arrived. Both boys enjoyed watching their father torture slaves.

Arrah, finished with her daily duties, walked up to find her husband and oldest son being tied up. An emotional terror penetrated her body as she collapsed. Dayhoe, Cy, and Tinah embraced their fearful mom. Tinah, looking shamefaced, started to weep as she curled up in Arrah's arms for needed comfort. Arrah gathered herself, and examining the situation, asked Dayhoe what was happening. Dayhoe, still terror-stricken, gave his account of seeing Cassius leaving the shack, then finding Tinah abused and soiled in their shack, crying on the floor. He went on to tell Arrah how Dred fought Cassius, explaining that Banjoe was trying to pull Dred off. Arrah took in the explanation while searching for a solution.

Cassius, still covered with blood and shirtless, stepped from the crowd, kicking Banjoes face as he turned to Dred. "Boy, ya 'bout done it! Now you and your boy are gonna pay."

"The fight had nothing to do with Banjoe, I was the one who attacked you," Dred begged. Cassius ignored Dred as he shoved a seven-foot long metal spike six inches up Banjoe's anus canal. Banjoe let out a piercing cry, pleading for him to stop as he was hoisted up the tree by one of his feet, dangling naked. The end of the spike was secured at an angle to the tree. Banjoe clenched down on the spike, struggling to keep it from moving further into his body. Cassius and his boys took turns punching Banjoe in his face as he fought to keep the spike from moving.

Dred, emotionally overwhelmed, screamed at Cassius as he watched the morbid horror, begging for his oldest son's life. "It was me, Cassius, it was my fight. It's me, Cassius, it was my fight. Please stop!" Dred yelled. Fighting his restraint unsuccessfully, Dred wore down, becoming exhausted from the emotional outburst. He turned to Dayhoe, and demanded that he take the family back to the shack and not return. Dayhoe did as he was told, forcefully removing his hysterical mom and siblings from the awful sight.

Banjoe, still fighting the cold, sharp spike, cried out to his dad for help. "Make it stop, dad, please make it stop." The weight of his body was pushing down on the spike. Dred struggled with the rope, still trying to free himself with no success. Dred looked at his oldest son hanging from the tree. Banjoe started to lose the fight with the spike as it inched painfully, slowly tearing his flesh as it forced its way into his intestines.

In their native tongue Dred calmly called out to Banjoe, "I love you, it is okay to let go. You have fought enough. Let go, son. We are proud, I love you!" Banjoe continued to fight gravity as his body slipped slowly down the life-taking spike, dark red blood seeped down the spike towards the tree holding it in place. The spike inched through the intestines, then into the liver, moving to life's end. Banjoe, exhausted, had stopped fighting and just stared into his dad eyes for comfort. Dred continued to say, "I love you Banjoe, I love you Banjoe." The spike punctured his lungs and blood bubbled from his lips.

Cassius, noticing Banjoe starting to fade, walked over behind the defeated Dred and lifted his sweaty head up by the hair. He un-emotionally sliced Dred's throat. Dred fought the pain of the razor sharp knife sliding across his neck, burning as it separated the tissue protecting his soul from the outside world. Cassius held Dred's head up for everyone to see as blood pumped onto the ground. Dred struggled to stand proudly, keeping his dying body from showing weakness. Air gargled from his throat as blood gushed down his chest. Cassius let go of Dred's lifeless body, walked over to Banjoe, and stabbed him in the heart, twisting the knife before pulling it out. Cassius turned to the horror-struck Boo, "Clean this mess up, boy."

"Ya, yes sir, boss," Boo answered. Boo jumped up yelling at the slaves to start cleaning. Weak from the fight, Cassius climbed up onto the buggy to sit down. William and Thaddeus joined him by the buggy.

Cassius rubbed his face, feeling the blood oozing from his torn skin. "That savage put a whooping on me," Cassius confessed. Not knowing what to say, the two boys just starred at the dead slaves being lowered and taken off. "Before the both of you head to the house, make sure these savages settle down. I do not need any trouble tonight. Find Buckner and convince him that I did not touch that girl," Cassius told his sons. The two boys headed off as instructed. Cassius drove the buggy up to the house.

***

THE CURSE

Arrah watched the ghastly horror from their shack as she wept for her dead son and husband. Once the crowd of horrified slaves cleared out, she asked for the two corpses to be washed in the creek then wrapped to protect them from the elements until the funeral. She carefully took a sample of blood from both while trying to control her tearful emotions in front of the few slaves still watching from a distance. She returned to the shack with the blood of her dead loved ones, fighting the desire to release all the emotional energy built up inside. Cy and Tinah lay sobbing in the bed as Dayhoe paced the shack, expressing his intent for revenge. He was now the man of the family, emotionally unstable and unsure.

Arrah, realizing her strength, took over the shack. She became strong for her scared children. She calmly grabbed Dayhoe. "You will do nothing, boy. You will only protect this family. I will pray. I will pray to our ancestors. I will use the magic my grandmother taught me to curse this place of hate, to punish these people." Arrah used a wet cloth to clean the semen and blood off Tinah. She sent Dayhoe to fetch Cassius's blood soaked shirt. The kids sat in the corner praying silently, fearful of what was to come. Arrah waited for the community to become silent. Picking up charcoals from the fire pit, Arrah drew the Seal of Solomon on the shack's floor, then lit the candles that were placed circling the seal. Arrah poured the blood of her son and husband onto the Seal of Solomon, then she took the cloth from cleaning Tinah and smeared Cassius's semen across the seal. Cassius's shirt was soaked in water before Arrah squeezed out the blood onto the Seal. Reaching in her nation sack, Arrah mixed graveyard dust, snake skin, black pepper, salt, sulfur, and coon feces. She sprinkled the mixture across the seal. Pouring rust water finished the potion.

Taking off her clothes, Arrah went down to her knees, chanting "WOO-WAY-AH WOO-WAY-AH WOO-WAY-AH" as she bounced on her knees, calling out to the spirits of her ancestors. "WOO-WAY-AH-WOO-WAY-AH   WOO-WAY-AH." With both hands, she smeared the mixture across the center of the Seal of Solomon, "WOO-WAY-AH. WOO-WAY-AH, WOO-WAY-AH, as their feet run to evil, and they hasten to shed innocent blood, their thoughts of iniquity, devastation, and destruction are in their highway," she quoted Isaiah 59:7 with emotional hatred. "WOO-WAY-AH WOO-WAY-AH WOO-WAY-AH. Lay waste this evil, Shankpana. Lay waste this evil, unleash Shankpana wrath upon this blood and this seed, curse this man and his all branches for this be rotten. WOO-WAY-AH, WOO-WAY-AH, WOO-WAY-AH, SHANK-PANA, SHANKPANA, SHANKPANA, he shall therefore tear down the house, its stones and its timber and all the plaster of the house and he shall take them outside the city to an unclean place," she quoted Leviticus 26:31. "WOO-WAY-AH, WOO-WAY-AH, WOO-WAY-AH, SHANKPANA, SHANKPANA, SHANKPA-NA, WOO-WAY-AH, WOO-WAY-AH, WOO-WAY-AH."

Arrah stood up grasping a blade, slicing her hand, then squeezing her dark, red blood on to the Seal of Solomon. Falling down to her stomach, she spread her blood with her body across the seal, covering her body with the mixture. Her body trembled as her eyes rolled back into her head. Her body continued to tremble before becoming still in silent prayer. The shack became humid as moisture formed on the wall with a musky stench.

Jumping to her feet, she yelled while stretching her arms up towards the heavens, "I COMMAND YOU SHANKPANA, I COMMAND YOU SHANKPANA WITH EVERY DROP OF MY BLOOD, UNLOOSE YOUR WRATH UPON THIS EVIL, UPON THIS LAND, UPON THIS FAMILY OF HATE!"

Thunder rolled off in the distance as dry lightning lit up the clear night sky. Their wooden shack shook from the vibration coming up from below the earth's surface. A gust of wind funneled across the slave community onto their porch, opening then slamming the shack door. The wind circled in the shack before blowing the candles out. A dead smell engulfed the room causing the children to gag with disgust. A black smoke bellowed out of the seal, then funneled up to the ceiling, out through a crack in the roof. Arrah went down to her knees to gather the bloody paste from the Seal of Solomon. She then crept naked, covered with the mixture, up to the plantation house, marking columns, windows, doors of every structure with the mixture. Across the front entrance she wrote *YOU BE HOODOO!*

***

THE CURSE BEGINS

Cassius was up earlier than normal. He had not slept well due to his face being swollen from the beating he took from Dred. Sitting in his observatory room taking in the cool morning air, he had a moment of guilt, then shook it off. *Those boys deserved what they got. I had to set an example for all the slaves. I can't have the savages attacking their master. I have to be tough to keep control*, he thought, trying to justify himself. Cassius did not like killing his slaves, especially the top producer. He was mad at himself for the financial loss of the two slaves. He sat in silence rethinking the previous day's events. Anxiety moved from his stomach into his chest as the observatory temperature dropped for a brief moment. An uneasiness filled the room, becoming uncomfortable. He shifted his weight from side to side as he continued his thoughts. A soft drum beat started, and could be heard off in the distance. Cassius stood looking out over the slave community. *Why are those savages beating a drum?* He thought to himself.

Hearing the house come alive, Cassius went downstairs to start the day. Morning was Cassius's favorite part of the day. Everyone was full of energy and happy. The grandkids were easier to tolerate. He did not much care for the grandkids after lunch. Cassius again had to explain to Tanyia why he was attacked, then why he had killed two slaves. He left out the rape, although Tanyia had her suspicions.

The pounding pain in his head subsided enough after breakfast for Cassius to begin his day. Heading to the stable, he instantly noticed the dried blood marked around the house. *Those damn savages with their crazy beliefs,* Cassius thought to himself. His first reaction was to beat whoever was responsible but decided not to, due to the events of the day before. From past experience, he knew the tension in the slave community needed to settle down. He instructed a house slave to clean up the mess. Cassius decided to pittle around the homestead instead of his regular routine. Reaching the barn, he instructed the barn slave to fetch his old saddle from storage. He worked on his old saddle, making long overdue repairs. A soft drum beat stopped his work. Walking out behind the barn, he looked off in the distance away from his plantation. *What could that be?* He thought. Curious, Cassius saddled up William's horse before heading in the direction of the drum beat. Making his way through thick buck brush, Cassius followed a game trail deep into the hardwoods. After a short ride, the drum beat rose up into the treetops before stopping. Cassius stepped off his horse to investigate. The wind kicked up, blowing the treetops back and forth. Over the hollow, a deep, loud growl echoed out, stopping Cassius. "What was that?" Cassius whispered to himself. Slowly walking back to the horse, Cassius removed his rifle musket from the saddle. The growl floated in the wind every few seconds, making Cassius uneasy. He slowly peeked over a log, not seeing the source. *Sounds like a bear* he thought to himself. Carefully, he crept down into the hollow. Standing still, he heard the loud, deep growl up above his head. In a panicked burst, he swung around ready to fire. Cassius stepped back surprised. The tree was empty. Looking up into the tree, the deep growl again rumbled. Cassius laughed as he realized a fallen tree was wedged between two trees, making a growling sound every time the wind blew, wedging it further down between the two trees.

Returning to the top of the hollow, Cassius was surprised to find the horse gone. *Damn horse* he thought as he began his hike back to the barn. The wind became more intense, moving leaves and dust in a circular motion. The little wind funnels popping up made the hike difficult. He followed the game trail out of the woods to an unfamiliar area. Confused, Cassius looked around, not seeing anything he recognized. He looked back into the woods, wondering if he had gotten turned around. Following the game trail back into the woods, he arrived back at the hollow where he started. The wind had calmed down, not hindering his walk. Back in the hollow, he looked around for the tree that made the growl. Not finding the tree, Cassius began to get irritated. He hiked up to the other side of the hollow, still not seeing anything familiar. He looked up for the sun but only saw grey clouds. The soft drum beat again started. Not sure where he was, Cassius decided to follow the drum beat again. He walked toward the drum beat while searching for something familiar. The air pockets kept changing from cold to warm to hot, not abnormal in deep hardwoods. The drum beat again seemed to rise into the treetops before stopping. Frustrated, he sat on a partly rotten log trying to regain his bearings. The wind calmed enough for him to hear water running in the distance. Walking towards the sound, he came across a small, spring-fed stream. Cassius began following it downstream, expecting it to flow into Turkey Creek.

Hearing a strange language, he stopped to listen. Slowly, Cassius eased over toward the voices. He hid in the thick buck brush watching his slaves preparing for a funeral. The slaves rubbed oil on the forehead of their dead as they began singing religious hymns in their native language. The two bodies were wrapped in white cloth with only their faces showing. Cassius knew they were the bodies of the two slaves he had killed the day before. He sat back, rethinking his disciplinary actions. "Cassius, Cassius," a faint, dead voice whispered. Startled, Cassius turned his attention back to the funeral. Again, he heard, "Cassius, Cassius." Focusing in on the dead slaves, he noticed

Dred's eyes open wide, with a deep, dead stare right into Cassius's startled eyes. A long slow blink caught him off guard, realizing the corpse was indeed starring at him. Suddenly, a burning, tingling sensation crept up from his anus into his spine before spreading throughout his frightened body as a cold sweat overtook him. Looking away, Cassius gasped, not believing his eyes, and tried to control his rapid breathing.

Arrah, sensing Cassius's presence, continued with the ceremony, not bringing attention to him. She knew the curse had begun due to his presence. In denial, Cassius looked back at the dead corpse.

In a slow motion state, the corpses called out, "Cassius, Cassius," with both sets of dead eyes blinking while starring at Cassius. Falling onto his back, Cassius scrambled behind an oak tree. Sitting against the tree, he tried to control his rapid breathing and understand what he just witnessed. He could feel his heartbeat throughout his body. Arrah and her family heard the commotion, but kept their attention on the funeral. Settling down, Cassius peeked back around the tree seeing both corpses' eyes were closed. Still in a state of psychological shock, he sat there focused on the murdered bodies until they both were laid to rest. He watched as the grieving family finished the ceremony, then as they lowered the bodies into the ground. Their sorrowful prayers were in their native tongue, keeping Cassius from understanding. He sat there quietly watching the event until it was over. He reflected back on what he had done, regretting for a moment his excessive disciplinary actions. He waited for the grieving family to leave before exiting the buck brush. Cassius followed the trail back to the slave community, then back up to the barn.

Arrah watched as Cassius walked through the community looking confused and frazzled. "Wait until the fun begins," she whispered to herself, staring at him with vindictive hatred. William and Thaddeus had saddled up their horses, getting ready to go out searching for Cassius when they spotted him walking up the hill. Not wanting to talk, Cassius stormed past his boys, ignoring their questions.

After dinner, Cassius made his way to the quiet library so he could think. He could not decide what he saw, or if he saw what he thought he saw. Dozing off into a deep sleep, he curled up on the lumpy sofa. Being shaken, Cassius opened his eyes and looked over to see who was shaking him awake. He was surprised to see a little slave boy shaking him.

"Cassius, Cassius, Cassius," the little slave boy said with joyous excitement until Cassius sat up. Groggy, Cassius rubbed his eyes, making sure he really saw the little slave boy.

"What?" Cassius barked.

"Come see, come see, Cassius," the slave boy tugged on Cassius's hand.

"Come see? What?" Cassius said, still in disbelief. Cassius found himself walking behind the little slave boy across his plantation, through the slave community to the lonely, cold graves of the two murdered slaves. The little slave boy stopped between the two graves, looking up and extending his arm to be picked up. "I am not picking you up," Cassius said rudely, shocked that the little slave boy wanted to be picked up. Cassius stared down, noticing a resemblance in the slave boy's dark face. "Who are you?" Cassius asked. "You look like someone I know." The little slave boy continued extending his arm without making a sound. "Who are you?" Cassius again asked. The little slave boy only held out his arms, not answering. Carefully, Cassius picked the little slave boy up under his arms, holding him out away from himself. Staring into the boy's blue eyes, Cassius realized the boy was a dark, brown-skinned five-year-old Cassius. In disbelief, he dropped the boy while stepping back. "It can't be," Cassius said quietly.

Laughing, the little slave boy ran off into the thick woods, disappearing beyond the tree line. Cassius followed until he lost sight of the boy. The boy's laughter echoed through the woods as Cassius stood scanning the impenetrable darkness. The moonless night made it hard to see more than a few feet. Walking back across the small cemetery to the fresh graves, Cassius stopped to squat down. He grabbed a handful of the cold, loose dirt, again thinking about the two slaves he murdered. An uneasy feeling caused the hair on his neck to stand as he looked over his shoulder into the woods for the little slave boy. "Ha ha, he he," followed by giggling echoed in the dark woods as the little slave boy ran around just out of his sight.

A foggy, cold breeze blew across the slave graveyard causing an icy shiver down his spline. "Cassius, Cassius," a voice whispered in front of him. Before he could turn his head toward the voice, an unseen force grabbed him by the shirt, pulling him down into the freshly dug grave. The dead, cold dirt engulfed Cassius. Struggling to free himself, Cassius choked on the dirt filling his mouth and nose. He violently fought as he descended deeper into the dark, freezing grave. Eyes wide open, looking for anything to grab, he continued to be pulled deeper down. A hard, sudden thud stopped his descent.

Opening his eyes, Cassius did not realize where he had landed. Laying on the floor, frozen in fear, he looked around full of panic trying to figure out where he was. Freezing cold, his body shook, trying to shake the cold by shivering uncontrollably. The fear of being pulled into the grave was not easy for Cassius to shake. Finally breaking the frozen state of fear, he realized he was laying on the floor in his library. *Boy, I really thought the dream was real*, he thought to himself. Still shaken, Cassius lay quietly on the floor looking at the ceiling, rethinking what he had dreamt. A house slave stopped in the room to investigate the thud from the library. Seeing Cassius on the floor, the house slave quickly rushed over to assist him off the floor.

"You okay sir?" the slave asked.

"Yes, get me up," Cassius answered. Getting Cassius to his feet, the slave noticed Cassius's temperature.

"Why you so cold, sir?" the house slave asked.

"Because I am cold," Cassius barked. The house slave left the room after being dismissed. Realizing it was still early into the evening, he made himself a drink to calm his nerves before heading to his observation room. Cassius had never experienced guilt from killing slaves before. He was sure guilt was the reason for the strange events and the dream.

THE LAST GROUP

After dark, Glen the kitchen slave had his family ready to depart for freedom. Glen had no idea where to meet the wagons, but knew how to get to the old dirt road. If they could not locate the wagons, Glen and his family could sneak back into their shack. Boo was on duty patrolling the community through the night. Glen watched Boo while counting the seconds that his family would have to make the tree line. As Boo turned the corner, Glen lead his family the fifty yards to the tree line and took cover in a dry, dark ditch before Boo reappeared. Boo marched his route, again turning the corner. Once Boo was out of sight, Glen and his family headed toward the old dirt road. Hearing shuffling from the woods behind him, Boo reversed his route to investigate. Coming back around the corner, Boo spotted Glen's family scurrying away from the slave community through the woods. Boo froze for a second in panic before shooting his rifle musket in the escaping slaves' direction, not hitting anyone.

Cassius, sitting in his observatory, stood after hearing the blast from down the hill. He looked out toward the commotion to see Boo running toward the plantation house yelling, still carrying his rifle musket. Realizing something was wrong, Cassius ran down the stairs yelling for his boys to join him outside.

Boo, out of breath, informed Cassius there were slaves escaping through the woods. "They running boss, they running away. I sh . . . sha . . . shot boss, I don', do not think I hit any," Boo said bouncing on his toes, looking for praise. Deep red anger came across Cassius's face as he looked out toward the woods. *I will kill every last one of them*, Cassius thought to himself. He yelled for William to saddle the horses. Cassius sent his three boys out on horseback with the dogs while Boo and the other drivers followed on foot.

The lead from the rifle musket was heard above Glen and his family's head, followed by the sound of the blast as they raced towards the old dirt road. The backup plan of returning to their shack was no longer an option. Praying as he ran, Glen knew Cassius and his boys would soon be hot on their trail. The reality of his family dying on the whipping poles caused a gut-wrenching feeling down in his stomach as he second-guessed his decision to escape.

Reaching the old dirt road, Glen, not knowing the exact spot to meet the wagons, decided to search the direction away from the plantation. The oddly still, cool night did not help the desperate situation. Down in the woods, voices yelling and barking could be heard from the search party as the family hurried down the old dirt road in search of the escape wagons. As the search party moved closer, Glen began urging his family to hurry. Rounding a turn on the old dirt road, Glen saw the two wagons pulling out from the meeting spot. Glen began yelling and waving his arms, praying to attract the driver's attention. The second wagon driver noticed the group of slaves, stopping for them to climb into the wagon. "We are in, we are all in," Glen yelled as the driver pulled away.

"Where are David Ray and the other slaves?" Nathen, the second driver, asked.

"Dead, they all are dead," Glen answered. Nathen shook his head with sadness as he drove the last group to their freedom.

***

THE CURSED FAMILY

Losing another six slaves caused Cassius to wake up in a foul mood. He stumbled down for breakfast, barking at anyone willing to speak to him. After a silent breakfast, he made his way to the barn to start the day. Unlike most plantation owners his age, Cassius was involved in the daily operations, controlling everything on the plantation. He did not trust anyone. He firmly believed the only person you can trust is yourself. Over time, Cassius had learned his boys were more likely to screw up than the slaves. The oldest two boys would torture and kill all the slaves if he let them. Without his control, the two were worthless. Cassius enjoyed patrolling the plantation barking orders on Old Bob, his faithful horse. His horse he could trust. Cassius only bought Appaloosa horses. He liked their colorful, spotted coat pattern and unique markings. Familiar with the route, Old Bob carried Cassius from field to field without a command. Cassius checked with the drivers, making sure each field was being worked correctly.

Riding up to the last field, Old Bob suddenly stopped, becoming nervous and not wanting to continue the route. The abnormal behavior caused Cassius to dismount to check Old Bob. Inspecting his hooves and legs, Cassius did not find anything that would cause discomfort to the horse. Cassius rubbed the side of Old Bob's head, gave him a few words of encouragement, then continued down the trail. Again uneasy, Old Bob stopped and neighed, backing up with his head down away from the woods. Cassius began scanning the area, curious to know what was agitating the horse. He noticed a shadow prowling just behind the tree line. He pulled out his rifle musket as he guided Old Bob toward the shadow. Old Bob refused to go, backing up, again neighing. Cassius tried encouraging Old Bob with no success. Cassius stepped down off the horse to investigate. He crept into the wooded area, squatting down and listening for movement. Not a sound. No squirrels moving or birds chirping. A lone crow squawk echoed up in the trees, breaking the silence. *Must be a panther,* Cassius thought as he returned to the trail, mounting Old Bob. Cassius kept catching glimpses of the shadow as he continued his patrol.

Having had enough, Cassius gathered up his boys and the drivers before he returned to the stable. The panther needed to be dealt with before livestock or slaves came up missing. The strategy was to push the panther with a line of slaves and dogs to the shooters. William and Thaddeus took the slaves and dogs to the other side of the sixty-five acre patch of hardwood. Cassius, Buckner, and the drivers waited thirty to forty yards apart. When the panther was flushed out of the woods, they would shoot. William and Thaddeus stayed back behind the line of slaves in case the panther attacked a slave or ran through the line to escape. As the line grew closer, Cassius spotted the shadow darting from tree to tree. Losing sight of the shadow, Cassius repositioned himself to the side of the wooded area. As the line started to exit the woods, Cassius saw the shadow easing up the side of an oak tree. Cassius raised his rifle musket to shoot. *Boom!!* Everyone stopped as the blast echoed through the wood. A loud whimper of excruciating agony was heard flopping around in the brush. A horrible sound, gasping for air, screeching an unfamiliar sound. Cassius cautiously approached the target finding no signs of the panther. Following the choking, air-gasping sound of death, Cassius found Thaddeus's body fighting for life. The slug struck the corner of his chin, destroying the mouth and back of his head. Cassius hit his knees as Thaddeus, big-eyed, looked up at his father for help as he fought from choking. Cassius held Thaddeus's body tight, knowing there was nothing that could be done. Thaddeus's quivering body jerked and kicked violently as dark blood spewed from his dismembered face, covering Cassius. Slowly, his entire body became still as his soul left. A hollow feeling rose from deep in Cassius's stomach, a tightening around his lungs then burning his throat as the silent scream left his mouth. The emotional burst stopped his breath as he fought to regain control. Cassius released the corpse to the cold ground as he stood, walking away with his head down in silence, not looking back as William reacted to his dead brother's corpse. William's screams of sorrow echoed through the woods as the rest of the group stood watching. Cassius began the silent march to inform his family.

For the second time in three days, Cassius arrived home blood-soaked with the stench of death. Irritated with her husband, Tanyia asked in her sour tone, "How many slaves did you kill today?" The dazed Cassius did not acknowledge the question.

"Where is Harriett?" Cassius asked his wife. Caught off guard, Tanyia questioned his concern about Harriett. Raising his voice,

Cassius demanded, "Answer the question, woman!" An uneasiness came over Tanyia as she directed Cassius out front where Harriett was sitting with Buckner's wife Sarah. Both women instantly sat up as the blood covered Cassius approached with Tanyia in tow. Stopping before the two women, Cassius turned his focus to Harriett.

"Uh, Thaddeus was, um, shot," Cassius said unemotionally, still in shock. "He was shot in the face, then he died," Cassius continued. Unheard, he went on to recount what had happened as Harriett and Tanyia began sobbing uncontrollably. Not knowing what to do, Cassius stood quietly, watching the two ladies deal with their uncontrollable emotions. After the initial burst of emotion ceased, Sarah escorted the ladies into the house, trying her best to console the two.

Cassius sat down on the concrete bench covering his expressionless face with blood-covered hands as he began to softly weep. A cool breeze blew, causing a slight chill. Unable to stand, he continued to sit there in painful silence, blocking out the world around him. Regaining control of his raw emotions, he retreated to his observatory to sip whiskey in an attempt to escape the emotional pain. He replayed the day's events, trying to make sense of the accident. "Cassius, Cassius," a faint voice called. Still sipping whiskey, Cassius sat up with his eyes opened wide. Looking around the observatory room he heard, "Cassius, Cassius," the faint voice again whispering. Spinning around and jumping out of his chair, Cassius stood in defense.

"Who is there?" Cassius demanded. The empty room stared back. Heart pumping fast, Cassius backed towards the door. A dark silhouette moved from the shadow, again whispering "Cassius, Cassius." Frozen in supernatural terror, Cassius stared intensely at the dark silhouette. Jerking right then left, the silhouette faded from view. Putting his hands on the top of the chair for balance, he took a deep breath and a moment to regain control of his senses. Cassius examined the observatory room, searching for a logical explanation and finding none. A soft drum beat started off in the distance. Cassius stared out over his plantation, only seeing a few fires in the slave community. Emotionally drained, Cassius dismissed the encounter as exhaustion, then headed for bed.

Before daybreak, Cassius woke to sounds of moans, groans, and fretful whimpers. Still spooked from the observatory encounter and a bit edgy, Cassius leaped from the warm bed to investigate. He cautiously moved through the halls toward the painful sounds. Spotting William's wife Lilly, Cassius inquired about the sickening sounds. Visually upset, Lilly explained that Joe Jack and Wilma were up most of the night sick. Tanyia and a house slave were seeing to them, due to her being with child. Both had fever, headache, throwing up, and jaundice. Joe Jack was bleeding around his mouth, eyes, and occasionally throwing up blood. They just started to see blood in Wilma's throw-up. Concerned, but not wanting anything to do with sick kids, Cassius told Lilly he would send for Doc Beshear and excused himself.

Once downstairs, Cassius instructed Buckner to ride to town and fetch the doctor. William was ordered to oversee Thaddeus's funeral preparations. Cassius did not care to spend much time dwelling in sorrow. "I want him in the ground this afternoon," Cassius ordered.

Feeling a sudden loss of breath, Cassius sat down on the old mossy stump outside the stable. He closed his eyes, bowing as if to pray, taking deep breaths, trying to control emotions he often ignored. Again, a soft drum beat could be heard off in the distance. A burst of energy rushed up his spine as he was lifted off the stump, landing on his chest some ten feet from where he sat. The stable slave ran over to assist. "Leave me be," Cassius yelled for the stable slave to stop. A burning sensation up his spine and across his shoulder lingered as Cassius lay on the ground confused. "What the hell threw me off the stump?" Cassius asked the stable slave who arrived to help.

"I thought you jumped from that stump, boss!" the stable slave nervously answered. Standing up, Cassius removed his shirt revealing deep, blood dotted scratches along his spine and shoulder down his arm. The stable slave examined his back. "There's a red hand print marked on your lower back, boss," the stable slave pointed out.

"Yes, sir dat's a hand print," the stable slave confirmed.

Feeling weak and still suffering from the burning sensation, Cassius got back down on the cold ground, laying on his back. The burning feeling still pulsated through his body lying there on the ground. He excused the stable slave while he stared at the blue sky, watching random clouds fly by. The few minutes of solitude allowed him to regain his strength. Standing, Cassius inspected the stump, not finding anything unusual. He headed to the horse stable so he and Old Bob could make the daily rounds. Taking a moment to speak with Old Bob, Cassius heard one of the house slave girls yelling, "Master Cassius! Master Cassius!" Irritated, Cassius stepped from the stable, barking loud at the house slave, "What do you want?"

"It is Master Joe Jack!" Cassius could see tears streaming down from the young house slave's face. She continued, "Master Joe Jack is dead."

"Dead?" Cassius asked.

"Yes sir, he dead."

Unable to speak, Cassius went back to mount Old Bob then rode out across the plantation. He needed to get away from the house. He was not much for showing emotion. Throughout the day, Cassius kept replaying the events leading up to Thaddeus's violent death and everything that followed. *What was the shadow? What threw me from the stump?* He stopped by the woods to look around, trying to figure out what he saw on the tree. Standing in the spot where he pulled the trigger, he stared at the oak tree. Nothing odd stood out. He walked down to the spot where Thaddeus was killed. Cassius squatted, then stood a couple of times, looking back to where he pulled the trigger. He realized there was no way the slug could make it through the thick, overgrown hardwoods to strike Thaddeus. Looking at his son's blood covering the forest floor, Cassius knelt down, rubbing his finger around a dried puddle of blood. He began fighting the tears that swelled around his eyes. "I am sorry son," he whispered. For a moment, he allowed emotions, making himself human. A creepy feeling of being watched overtook him. He took a long, hard stare into the woods, looking for anything out of place. Up on the hill, just inside the tree line, Cassius spotted a black panther trotting away from him. Anger rose up from within his stomach, seeing the cat that caused Thaddeus's death. *I will get you,* Cassius thought to himself. He watched the panther until it was out of sight. Content with his investigation, he headed back to the trail and mounted Old Bob.

Finishing his rounds, Cassius returned Old Bob to the stable. Preparing himself, Cassius slowly walked toward the pain-filled house. Cassius stopped, then backed up to focus to the top of one of the columns. A dark silhouette hovered against the column. Cassius again backed up, trying to make sense of the silhouette. Second guessing himself, he continued inside. Tanyia greeted Cassius with the news that Joe Jack and Wilma had both died. She went on telling him that Doc Beshear said he had never seen yellow fever move so quickly. What happened in hours usually took a couple of weeks.

Weary and drained, Tanyia began to cry. "How could this be happening? We have lost a son and two grandkids in two days. Doc said there is a good chance the yellow fever has spread. He said to keep everyone on the plantation and he will return in a couple of days for a follow up." Cassius gave her his handkerchief as he gently hugged her. "I can't take much more," she cried. Cassius held his wife while she released her sorrow.

After dinner, Cassius and Tanyia strolled down to Turkey Creek in silence. Taking a moment, they enjoyed their twins fishing the creek. "How do we protect our family?" Tanyia looked at Cassius for a solution. Not having an answer, Cassius just shook his head. The couple finished the moment before heading back to the house.

The following morning, Cassius woke to a quiet house. His face was still sore with some swelling, but it was nothing to worry about. *A well-deserved good night's sleep*, he thought. Although he dreaded the funeral for the three deceased, he felt pretty good.

While Cassius was eating breakfast alone, Buckner stumbled into the room, using the wall to hold himself up and having difficulty breathing. Dropping to his knees, Buckner explained the obvious, "I can't breathe." Cassius instructed a house slave to lay him down onto the ground. Tanyia, hearing the commotion, came to investigate. Buckner pointed to his ulcerous sores. Tanyia quickly examined him, finding oozing tumors on his neck and under his armpits. She questioned him about the sores. Struggling to breathe, Buckner explained he had just noticed the sores. He claimed a sharp pain shot through his head before the sores swelled and started to ooze. Sweat started to pour off his head as he continued struggling to breathe. Cassius had two house slaves help Buckner to his bedroom. Tanyia forced Buckner to drink water as Doc Beshear instructed. She wiped him down with a cold cloth, trying to ease his pain. Noticing more sores forming, Tanyia knew the disease was moving fast. She instructed a house slave to continue wiping him down with a wet cloth. Trying to kill the bacteria, Tanyia poured whiskey into his sores. Buckner screamed in pain from the alcohol burning his open sores like an intense fire. Tanyia apologized as she continued to treat the other sores with the whiskey. Buckner finally passed out from the excruciating pain.

Tanyia, leaving the room, sent a house slave to round up the family to the parlor. Cassius stepped into the quiet library to make himself a stiff drink while he waited for the family to be gathered. Sitting back and closing his eyes, he realized Thaddeus's death was just two days before, but seemed like weeks ago. They had not even put him in the ground.

"Cassius, Cassius, Cassius, Cassius," the voice whispers softly.

Cassius forcefully stood and looked around. "Show yourself," he demanded. The dark silhouette hovered in full view. Cassius stood confidently staring intensely. "What do you want?" Cassius yelled.

"Yoooouuuu Cassius, yoooouuuu!" The silhouette flashed across the room disappearing into the wall.

"Come get me! Come get me you son of a bitch!" Cassius yelled as Tanyia entered the library. "Who are you yelling at?" she asked.

"I do not . . . ah, nobody," he said lowering his head. Confused,

Tanyia summoned him to the parlor. With the family together, Tanyia informed everyone about the yellow fever and advised all to be aware of any signs of sickness. Doc Beshear would return in a couple of days. Until then, she wanted everyone to stay clear of each other. Buckner's wife Sarah brought to Tanyia's attention that Little Lorre had sores on her legs. Tanyia took a quick look at the lesions and small reddish spots. She decided it was not abnormal. Tanyia advised Sarah to keep checking on Little Lorre. Tanyia again told everyone to stay clear of each other, then she left to check on Buckner. His sores were oozing bloody puss and he had started throwing up blood. The house slave pointed out the blackness of his fingertips. Tanyia found it odd that his symptoms were different from Joe Jack and Wilma. The lethargic Buckner continued to struggle breathing and was soaked by his sweat. Staying calm, Tanyia left the room, taking a moment to gather her strength in the hall.

In the library, Cassius was feeling around the walls, looking for something to explain what he had heard and seen. Tanyia startled him as she entered the library. Not paying attention to Cassius feeling up the wall, she informed him that Buckner had gotten worse. Cassius took a moment to console Tanyia before he turned his attention back to the wall. Preoccupied with her family dying, Tanyia left the room. Cassius sat in the library on the sofa as he tried to figure out the shadow he kept seeing and the voice he kept hearing. Not being able to make sense of it, he fell asleep. Shivering, he awoke, finding the library cold. Cassius sat up looking around and gathering his senses. An awful aroma billowed up in a black fog. Anxiety raced through his veins as he stood and backed away. "Cassius, Cassius," a voice whispered as Cassius felt a push on his lower back. Panic joined the anxiety as he raced from the library, then out of the house. Away from the house, he looked back to see if anything followed. Taking deep a breath, he began to wonder if he was going mad. Finding a spot under an oak, Cassius sat lost in thought, not sure what he had encountered. He sat there undisturbed.

Keeping his experience quiet, Cassius attended the funerals, still unsure of what he had witnessed. Afterward, he walked with his family back to the house. Tanyia, curious to know if the yellow fever was attacking the slaves, demanded Cassius escort her to the slave community to inspect each slave. One by one, each slave stood for Tanyia to inspect. "They all look healthy," Tanyia shared with Cassius. Gathering a few of the older slave women, Tanyia explained what to look for and when to send for her. Satisfied, she was escorted back up the hill. Arrah watched as the couple walked up the hill. Her eyes still filled with vindictive hate, she whispered, "Your time is coming Cassius, your time is coming!"

***

SHAK

After dinner, Cassius retreated to his observatory room. On guard, he cautiously sipped his whiskey, waiting for the silhouette to appear. After a few hours, Cassius became irritated the silhouette had not shown. With the house asleep, he decided to check the library again and try to clarify the day's events. Approaching Clifton's room, he heard odd chatter. Cassius paused to listen. Clifton was speaking to someone about his uncle and cousins dying. Finding it strange not hearing a response to Clifton's question, Cassius entered his room expecting to encounter another adult. To Cassius's surprise, Clifton was alone.

Startling Clifton, Cassius asked, "Who are you talking too?"

"Shak," Clifton answered.

"Who is Shak?" Cassius asked.

Clifton explained, "Shak is my friend. He visits me sometimes at night. He tells me stories and answers my questions. Curious, Cassius asked what he looked like. Clifton described Shak as black, with a head full of blonde hair to his waist, long blonde hair around his neck to his waist, long blonde hair from his waist to his knees, and intertwined hair around his wrists and ankles.

"Where is he?" Cassius asked, looking around the room.

"Right there by the window," Clifton answered.

Not seeing anything, he turned back to Clifton. "Go to sleep," Cassius demanded as he stormed out of the room. Forcing himself into the library, Cassius again searched the walls and floors with an uneasiness. He needed answers to explain the madness but his search came up empty.

Not able to sleep, Cassius decided to walk outside. Followed by his dog Topaz, he walked down to the slave community carrying his whiskey bottle. Sitting on a stump just outside the community, he watched Boo patrol, looking for runaways. As Boo rounded the corner, Cassius called his name, startling the driver. Cassius laughed as Boo hurried over.

"Sit there on that stump," Cassius invited Boo.

"Yes, sir boss." Not sure what was happening, Boo sat nervously.

"How long have we been together?" Cassius asked.

"Ah, since we at Master Silas, Boss," Boo answered.

"That right, but I would say over 30 years," Cassius added.

"Yes, yes sir Boss, that, ah sound 'bout right," Boo agreed.

"Since you have always been loyal to me, I have decided let you be the boss over the drivers. You need to pick someone to replace your position as a driver." Boo's eyes opened wide with excitement once he realized what Cassius was saying. "The drivers will report to you. You will report to me," Cassius clarified. "I am also going to give you a horse to ride from field to field." Bouncing on the stump, Boo answered, "Yes, yes sir, boss!" Cassius took another drink of his whiskey. "Next week, we will build you a nice little house to overlook the community," Cassius decided. Happiness overcame Boo as his eyes filled up with tears. "Well, go on about your last night patrolling," Cassius said with a laugh. Boo walked off, whistling a happy tune.

Cassius continued sitting on the stump while watching over his plantation and thinking back over the years. Proud of his accomplishments, he began walking back up to the house. Looking up at the house, Cassius noticed the silhouette standing in his observation room. He hurried up the stairs to confront the nemesis. Arriving to the observation room, Cassius found it empty. Pouring another shot of whiskey, Cassius sat waiting for the silhouette to show itself.

Lying in bed the next morning, Cassius felt the swelling around his eyes had gone down, but his face was still slightly sore. Too much whiskey left his head pounding. He had laid awake most of the night thinking about the silhouette and wondering if he was going out of his mind. Never in his life had he had such encounters. Then he wondered if the silhouette was responsible for the death of Thaddeus, Joe Jack, and Wilma. Uncharacteristically, Cassius prayed for a better day before getting dressed. He eased from his room hopeful for a normal morning. Making his way into the kitchen, Cassius scarfed his breakfast down then quickly made his way out to the stable. A stable slave was leading Harriett's kids Billy and Martha around the pasture as Harriett watched Jouble play in the brown mud. Harriett normally did not watch her kids, but since Thaddeus passed away, she felt it was best to be around. The stable slave was busy with his grandkids, so Cassius saddled Old Bob himself and walked him out of the stable. Mounting his faithful horse, Cassius paused to enjoy his grandkids learning to ride.

Old Bob trotted across the green pasture headed for the fields as something caught Cassius's eye. From the wooded area, Cassius saw the dark silhouette streak toward his grandkids. Before Cassius could process and react, the Appaloosa carrying his grandkids reared up, causing the two kids to fall back as the horse began bucking uncontrollably. Harriett looked up from Jouble in time to see the back of Billy's neck snap from the force of the Appaloosa's kick. The dark silhouette paused briefly before turning toward Cassius. Charging Old Bob, the silhouette gained speed as Cassius tightened his grip for what was to come. Just as Old Bob began to buck, the silhouette disappeared. Cassius rode out the bucks until he was able to regain control.

Cassius turned toward Harriett, ordering her to take Jouble inside as he rode toward the scene to investigate. The horror was too much for the grandfather, discovering Martha's crushed skull halfway smushed into wet ground from the horse's hoof and Billy's spine bulged out of his broken neck. Cassius slid off Old Bob, grabbed his rifle musket, and aimed at the guilty horse. Before pulling the trigger, Cassius thought about the dried blood around the house, the *You Be Hoodoo* across the door, the shadow in the woods, the dark silhouette around the house, the voice speaking his name, the awful smelling fog, and Clifton's invisible friend Shak. Everything started to piece together and make sense. *A witch*, Cassius said to himself. *Must be a witch down in the slave community. A witch has cursed my family.* Cassius dropped his rifle musket to gather his dead grandkids. He took a moment to pray before instructing the stable slave to take the corpses to the stable.

Cassius rode to the house looking for Clifton. Tanyia met Cassius outside the house looking for information about Billy and Martha. Cassius ignored her questions, asking the whereabouts of Clifton. Tanyia stood her ground, demanding to know about her grandkids. Pushing her aside, Cassius went inside yelling Clifton's name. Avoiding Harriett, Cassius made his way upstairs to Clifton's room. Tanyia and Harriett followed Cassius, hysterically begging for information about the two kids. Not finding Clifton in his room, Cassius turned to the two women and blurted out, "They are both dead!" Not wanting to share the stomach-churning details, he asked again, "Where is Clifton?" The dreadful news knocked both women to the ground. Cassius asked again, "Where is Clifton?" Without looking up, Tanyia said, "Playing at Turkey Creek with Malley." Not having time to deal with the dead and their mourners, Cassius rushed out to Turkey Creek looking for the twins. He found the boys swimming in the creek. Cassius waded into the creek, snatching Clifton out while ordering Malley to the house. Propping Clifton on a half rotten stump, Cassius demanded to know more about Shak. "What is Shak?" Clifton, realizing his dad's intense anger, started to cry.

"Stop crying," Cassius insisted.

Obeying his father, Clifton regained control before explaining. "I have only talked to Shak a few times. Shak appears at night and talks with me," Clifton answered. He tried to assure his father that Shak was nice.

Cassius calmly explained, "Shak is evil and I want you to stay away from it." Cassius finished his interrogation and sent Clifton to the house. Cassius rode Old Bob out to the fields. Finding Boo, he quietly instructed Boo to find the witch.

Not wanting to get involved with a witch, Boo said, "I, ah, I do not know nothing about no witch, Boss." Cassius snatched Boo by the throat, pulling him face to face.

"You find the witch or spend your last days on that pole, do you understand me?"

"Ye... Yes sir, Boss," Boo answered, understanding the seriousness and not wanting anything to do with the whipping pole. Boo started his investigation the next morning when the slaves were off doing their daily work. Trying to stay unseen, Boo went from shack to shack to investigate. After searching all the shacks in the slave community, Boo reported his findings. He described the Seal of Solomon drawn on the floor in the shack that once housed the two dead slaves Dred and Banjoe. Cassius dismissed Boo as he headed to the observatory to think. Sipping his whiskey, Cassius, for the first time in his life, thought about curses, witches, and ghosts. He had read stories in his youth about ghosts and witches, but never gave them much credibility. Not knowing anything about curses or witches, Cassius knew he would need help.

***

THE WITCH

The next morning, Cassius rode to town in hope of finding someone to help with getting rid of the witch. Not sure who to ask,

Cassius stopped in at the local brothel. He was greeted by Madam Emily Maples, a tall, pale woman with her hair pulled up away from her face. She wore a low-cut dress showing off the two black moles on her left breast and her ample cleavage.

"What can I do for you Cassius?" She asked in her little girl voice as she squirted her perfume into the air to walk through. Madam Emily walked around Cassius as she rubbed her hand across his chest and down to his hip.

"I am not here for fun," Cassius pushed her hand away rudely. "I need to know who around town can get rid of a witch."

"A witch?" She asked for clarification.

"Yes, we have a witch in our slave community," Cassius said politely, not wanting to make the Madam mad. The bell above the entrance rang as a customer looking for services entered the brothel. "Have a seat in the parlor. Someone will be right with you," Madam Emily Maples directed the customer.

Turning her attention back to Cassius, the Madam said, "Well, go behind my building, follow the stairs down to the door, and ask for Courtney Mariea. She reads some sort of cards that might help you." Thanking the Madam, Cassius left the brothel and made his way around back to the green stairs.

A little sign on the wall said "Tarot Reader." Knocking on the freshly painted green door, Cassius asked the lady to see Courtney Mariea. The lady escorted Cassius to a room to be seated at the table. A polished grand piano sat up against the wall with two oak rocking chairs to one side and a clean brass spittoon to the other. A small pink Venetian chandelier holding four lit candles hung just above the black painted oak table. The purple and black walls were covered with white lines and circles representing planets and stars. Cassius sat silently, waiting to be seen.

A few moments later a short, round, bald-headed woman entered the room dressed in an orange robe trimmed in green. As Cassius tried to speak, she held her hand up for him to be quiet. Courtney Mariea sat down and dealt out three stacks of cards before flipping over the top card from each stack. She revealed the judgement card, the hanged man card, and the death card. After she looked over the cards, she looked into Cassius's eyes. "Souls will leave you to be cleansed in the heavens. You must follow the painful path of your future. The end to your way of life is near. Have I answered your question?" she asked softly.

Confused and irritated Cassius growled "No! I just want to know how to get rid of a witch." "What? A witch?" Courtney Mariea asked.

"Yes, I have a witch in my slave community that has cast a curse on my family," Cassius grunted.

"No, I know nothing about witches, I read cards to predict your future," Courtney Mariea said with a sour attitude.

Pushing back from the table, Cassius stood to leave and threw a gold coin down on the table, mumbling "worthless woman" on his way out. Frustrated, he stormed back up the stairs and headed for Old Bob.

Not having any luck around town, he stopped in to ask the old barkeep. The early afternoon crowd sat without the music from the piano in the mostly empty, clean bar. After a short conversation about the witch, the barkeep told Cassius about an old native Indian conjurer just west of Clarksdale, Mississippi. The old barkeep had a cousin who lived in Clarksdale that could take him to see the conjurer for a price. Agreeing to the old barkeep's deal, Cassius was given a sealed envelope with the name Donald Browlski and an address. Cassius returned to his plantation to pick up supplies for the five-day trip. With Thaddeus dead and Buckner sick, Cassius decided to take Boo to lead the pack horse, leaving William to oversee the plantation operations.

After the day and a half journey, Cassius and Boo arrived in Clarksdale. They found the address on the envelope just inside the town limits. The old stone house was surrounded with a dirty white picket fence connected to a big front porch with a swing. Cassius left Boo to tend the horses as he walked up, knocking on the front door. An older guy looking to be in his late sixties, clean cut and freshly shaven, opened the door in dress pants and suspenders.

"Are you Donald Browlski?" Cassius asked.

"Yes! Yes, I am," replied the man.

Cassius handed him the sealed envelope from the old barkeep. After a couple of chuckles about the letter, Donald invited Cassius into his house. The two men sat down as Donald motioned to his house servant for some drinks.

"So, my cousin says you have yourself a witch problem?" Donald asked, still holding the letter. "Yes, one of my slaves cast an evil curse on my family after I killed her husband and son. The curse has killed one son, another son is dying, and four grandkids have died," Cassius tried not to seem irritated.

"Well, that only seems fair. Eye for an eye is what the good book teaches us," Donald laughed, being sarcastic. Cassius just grinned with no response. "Well, my cousin says you are not much of a talker, so I will just get down to business. The old Indian woman will want a couple of gold coins, and I will need a few for myself. The letter mentions you have already paid my cousin a couple of gold coins also?"

"That is right, I can give you a couple now and the rest when we return to town," Cassius said, still trying not to act irritated. With a handshake, Donald gathered the supplies needed for the overnight stay. The two men went outside to begin their trip to see the old Indian woman. They rode side by side through town, with Boo following with the pack horse. Donald, a friendly, talkative man, carried on a one-sided conversation as Cassius just grunted, trying to be polite. Heading northwest of town, the three traveled four hours before arriving at the Mississippi River just before dark.

***

THE OLD INDIAN WOMAN

The old Indian woman lived on an overgrown, wooded, twelve-acre island on the edge of the Mississippi River before a big bend.

"Just across the wooden bridge is a trail leading up to the Indian woman's shack," Donald pointed out. "I will sit here with your boy while he sets up camp for the night." Cassius nodded his approval as he turned Old Bob towards the bridge.

"Hey, one more thing before you go. The old Indian woman is old. I mean, she was old when I was a boy. Do not act surprise when she opens the door. Her name is Nekki," Donald finished. Cassius nodded again as he rode across the narrow wooden bridge. He slowly rode Old Bob down the dark dirt road. The thick, overgrown trees and brush made the night darker. A feeling of being watched caused Cassius to stay alert, looking for trouble. He could hear something shadowing him just inside the woods. Every time he stopped Old Bob to listen, whatever was shadowing him would also stop. Cassius pulled his revolver, expecting a panther to pounce on him at any moment. Finally, up the trail in the distance, he faintly saw light flickering from a fire. He carefully followed the rutted dirt road until he arrived at the shabby shack. The old shack was up on stilts to protect it from river floods, and it looked to be falling apart. Light from inside the shack flickered through the cracks and holes up and down the outside. A rotting wooden ramp, covered with vines that held it together, showed the way to the door. Cassius carefully walked up the ramp as it let out a creak with each step. Unfamiliar animal sounds could be heard up in the treetops, jumping from tree to tree, making a fuss about the intruder. The smell of freshly turned up delta mud made his stomach turn with disgust. Mosquitos buzzed around his head looking for a fresh meal. The Mississippi River's mighty current could be heard rushing water and debris down river. From just beyond the trees, he could feel a pull from the old muddy river daring him to jump in for a swim.

He firmly knocked on the splintered door as he looked down at the decaying porch, praying it would hold his weight. After a few moments, Cassius heard slow footsteps moving closer. The old splintered door slowly squeaked opened to reveal the old Indian woman. With her shrill voice, she said, "Come in Cassius, I have been expecting you," Nekki caught Cassius off guard. "Please remove your muddy boots before entering," she requested. The five-foot tall woman was dressed in an old white robe, with a matching scarf covering her oily white hair. Her face was sunken in, covered with wrinkled, leathery skin. She had one green eye and one solid black eye that did not move, it just stared forward without blinking. Nekki placed a pinch of tobacco snuff into her mouth as Cassius stepped into her shack. Trying not to show his discomfort, Cassius nodded as he politely said "Ma'am" and removed his hat. The front room of the shack was filled with stacks and boxes of old newspapers, covered with dust and spider webs. Cassius could not tell if there was any furniture behind the stacks of newspapers. A Sticking Tommy miner's candle was shoved into the wall for light in the small room. The smell of dead fish filled the shack, making it hard for Cassius to breathe. Nekki's overly long toenails made a tapping noise on the floor as she walked. Cassius followed Nekki through the clutter into a small kitchen with a cutting table full of old fish heads next to a wood burning stove. There was a grimy oak table in the center with four chairs and two lit candles for light. Nekki motioned for Cassius to sit while she dipped a steel ladle into the iron pot boiling on the wood burning stove, and poured the liquid around the top of the table. She coughed up a mouthful of mucus, spitting it into a rusty bucket before sitting across from Cassius. The cracks in the walls let bugs fly back and forth at will and the breeze from the muddy river cooled the room. Cassius witnessed two large rats fighting over a fish head down the short hallway toward the back room. His fear of rats made him more uncomfortable. The back room had a 13-inch tall red crowned parrot sitting on a stand also watching the two rats fight over the fish head. The parrot squawked random words every few minutes.

"How did you know I was coming to see you?" Cassius asked, still amazed.

"I saw you in my dream last night. You have a witch killing your family and you need my help," Nekki again surprised Cassius.

Staring at her old face, Cassius bluntly asked Nekki, "How old are you?"

Her long yellow and brown teeth protruded from her mouth when she talked. "Well, I stopped counting over twenty years ago when I turned ninety-nine."

Shaking his head in disbelief, Cassius went on with his business. He dropped two gold coins onto the table as he asked how to get rid of the witch. Removing the gold coins from the table, her robe turned from white to yellow as she smiled.

"Why did your robe just change color?" Cassius asked, not believing his eyes.

"Oh, it changes with my mood," Nekki shared like it was a normal occurrence. "Why did this witch curse your family?" she asked.

Not telling the complete story, Cassius just mentioned he killed her husband and son for attacking him. "I can't let my slaves get away with attacking me."

Not believing his story, Nekki went on to inform him the witch will have to be convinced to reverse the curse. "You will have to ask it to reverse the curse or torture it to do so. For another two coins I can tell you how." Not in a position to argue the fees, Cassius dropped another two coins onto the table.

After picking up the two coins, she began chanting a native Indian ritual song under her breath. A sharp pain from Cassius's left Achilles tendon caused him to jump out of his chair, yelling in pain as he ran to the other side of the kitchen behind Nekki for protection. "What the hell was that?" Cassius yelled with anger, looking for what bit him.

Nekki laughed as she picked up her pet parrot. "That's just old Willie, he just wanted to taste you!" Nekki laughed. She picked up the parrot. The beautiful bird was green with a bright red forehead. Willie laughed as he fluttered his wing, saying "Willie don't like" over and over. Nekki returned the bird to its perch and attached a string to its leg. "He is tied to his perch," Nekki assured Cassius he was out of danger. Cassius returned to his chair, rubbing the sore

Achilles tendon. After Cassius had calmed down, Nekki continued the native Indian song under her breath. Her robe turned blue as she reached across the table and grabbed his hands. She poked her pinky nails into each of his palms, causing Cassius's blood to drip out onto the table. With a wipe of her frail thumbs the poke holes disappeared.

She took a deep breath before she slipped off into a spiritual trance with her good eye closed and the black eye still looking forward. Her little body began shaking as she struggled to hold onto Cassius's rough hands. Nekki's black eye began glowing white from its core as her robe turned black. She began to moan and groan while watching the torture Cassius had inflicted on his slaves, followed by the rape of all the past slaves and the young Tinah, then the murder of Dred and Banjoe. Nekki watched as Arrah cast the revengeful spell, and as Shankpana rose up through the Seal of Solomon. Nekki's one good eye opened, looking directly into Cassius eyes. Without saying a word, she realized the seriousness of Cassius's situation.

Not sure what to do, Cassius sat silent staring back at her, trying not to look at the glowing black eye. Time seemed to stop while he waited for her to say something. The only noise came from the river behind the shack and the rushing sediment.

Nekki broke the silence when she let out a loud screech, causing Cassius to fall back out of his chair onto the floor. He held both ears, trying to protect them from the piercing screech. The rats vacated the shack as the parrot squawked, still tied to its perch. The loud screech from Nekki was heard by Donald and Boo sitting out by the campfire. The ground trembled as the two men stood, expecting someone or something to run across the bridge. Boo started to run toward the bridge to find Cassius but Donald called him back. "Cassius has to get the answer he is looking for by himself."

The loud screech ended when Nekki's dead body hit the wooden floor. Cassius stood up, dusting himself off before walking over to check on Nekki. *The old Indian is dead*, he thought as he reached down to take back his coins. The nasty smell of her bowels releasing caused him to step back, leaving the coins. Cassius covered his nose and mouth as he headed for the exit, trying not to throw up. A few moments after Cassius left the shack, Nekki opened her good eye and listened before getting up. She cleaned herself up before peeking out the dingy window, checking to make sure Cassius was gone. *What a nasty curse that boy is up against. I am sure not getting involved with that barbaric angel,* she thought to herself as she counted her gold coins. She walked into her bedroom to hide the coins in an old mason jar and gave Willie a cracker. She sat on her bed wondering if she needed protection after seeing the angel. That angel looked right into my eye. "I better protect myself to be safe," she told Willie.

Cassius, a little confused, followed the overgrown trail back to camp. His ears were still ringing from the loud screech. Donald and Boo stood up when they saw Cassius ride across the rickety bridge. "What happened over there?" Donald asked when Cassius was in range.

Getting off Old Bob, Cassius still looked dazed and confused. "She went into a trance then stood up, letting out a loud screech. Then she dropped dead," he explained.

"We ah, we heard the loud screech Boss. I was ah, coming to help but um, Mr. Donald stops me," Boo shared while bouncing on his toes.

"That was a loud screech. We also felt the ground tremble," Donald added.

"I am not sure what happened in there. She did say I needed to get the witch to reverse the curse. By torture if needed," Cassius shared.

"You good at torture, Boss," Boo happily pointed out.

"She died?" Donald asked in disbelief.

"Yep, right there in front of me. An awful smell came out of her," Cassius added.

Cassius allowed Boo to join in with the whiskey as they sat by the fire listening to the Mississippi river play its mighty tune. After finishing the bottle, the three men passed out.

Nekki waited in the shadows until they were peacefully in deep sleep. She eased up to their camp and carefully took a hair sample from Cassius. Returning to her shack, Nekki retrieved her sacred bag to begin the mixture while chanting a prayer. She wanted to remove herself from any connection with the curse that Cassius was fighting. Nekki poured a bag of fish eyes into her spell kettle along with snake skin, river water, squirrel tongue, and various roots and spices. After the concoction was complete, she returned to the camp site to pour a circle around Cassius.

About an hour later, Cassius woke up gagging from the dead fish smell surrounding him. His stomach rolled back and forth as nasty, thick saliva filled his mouth. The pain from down deep in his bowels began as he lay propped up on his saddle bag. A cold clamminess overtook his body as his stomach muscles began to cramp, followed by severe ache. Cassius violently vomited pink slime filled with what looked to be fish eyes three times, waking up the other two men. After vomiting, the symptoms quickly went away. As Cassius went over to the water to clean up, the other two men began moving the camp over away from the foul mess before they laid back down to finish their sleep. Nekki lay in bed confident she was safe from the curse. The three men woke up early the next morning and headed back to Clarksdale. Cassius paid Donald the rest of the payment before heading back to Skuna Valley.

***

REVERSE THE CURSE

Cassius sent Boo to fetch William to the stable. He went over the whole plan with William and Boo. Once the slaves returned from their workday, Boo found Dayhoe and Cy. As ordered by Cassius, he shackled both and escorted them to the whipping poles. William hung the shackled hands of the scared slaves from the overhead hooks, then pulled each up onto their toes before securing the rope.

William began punching each slave in the ribs to remove their fight. As the slaves gathered to watch, Boo spotted Tinah. He grabbed Tinah from the crowd, hiding her from sight as Cassius instructed.

Like a few days earlier, Arrah walked down the hill to the slave community, having finished her house duties, to find her family being prepared for punishment. Panicking, Arrah ran to the whipping poles. Cassius spotted Arrah moving across the crowd. He grabbed her by the hair, pulling her to the pole where he had killed Dred. Boo secured her neck, hands, and feet to the pole.

Looking at Arrah, Cassius asked, "Did you curse my family?" Not answering, she stared at the ground. He punched her in the face before asking again, "Did you curse my family?"

Spitting blood from her busted mouth, she answered "No!" Arrah stared forward, away from Cassius's eyes. Cassius nodded for William to start the whipping of both boys. Tears filled Arrah's eyes as she watched the rough leather slice her sons' backs. The two boys tried to stand proudly and fight the pain like their father. After 10 painful lashes each, Cassius stopped William and motioned for Boo to turn the boys facing the front. Both boys tried not to cry as blood dripped from their torn backs. Cassius asked again, "Did you curse my family?" Tears ran down Arrah's swollen face as she stared forward, ignoring Cassius's question. Again, she was asked the question, "Did you curse my family?"

"No!" she softly said.

Cassius nodded for William to begin whipping the slaves' front side, tearing the skin on the face and chest. The two boys screamed from the extreme pain the leather caused as it sliced their skin.

In desperation, Arrah screamed, "YES! Yes, Yes, I cursed your family! I cursed your family! You killed my husband and my son. You took my daughter's innocence away. Yes, I cursed you and your evil family!"

Turning his attention to Dayhoe, Cassius took out his knife, shoving all nine inches down into his thigh and pulling it back out. Dayhoe screamed in horror, eyes big, shaking with dreadful fear.

Pushing Dayhoe's head to the pole, Cassius starred into Dayhoe's panicked eyes.

"Say hi to your dad," Cassius said as he slammed his knife through the left ear into Dayhoe's skull. His eye bulged out as his body flopped around on the pole before going limp.

Arrah screamed with horror as she struggled to get free. Realizing Cy was next, she pleaded with Cassius to stop. "Stop Cassius, please do not kill my last son!"

Leaving the knife in Dayhoe's head, Cassius walked over to Arrah, again punching her in the face. "Stop the damn curse," he growled. Tears ran down her face as blood oozed from her mouth. "I can't," she mumbled.

"Make it stop" he yelled again. Walking back over to Dayhoe, Cassius removed his knife from the ear, wiped the blood on Dayhoe's clothes, and turned his attention to the terrified Cy.

"I will do anything. I will do anything," Arrah cried.

Walking slowly to Cy, Cassius raised his knife, deeply slicing the skin across Cy's chin and exposing the bone. Standing bravely, Cy was still, trying to fight the pain. Cassius could see the overwhelming fear in the young boy's eyes.

"I will do anything," Arrah continued to cry.

"Make it stop, witch," Cassius yelled at the begging Arrah.

Shaking her head, Arrah whispered, "No, I can't."

"What did you say, witch?" Cassius yelled.

"I can't stop the curse. What is done, is done!" she yelled.

Stabbing Cy in the upper left shoulder down toward his chest, Cassius demanded again, "Make it stop." Cy yelled in excruciating agony as Arrah continued to shake her head saying, "I can't." Cassius shoved his forearm into Cy's face as he removed his knife from the shoulder. "Make it stop," Cassius yelled again.

Arrah cried "I can't. What is done is done."

Cassius swung around, stabbing Cy mid chest, just below the throat, pinning him against the pole. Cy let out a silent scream as he looked at his mom in disbelief. Helplessly, Arrah watched her final son's body go limp. Again, Cassius removed his knife and wiped the blood onto the slave's clothes. Cassius, picking up the seven-foot spike, began walking around the whipping poles holding Arrah's two dead sons. Arrah, no longer caring for her own life, began to pray. She was expecting the spike that ended Banjoe's life. Cassius calmly walked around with the spike in his hands. "What can I do next to get you to stop the curse?" he said loudly. "Bring her to me, Boo," Cassius yelled.

Arrah heard the cry from her baby girl Tinah. She watched again in horror as William tore off Tinah's clothes, exposing her young body before pushing her to the rock covered ground. Boo tied the rope around her ankle as William hoisted her up the oak tree. Cassius again commanded Arrah, "Make the curse stop." Arrah started to shake her head no when a deep, venomous hate filled her desperate soul, causing a total collapse of human emotions as she responded, "Okay."

"What did you say, witch?" Cassius asked for clarification.

"Okay, I will stop the curse," Arrah answered with a vengeful smile.

Cassius instructed Boo to release Arrah but leave Tinah hanging from the tree. Arrah walked with William and Boo down to her shack as Cassius waited to see if he would use the spike on young Tinah.

Arrah grabbed a bamboo stick from outside the shack before going inside. William and Boo watched as she took her nation sack and sprinkled spices and graveyard dirt around the Seal of Solomon. Arrah slit her hand, squeezing blood onto the seal. She took off her clothes before going down to her knees. She snapped the cane pole in half, using both sides to stir her dark red blood into the mixture. Arrah started a mumbled chant, swaying back and forth and collapsing in the center of the seal. Lightning struck a tree across Turkey Creek as the wind kicked up dust. A shower of large hail began pounding the plantation causing the slave community to run for cover. Arrah slid her naked body across the seal covering herself in the bloody mud. She stood up holding a half of the bloody cane in each hand. She began dancing counterclockwise around the seal chanting, "Uba uba uba yah yah, uba uba uba yah yah!" Thunder rumbled from across the plantation causing Cassius to look up confused. There were no storm clouds. A devilish smile came across Arrah's bloody face as she swung around, shoving a cane pole into William's throat and the other into Boo's forehead. William grabbed his throat as he dropped to his knees. Gasping for air, William fell forward, shoving the cane pole through the back of his neck. Boo fell dead backwards out the door and onto the porch with the cane pole sticking out of his forehead.

Surprised, Cassius grabbed his musket rifle before running over to the witch's shack. Stepping over Boo, he gasped, finding William's blood covering the wooden floor as he gargled his last breath. Cassius raised his rifle musket to Arrah, who was still dancing naked around the seal. Another rumble of thunder shook the shack. Cassius noticed Arrah's hair turning yellow and her eyes bulging dark blue. She stared into his eyes, beginning to speak with a deep African growl, "Uba uba uba yah yah, uba uba uba yah yah! Die Cassius Die!"

"Shak," Cassius said, pulling the trigger. Arrah's body flew back from the impact, although the bulging, dark blue eyes stayed, becoming the dark silhouette chanting, "Uba uba uba yah yah, uba uba ub, yah yah," as Shak revealed itself! Standing still in a trance, Cassius locked eyes with the dark silhouette trying to understand its dark soul. "Shak," Cassius said out loud again, finally standing face to face with the demon terrorizing his plantation. "Uba uba uba yah yah, uba uba uba yah yah," Shak chanted until it disappeared.

A swarm of mosquitoes filled the shack as Cassius kneeled down to check on William, making sure there was nothing he could do to help him. Fearing for his family, Cassius raced to the plantation house.

***

END OF HER ROPE

Tanyia sat on the porch as she watched Cassius scurry up the hill toward the house. Deep in her gut, she knew he was not hurrying to share good news. Cassius spotted her as he was approaching the porch. "What is wrong?" she asked with a sour tone. Noticing her red eyes and puffy cheeks, Cassius could tell she was at the end of her rope. Sitting down in the wooden rocker across from her, Cassius stared at the porch floor not knowing how to start. "Just say what you need to say. I am not sitting here any longer waiting for your bad news."

Startled, Cassius looked up. Trying to be sympathetic, he said "William is dead."

Tanyia looked away, holding back tears. Emotionally irritated, she asked, "How?"

"The witch has killed him," Cassius replied.

"The witch? When did we get a witch, Cassius?" she asked, raising her voice.

Leaving out raping Tinah, Cassius told her about the past few days of hearing voices calling his name, the dark silhouette in the house, the shadow in the woods, and Clifton talking to Shak. He went on to tell her how Arrah was the witch who cursed the family.

Full of rage, Tanyia asked, "Why Cassius? Why would this witch want to curse our family?" Shaking his head, he lied, "I do not know." Suspicious that Cassius was not being truthful, Tanyia asked if it had anything to do with the two slaves he killed earlier in the week. Shaking his head, Cassius said, "Maybe."

The two sat in silence as they absorbed the other's mood. A sudden burst of anger broke the silence as Tanyia jumped up out of her chair, slapping, kicking, and punching Cassius. Not defending himself, Cassius sat with head down and absorbed the blows. Exhausted and out of breath, she sat back down. After catching her breath, she asked, "These slaves you killed, why did they attack you?" Lying, Cassius said he did not know. "You do not know?" Tanyia jumped up, again slapping, kicking, and punching him. "You lie Cassius, you lie," Tanyia yelled. She sat back down again in silence. Looking for his reaction, Tanyia asked about Tinah, "Is this the family of the girl you forced yourself on?" Cassius's head snapped up, not expecting the blunt question. "That is right Cassius, I know, like I have known for years about you laying with strange women. I have known for years about your mid-afternoon trips down to the slave community."

Before Cassius could defend himself, a house slave ran onto the porch. "It is Master Buckner! Master Buckner not have much longer." Tanyia raced up to his bedside. Cassius followed, but stayed back at the door. Buckner struggled to breathe. His hands and feet had turned solid black and hardened. Tanyia affectionately sat by his side, gently rubbing his head. He was not looking good, but he was still alive. "Doc Beshear will be here in the morning," she whispered to her sick son. Afraid of catching his deadly disease, Cassius stayed back until enough time passed for him to excuse himself. He found Clifton to again go over the danger of Shak. "If you see him, come get me," Cassius ordered.

***

CASSIUS MEETS SHAK

Grabbing a fresh bottle of whiskey, the defeated Cassius made his way to the observatory room. After the whiskey began working, Cassius stood to look out over his cursed plantation. His deep thoughts were interrupted when he felt the powerful presence of Shak.

Not turning, Cassius spoke. "Why not just kill me and be done? Why must you kill my family? I deserve what I have coming. I know my final breath will be horrible but why, why must the devil punish my family?"

Not expecting a response, Cassius heard, "Devil? Shak no devil. Shak follow God's plan," Shankpana corrected Cassius in its African accent. "Cassius is the devil. Everything Cassius do is evil. God send

Shak to destroy the devil. Rid this land of the devil."

Surprised to hear a response, Cassius fought the urge to turn around. Instead he asked with disgust, "God's plan? You say this is God's plan? When did killing innocent children become God's plan? This is not the work of my God." Cassius became angrier.

Shak laughed out loud from the bottom of its stomach, "God? You got no God. In Cassius's world, you create evil. You teach your kids evil, then their kids evil. You break all God's law. God send Shak to destroy your evil. You the devil." Cassius spun around to confront Shak. The two stood locked eye to eye. The dark blue eyes sent chills down Cassius's spine. The loud tick of the red marble carved clock filled the room as the opponents stared at each other.

"Kill me now and leave my family alone," Cassius demanded with a rage of hate. "End it now!" Cassius yelled. The two continued the eye-lock stare. "NO!" Shak responded as it disappeared. Exhaling, Cassius stumbled before he collapsed into his chair, more defeated than before. He raised his bottle and took a few gulps. The whiskey made the emotional pain worse. He stumbled his way down from the observatory and out of the house, then down the hill to the slave community, finding the death shack that bore the curse. He kicked open the wooden door to find it empty, with dried blood covering the floor. The dark shack reeked of death. Cassius yelled out for Shak to show himself. He continued cursing out loud, waking the sleeping slaves in the nearby shacks. Cassius began destroying the shack, ridding himself of the built up rage. The community of slaves circled the shack, watching the display of uncontrollable anger. Cassius, unaware of the audience, continued his tirade, turning his bottle up, finishing his whiskey and slamming the empty bottle against the wall. The defeated Cassius went down to his knees and began to cry. He again yelled for Shak to appear. Overcome with emotions, Cassius cried loud, long, and hard, losing control of his breathing. Suffocated by his own emotions, he gasped for air. Exhaustion helped him as he regained control, then passed out in the center of the dried blood-covered Seal of Solomon. The next morning, Cassius opened his eyes face first on the crack-filled wooden floor of the shack. His alcohol-laced sweat caused a mushy, bloody mud that covered his body and face. Confused about where he was, Cassius raised his head to look around the shack. He rolled over, wishing the pounding in his head would stop. Thousands of black butterflies covered the shack. Looking at the butterflies, he thought back and wondered if he actually had a conversation with Shak, or if it was just a drunken dream.

The lightheaded and dizzy Cassius stumbled his way over to Turkey Creek to dip his head under the cold running water and wash the bloody mud off himself. He laid back on the sand collected on the creek's bank, reflecting back over the past few weeks. The cold sand made his pounding head feel better. His short encounter with Courtney Mariea flashed into his head: "Souls will leave you to be cleansed in the heavens. You must follow the painful path of your future. The end to your way of life is near." The words she spoke continued to run through his pounding head. Cassius decided he needed to know the meaning behind Courtney Mariea's words, and how she could help his situation.

***

TAROT READER

After cleaning up, Cassius rode Old Bob back to town to see the Tarot reader. He was seated at the table again. Courtney Mariea, dressed in a blue robe with pink trim, entered the room and across from Cassius. Looking up, she recognized the man from a few days earlier.

"What do you want? I have already told you that I know nothing about witches," Courtney Mariea asked with attitude.

Understanding her attitude, Cassius politely apologized for being rude.

"I am sorry for the way I treated you," Cassius said while removing his hat. I need to know what you meant the other day when you said "Souls will leave you to be cleansed in the heavens. You must follow the painful path of your future. The end to your way of life is near."

Staring quietly for a moment, Courtney Mariea held out her hand. "I need three gold coins for the other day and five gold coins for today." After Cassius dropped eight gold coins into her extended hand, Courtney Mariea left the Tarot room to clear her head before starting over. Returning to the room, she shuffled the Tarot cards. Making three stacks, she flipped three cards onto the table: the judgement card, the hanged man card, and the death card. Interestingly, those were the same three cards he received last time. The Tarot reader closed her eyes to think. Cassius, once skeptical of spirituality, sat on the edge of his seat waiting for an answer about his uncertain future.

Courtney Mariea opened her eyes with concern. "I see trouble for you and your family, God has sent for your souls by a painful force," Courtney Mariea finished with a sigh. She reached across the table and took Cassius's hands into her own, closing her eyes again. She said a soft prayer before revisiting the reading of his future.

Opening her eyes, she confirmed his doomed outlook. "I am sorry, but the cards are angry with you. I still see trouble for you and your family."

Cassius dropped his head in sadness asking, "Is there anything we could do to change our outcome?"

Looking up with a positive smile, Courtney Mariea said, "Yes, change your ways. There is always a way to change your future." Courtney Mariea quoted Jeremiah 29:11, "'For I know the plans I have for you,' declares the LORD, 'plans to prosper you and not to harm you, plans to give you hope and a future.'"

"We can always change our future."

Thanking Courtney Mariea for her time, Cassius left.

Desperate, not knowing what to do or how to protect his family, Cassius walked quietly down the road before sitting down on an iron bench in front of a stable. He sat on the cold bench and stared at the rock-covered ground, not noticing the busy town going about its normal routine. A nauseous feeling started deep in his stomach and moved up to his throat as he wondered what Shak had in store for his remaining family. Normally disclaiming blame or fault, Cassius accepted the full responsibility for the hell his family was encountering. Everything he had worked for since leaving his parents' house in Savannah, Tennessee was being destroyed due to the shortcuts and bad decisions he had taken throughout his life.

Still in emotional deep thought, Cassius noticed the life-size crucifix hanging above the entrance of the Catholic church across the street. Sitting in silence, Cassius stared at Jesus hanging on the wooden cross. A warm, religious feeling overcame his cold heart before branching out across his body as the statue of Jesus stared down back at him. An unfamiliar, shameful guilt caused moisture to fill his eyes, and he openly cried as people walked by staring at the scene. For the first time in his life, he felt the warmth of Jesus in his heart. Never taking the time to investigate Jesus for himself, Cassius normally avoided religion and any talk about an afterlife. The spiritual pull on his heart became too much for Cassius to ignore. As he sat alone on the cold bench, he opened himself up to God.

***

WARMTH OF JESUS

Needing to save his cursed family, he slowly walked across the road to the church entrance and opened the heavy walnut door. The smell of frankincense warmly invited him into the house of God. The white terrazzo marble floor led the way through the Roman basilica-designed church. In the north and south walls were six stained glass windows depicting events involving Mary in the life of Jesus.

Cassius slowly walked down the aisle towards the unfamiliar marble altar with the Last Supper carved across the front. He looked up, admiring the beautiful design. He sat down in the walnut pew in the second row, taking in the statues of Mary praying at the foot of the cross, looking up at her dying son. He looked around the church for witnesses before carefully removing a worn Bible from its holder attached to the back of the pew. Cassius opened God's book, beginning to read from the Acts of the Apostles:

3 As he neared Damascus on his journey, suddenly a light from heaven flashed around him. 4 He fell to the ground and heard a voice say to him, "Saul, Saul, why do you persecute me?"

5 "Who are you, Lord?" Saul asked. "I am Jesus, whom you are persecuting," he replied.

6 "Now get up and go into the city, and you will be told what you must do."

7 The men traveling with Saul stood there speechless; they heard the sound but did not see anyone.

8 Saul got up from the ground, but when he opened his eyes, he could see nothing. So, they led him by the hand into Damascus.

9 For three days he was blind, and did not eat or drink anything.

10 In Damascus there was a disciple named Ananias. The Lord called to him in a vision, "Ananias!" "Yes, Lord," he answered.

11 The Lord told him, "Go to the house of Judas on Straight Street and ask for a man from Tarsus named Saul, for he is praying.

¹²In a vision he has seen a man named Ananias come and place his hands on him to restore his sight."

¹³"Lord," Ananias answered, "I have heard many reports about this man and all the harm he has done to your holy people in Jerusalem.

¹⁴And he has come here with authority from the chief priests to arrest all who call on your name."

¹⁵But the Lord said to Ananias, "Go! This man is my chosen instrument to proclaim my name to the Gentiles and their kings and to the people of Israel.

¹⁶I will show him how much he must suffer for my name."

¹⁷Then Ananias went to the house and entered it. Placing his hand on Saul, he said, "Brother Saul, the Lord—Jesus, who appeared to you on the road as you were coming here—has sent me so that you may see again and be filled with the Holy Spirit."

¹⁸Immediately, something like scales fell from Saul's eyes, and he could see again. He got up and was baptized, Acts, 9:3-18.

Putting the Holy Bible back into its holder, Cassius began to silently weep as he looked up at the Crucifix. Heavy guilt pressed against his chest, realizing God knew every horrible action he had taken throughout his life. In the dark moment, Cassius felt God's hand reach for his soul, and as self-sorrow overtook the evil within, he realized his soul was doomed.

With a broken voice, Cassius asked out loud to the empty church, "Can someone like me be forgiven?"

Cassius sat all alone in God's house, waiting for the answer. Over an hour of solitude reflecting on his sinful life, he realized how horrific his life decisions had been and how much harm he had caused others. Cassius cried out again to the empty church, "Oh God, I am so sorry, I have persecuted you over and over my whole life. Why did you give me this life that I did not deserve?"

"Because he loves you," a warm, loving voice startled Cassius. Looking up, Cassius saw the older, bald man with brown eyes and grey mutton chops, dressed in all black with a white collar, staring down at him with a smile.

"Who are you?" Cassius nicely asked, wiping the tears off his face and out of breath from all the emotions he had just released.

"I am Father Harold Hill and this is my church. I have been sitting off beside the altar watching you and praying for you for over an hour." Cassius raised his hands over his face, shaking his head with awkward embarrassment. "No need in being embarrassed, son, we all hit rock bottom at some time in our life. Life is hard and God understands our challenges," the priest sat down next to Cassius, putting his hand on his upper back for comfort. "I have met many of God's children right here in this very spot over the years. Most importantly, you have found your way into God's house. Are you Catholic, son?" the priest asked.

"No, I am ah, I do not know what faith I am." Cassius shamefully answered, still fighting the raw emotions.

"That is okay. Now tell me, how have you persecuted Jesus?" the priest asked.

"I can't, I can't say all the bad things I have done," Cassius said with shameful fear. "Everything you tell me will be between you, me, and God," Father Hill assured.

Still not looking up, Cassius confessed to the priest, "I have killed for money, I have killed for land, I have killed for punishment, and I have killed because of the wrong I had done." Embarrassed by his past, another burst of guilt-filled emotions again overtook Cassius as he began to cry like a child. Father Hill sat patiently, encouraging

Cassius to let it all out.

Once the emotions stopped, Cassius continued, "I have laid with strange women, I have forced myself on helpless slave women, and I have tortured and beaten slaves." Another episode of emotions rushed up from deep inside, where Cassius had never visited. Father Hill patted Cassius on the back, trying to console him. Calming down, Cassius turned toward the priest with a wet face, "Can someone like me be forgiven?"

"Yes, my son," Father Hill said with a loving smile. "God never turns his back on us! If you are honestly sorry and are willing to change your ways, God will forgive you. But you have to be willing to accept his punishment," the priest answered. Father Hill placed his hand on top of Cassius's head as he began a prayer, "God, the Father of mercies, through the death and resurrection of his Son, has reconciled the world to himself and sent the Holy Spirit among us for the forgiveness of sins; through the ministry of the church may God give you pardon and peace, Amen." The priest stopped the prayer short without finishing the absolution, due to Cassius not being Catholic. The two men stood and embraced, "Go my son. Change your ways and bring Christ into your life. God knows how sorry you are for all the sins you have committed against him."

Cassius walked toward the exit, but turned around to confirm he had actually spoken to Father Hill. He watched the priest walk around the altar to the sacristy. Cassius looked over the church, taking in its beauty before turning back toward the exit. Cassius left the church feeling the burden of life-long sin lifted off his heart.

**

DOC BESHEAR

Doc Beshear arrived mid-morning to check on the dying family. Before going up to examine Buckner, Tanyia filled the Doc in on Billy and Carrie being killed in the horse accident, about William being stabbed by a slave.

At a loss for words, Doc Beshear sat quietly, counting the deaths to six in less than a week. "My God," the doctor said before asking Tanyia how she was holding up. She confessed that she had focused on keeping what family she has left safe, not taking time to grieve, and had not slept much.

Doc gave her some opium to mix with alcohol. "Drink this before bed. It will help you sleep." He told her to follow his instructions. "Too much opium could be toxic," the doctor warned. Doc went up to examine Buckner. To the doctor's surprise, Buckner did not have yellow fever. *Black Death?* Doc thought to himself. After further examination, he was right. All the signs were there. From the way he looked, his time was short. He turned to Tanyia and gave her the news. Not showing any emotions, Tanyia asked the Doc if he could check the rest of her family. The Doc examined the family, finding some lesions and red spots on Little Lorre and what looked like honeycombs under the dry skin all over Patty Lee's legs. "Do these hurt?" the Doc asked.

"No, I did not even notice until you pointed them out to me," the ten-year-old answered. Surprised by the odd honeycomb pattern under her skin, Doc Beshear went out to his buggy to retrieve his new medical research book. Not able to find any information on the unique pattern, Doc went back inside for a better inspection. Rubbing his hand over the pattern, he could feel the holes inside. A couple more formed while he was examining her legs. Trying not to show his uneasiness, the doctor pulled out his surgical knife. He carefully sliced the skin atop an older looking honeycomb, causing the skin to open up an inch diameter gap and exposing the hollow holes in her flesh. The rotten flesh smell caught Doc off guard. He gagged as he quickly covered the opening up with a piece of cloth. Patty Lee, watching, started to cry as she realized her legs were rotting away. Doc wrapped the sore before exiting the room.

He found Tanyia down in the Library sitting in silence. "Uh, I have found some honeycomb shaped sores on Patty Lee's legs. I believe her tissue is rotting," Doc described. "I have never seen or heard of anything like this before." Tanyia stood up to follow the doctor into Patty Lee's room.

Before entering, Doc prepared Tanyia for what she was about to see. "It smells like rotted meat that has been sitting in the hot sun for a few days," Doc Beshear said to warn Tanyia. The two entered the room to inspect Patty Lee's legs. The frightened girl lay crying on the bed. Doc removed the bandage for further inspection. The rotten smell again gagged the doctor as Tanyia looked away to gather herself. The holes of the honeycomb shaped sores went down to the bone. The holes were dry, without any sign of blood or infection. The Doc poured a little whiskey into the hole. "Does that hurt?" he asked the scared girl.

"Does what hurt?" she responded.

Again, the doctor rubbed some salve on both legs and wrapped them with cloth. "The salve will help heal your sores," the doctor lied to Patty Lee before exiting the room.

Tanyia kissed her granddaughter on the forehead and followed Doc to the library. "So, the salve will help?" Tanyia asked the Doc.

"Ah, no," the doc answered. "I have never seen anything like those sores. I am going back to town for further research. Keep rubbing salve on her legs every few hours until I return." He also suggested making some rub for little Lorre's lesions. Lillie's baby should come within the next couple of weeks. Everything with her looked good. Doc Beshear insisted they not leave the plantation, and reminded them to keep eye on the slaves. He did not want an epidemic. He assured Tanyia that he would be back in a few days.

Not long after Doc left, a house slave informed Tanya that Buckner passed. Needing fresh air, she went out to join Cassius, who had just returned from town and was sitting on the porch.

"Buckner is dead" she said. Cassius looked up to pray then softy said, "I'm sorry."

"Patty Lee has a flesh-rotting, maybe flesh-eating, disease that Doc has never seen or heard off. He is riding back to town for further research." Tanyia sat on the chair with her puffy eyes closed, wondering what would happen next. "I hope you are sorry," Tanyia said bitterly. "You have brought this hell down onto our family." Not being able to look at her husband, Tanyia removed herself into the house. Cassius sat in silence as he thought back over his conversation with Father Hill.

Two days later, Doc Beshear returned with a colleague, Jonathan Jacob from Memphis, a young doctor not far removed from medical school up in the northeast. The two sat down with Tanyia. "We think it best to remove both of her legs," the doctor suggested.

Tanyia slowly stood, asking the doctors to follow. She escorted the two doctors up to Patty Lee's bedroom. Both doctors gasped at the sight of her. The honeycomb pattern sores had overtaken her entire body up to her neck. "I not sure she is even alive," Tanyia confessed.

Doc Beshear pulled back the blanket, exposing the girl's stomach. Carefully, he rubbed his hand across her torso. The brittle skin turned to dust, exposing the holes and releasing the foul smell of rotting flesh. The three gagged, fighting off the urge to throw up.

Turning back to his colleague, Doc was caught off guard when Patty Lee suddenly sat up, letting out a terrific scream followed by painful moans before collapsing back down on the bed. Doc Beshear felt for a pulse in her neck, and did not find any. "She is dead," he confirmed.

Tanyia closed her eyes, saying, "It is for the best," as she covered her dead granddaughter. With permission from Tanyia, the doctors instructed the house slaves to remove everything in her room to burn with her. The house slaves carried her corpse down to a field, along with her bed, clothes, and furniture. They filled in the gaps with brush before setting it all on fire. Tanyia, and her family watched from a distance, praying for God to have mercy on them all.

Sunday morning, Cassius rode Old Bob down to the slave community. He walked around until he reached the little slaves' church.

With a deep breath, he opened the splintered wooden door, causing all the slaves in attendance to turn around. The preacher slave froze in shock, not knowing why Cassius had entered his church. The congregation sat anxiously, wondering what was going to happen. Cassius walked into the church and found himself a seat in the back row. Before sitting, he motioned to the slave preacher to continue his sermon. An uneasy feeling overtook the preacher as he continued his sermon, not sure what hell Cassius was planning to unleash on his congregation. Cassius sat quietly with his eyes closed and arms folded, listening to the slave preacher discuss Isaiah 55:7, which spoke out to Cassius.

"7 Let the wicked forsake their way and sinners their thoughts; Let them turn to the LORD to find mercy; to our God, who is generous in forgiving."

After the service ended, Cassius sat in the pew, still with his eyes closed, waiting for all the slaves to exit. Once the church was empty, he approached the preacher slave who was cleaning up the plain wooden altar. Not sure why Cassius was approaching him, the preacher stood, frightened for what was to come.

"What is your name, preacher?" Cassius asked.

"Quee, sir," the preacher answered without making eye contact.

"Quee, I want to be baptized," Cassius said in a kind voice.

"Yes sir," Quee answered, still without looking up, not sure what Cassius wanted with him.

"Quee, I would like for you to baptize me. I would like to be baptized this afternoon in Turkey Creek."

Looking up, surprised, Quee asked, "Sir?"

"I found God this week and have prayed for forgiveness. Like Saul, I would like to be baptized." Still confused, Quee returned his stare to the ground, not sure what to do. "I am not telling you to baptize me, Quee. I am asking to be baptized by you. I would like for all the slaves and what is left of my family to witness me being baptized by you," Cassius said with a smile.

Looking up into Cassius's eyes, Quee answered, "Yes sir, I will baptize you." Later that afternoon, Quee stood waist deep in Turkey Creek reading from Matthew 3:13-17.

"¹³ Then Jesus came from Galilee to the Jordan to be baptized by John.

¹⁴ But John tried to deter him, saying, 'I need to be baptized by you, and do you come to me?'

¹⁵ Jesus replied, 'Let it be so now; it is proper for us to do this to fulfill all righteousness.' Then John consented.

¹⁶ As soon as Jesus was baptized, he went up out of the water. At that moment heaven was opened, and he saw the Spirit of God descending like a dove and alighting on him.

¹⁷ And a voice from heaven said, 'This is my Son, whom I love; with him I am well pleased.'"

Cassius then walked out into Turkey Creek to be baptized by preacher Quee in front of the whole plantation. The slave community stood in disbelief as they watched Quee dunk Cassius under the water. After the Prayer of Baptism was completed, Cassius and Quee exited the water, both smiling.

Not wanting any more attention, Cassius and his family returned to their plantation house. Cassius had two cooked hogs taken down to the slave community for the slaves to enjoy. After dinner, Cassius and Tanyia took a walk out across their plantation as he explained the past few days, and why he wanted to be baptized. Although she had a strong hate for Cassius, she was able to tell him she was happy that he found God.

***

SEVENTEEN PEACEFUL DAYS

Seventeen quiet, peaceful days passed after Cassius was baptized. No signs of Shak or any other sickness. Cassius had retreated to his observatory to reflect on the day's work. Adjusting to not having his boys or Boo to help was tough. He had to give more responsibility to the drivers, at least until Clifton and Malley were old enough to take over. He had all the whipping poles cut down and began managing the plantation with perks for good production instead of the beatings for low production. Cassius sipped his whiskey and planned for his future.

Screams echoed through the house, interrupting his silence. Cassius jumped from his chair, racing toward the loud horror. Sarah and Harriett stood outside Lilly's bedroom. Cassius, realizing Lilly was in labor, stopped and turned to go away. Wiping blood from her arms, Tanyia stepped into the walkway. She started to tell Sarah to fetch Cassius before seeing him herself. Hearing his name, Cassius turned to ask what she needed. "Lilly is bleeding profusely," Tanyia shared. She instructed Cassius to quickly ride to get Doc Beshear. Not wanting any more information, Cassius hurried to the stable to saddle Old Bob, then headed to town.

Almost two hours later, Cassius returned with the doctor. Tanyia explained how she firmly packed Lilly's vagina with cloth, then used very hot douches, trying to staunch the hemorrhage. Doc Beshear expressed his approval to Tanyia as they both entered Lilly's room. Grateful the screaming had stopped, Cassius headed to the quiet library for his whiskey. Into his second drink, Cassius heard Tanyia walking slowly down the hall. Noticing the sadness in her face, Cassius stood up to hear the bad news.

Starting to cry, Tanyia explained, "Doc could not stop the bleeding. She had lost too much blood and was starting to fade. The umbilical cord was wrapped around the baby's neck, strangling it during delivery. We lost both Lilly and a little girl." Cassius sat back down in his chair as he soaked in her explanation. Tanyia poured herself a whiskey and sat down. After cleaning up, Doc Beshear joined the sad couple for a drink before riding back to town. Doc Beshear informed them that he had reached out to colleagues in Memphis about the disease that killed Patty Lee. No one had ever seen or heard of anything close to the symptoms. Doc small talked about the war before leaving.

The next day, standing among too many fresh dirt piles, the dwindling family placed Lilly and her baby together in the ground. As the family prayed together, Cassius stood wondering if the deaths were due to the curse, or if they were natural. Since he had killed the witch and spoken with Father Hill, everything had settled down. Looking upon his family, he noticed Clifton seemed different. His eyebrows seemed to bend up and his head tilted a little to the left. His whole body looked out of shape. Thinking back to his older three boys, now dead, he remembered how they were awkward from time to time.

After dinner, Cassius sat on the porch with Tanyia, enjoying the twins and Jouble playing around the stable. Cassius and Tanyia watched Jouble, who had lost interest in the twins to play with Topaz, a beautiful Australian Shepherd. Topaz sat still as the three-year-old patted her on the head.

Hearing a scuffle, Cassius turned his attention back to the twins to see Clifton on top of Malley, punching him in the face. Malley had his arms up trying to protect himself. Normally Cassius did not interfere with their scuffles, but Malley was getting beat up pretty bad. Cassius walked down to pull Clifton off Malley. Tanyia came over to find out what happened. She did not like her boys fighting. Malley accused Clifton of hitting him for no reason. With no denial, Clifton just stared at the ground with a mischievous grin. Not liking Clifton's lack of response, Tanyia snatched him by the hair, pulling him inside and taking a wooden spoon to his backside. Staying out of her way, Cassius worked with Malley on how to protect himself, then returned to the porch.

***

SHAK RETURNS

Over the next few days, Cassius noticed Clifton keeping his distance from Malley and the family. He heard Clifton laughing out loud, then weeping uncontrollably in his bedroom at night. Occasionally, he appeared to be talking to himself. Not caring to get involved, Cassius left Clifton alone.

After another calm week, Cassius was lying in bed sound asleep, when he heard a chant in his dream. "Uba uba uba yah yah, uba uba uba yah yah! Cassius, Cassius! Uba uba uba yah, yah, uba uba uba yah yah! Cassius, Cassius! Uba uba uba yah yah, uba uba uba yah, yah!"

Realizing the chant was from Shak, Cassius tried to wake, but was paralyzed in a state of fear with adrenaline rushing through his body and eyes wide open, looking around the room for help. Suffocating with fear, Cassius fought to breathe. After a few moments, he was able to shake the state and sat up. A bit shaken, he rubbed his face. Sitting on the side of his bed, he looked around the room for the silhouette. Not seeing anything abnormal, Cassius said a quick prayer before he lay back down, listening to the silence until he fell back to sleep.

The strong thunderstorm shook Cassius from his sleep, still jumpy from his paralyzing dream. He lay in bed waiting for his heart to stop racing, then took a moment enjoying the sound of rain. He loved a good rainstorm. Although it stopped work for a day or two, he liked the way everything seemed clean afterwards.

Held captive by the storm, Cassius wandered up to his observatory for some quiet. He stood watching as the heavy rain formed small rivers of rushing water throughout the plantation. Sitting back in his chair, the soothing rain quickly put Cassius to sleep.

"Uba uba uba yah yah, uba uba uba yah yah!" The adrenaline burst

shook Cassius from his nap. Cautiously, he looked around the observatory. "Nothing," he muttered as he continued to listen to the heavy
rain. Late in the afternoon the rainstorm moved on. Cassius saddled
Old Bob and headed out to look over the rain-soaked plantation.
Moving from field to field, only finding a few fallen trees and flood-
ed fields, he stopped by the slave community to order the drivers to
remove the downed trees.

Headed back toward the house, Cassius heard Malley yelling his
name. Cassius directed Old Bob toward Turkey Creek to see what
the fuss was about. Malley ran up to meet Cassius, yelling about
Clifton, "He pushed Jouble off the bridge into Turkey Creek. He just
shoved him off. With the water rushing from the rain, Jouble was
swept away, down around the bend."

Riding up to the bridge where Clifton was still standing, Cassius
asked Clifton what had happened. With a devilish smirk, Clifton
explained, "Jouble lost his balance. I tried to catch him, but I missed."
Cassius sent the twins to the house as he gathered some drivers to
search the creek for Jouble. Hearing the news from Malley, Tanyia
and Harriett exited the house and headed for the creek as they saw
Cassius riding up on Old Bob.

"Where is Jouble?" Tanyia asked in a scared voice.

"We do not know. I have the drivers and some slaves searching
downstream for him." Cassius rode back down to assist in the search.
The two ladies waited by the bridge for a couple of hours until they
saw Cassius ride towards them with Jouble's limp body laid across
Old Bob's back. Both ladies stood motionless, waiting for Cassius
to confirm what they could already see. Harriett pulled her son's
corpse off the horse as she wept, holding his cold, wet body. Trying
to hold things together, Tanyia asked Cassius how it happened. He
relayed what he heard from Malley, then what Clifton said. He then
explained how one of the drivers found the boy's body lodged between two trees down the swollen creek. Tanyia asked if Cassius believed Clifton really pushed Jouble into the creek. Shaking his head,
Cassius said he did not know. The parents agreed that Clifton had

been acting different lately. Back at the house, Tanyia and Cassius stood outside Clifton's bedroom. Inside his room, they heard Clifton talking in an unclear mumble. Not looking up, Clifton continued to mumble as his parents entered his room.

"What happened out by the creek?" Tanyia asked. Not paying attention to his parents, he continued to mumble. Tanyia grabbed his arm, getting his attention. "What happened to Jouble?" Pulling his arm away from his mother, Clifton said, "I did not push him," without looking up. "He lost his balance and I tried to catch him. He fell into the creek." Clifton hid his amusement from his parents.

Not believing his son, Cassius grabbed Clifton by the neck and slammed him down into the bed. "What did you do?" Cassius again asked.

"He was falling and I tried to catch him," Clifton pleaded.

"I do not believe you, boy!" Cassius yelled. "Are you still talking with Shak?" Cassius asked with a stern voice

"No sir," Clifton lied. Letting Clifton up, Cassius stared into his son's red, tear-swollen eyes looking for guilt.

Not sure what to do, Cassius and Tanyia left his room. Walking down the hall, Tanyia confessed to Cassius that she did not believe Clifton. They both agreed as they continued downstairs. After his parents left, Clifton snuck into their room and found Tanyia's whiskey bottle for her medicine to help her sleep. With only about a cup of whiskey left in the bottle, Clifton poured four times the amount of opium Doc said to use into the bottle. Clifton put the bottle back and returned to his room. Later that night Tanyia, not able to sleep because of Jouble's death, sat up to drink her sleeping medicine. She added a little extra due to the emotional stress of the day.

Cassius woke the next morning, surprised to see Tanyia still in bed. Walking over to check on her, he noticed her lips and fingers were blue and her skin was pale. Reaching to wake her, he noticed her body was stiff. Realizing she was dead, he stepped back, not knowing what to do. He knelt down to move her hair out of her face before he covered her up, then sat on the side of the bed. This can't be an accident. Deep in his gut, he knew Clifton was responsible. *The boy has gone mad with all the deaths* Cassius thought, *or could it be the curse?* He made his way downstairs to get a house slave. The house was empty, not a house slave anywhere. Stepping out of the house, the plantation looked deserted. Back in the house and walking through the parlor, a wet drop splattered on his shoulder. He looked up and another drop hit him in the forehead. The dark red blood splattered across his face. Wiping his face, he saw the blood pooling on the ceiling. Cassius raced upstairs to find the source. Stopping at Clifton's room, he opened the door. To his horror, Cassius found Little Lorre dead, hanging from a noose. The emotional blast in his chest backed Cassius up. "What have you done?" Cassius demanded of the empty room. Racing to his room, Cassius grabbed his revolver and knife before going back to Clifton's bedroom. He gently cut down his dead granddaughter's body and removed the noose from around her neck. He said a quick prayer before covering her up with a blanket. Cassius knew this had to end as he checked the house for Clifton. Checking each room, Cassius discovered Harriett's body dismembered and scattered across the blood-covered floor of her room. Gagging, he carefully searched the room for Clifton. Not finding Clifton, Cassius slowly walked down the hall to Sarah's room. Standing outside her door, he heard a thud over and over and an unknown language being mumbled. Easing her door open, he peeked into the room and found Clifton covered in blood on top of Sarah, stabbing her mutilated, bloody corpse.

Cassius yelled as Clifton leapt off the bed and headed toward the open window. Clifton paused for a moment. Blue eyes, yellow hair, and black silhouette briefly revealed itself as Shak before exiting the window. "Shak!" Cassius yelled before running to the window. Cassius did not see which direction it ran.

Cassius quickly ran to Malley's room. Before opening the door, he said the *Our Father*. Taking a deep breath, he thought back to what Father Hill told him about forgiveness. "God never turns his back on us! If you are honestly sorry, and are willing to change your ways, God will forgive you. But you have to be willing to accept his punishment." Cassius leaned his forehead against Malley's door, "God, I am deeply sorry for all the wrong decisions I have made throughout my life, and I accept your punishment. Please direct me down the path you have chosen for me."

Cassius entered the room and found Malley tied to an old oak chair with his mouth gagged. When the gag was removed, Malley cried "Clifton has gone mad!"

"Where is Clifton?" Cassius asked as he approached the window. Malley's eyes were wide open, filled with crying panic. He was having problems talking from the emotional overload. Cassius looked out the open window for Clifton. Not finding him, he turned his attention back to Malley. As Cassius bent down to cut Malley free, Clifton came through the window, surprising Cassius by shoving the long blade through his back and dropping him to the ground. Clifton removed the knife before shoving the blade back into the side of Cassius's ribs. Losing a lot of blood, Cassius crawled toward his revolver before collapsing. Clifton again stabbed Cassius in the neck, just missing his spine. Cassius's body went limp as Clifton removed the blade, turning towards Malley. The unfamiliar, deep blue eyes stared at Malley as Clifton circled his twin brother. Speaking broken English with an African accent, Clifton explained to Malley, "Cassius brought this punishment onto this land. Cassius and all his roots must be removed." Malley was sobbing, not sure what was about to happen. "Cassius's evil ways must be stopped." Clifton kicked Malley's chair over, then stood over him positioning himself. He began chanting, "Uba uba uba yah yah, uba uba uba yah yah!" Clifton raised the blade above Malley's heart. "Uba uba uba yah yah, uba, uba uba yah yah!"

"Die you son of a bitch." BOOM! The blast blew a hole in Clifton's midsection and knocked him against the wall. Cassius dropped the revolver as he expired.

Doc Beshear arrived at the plantation to check on the sick when he heard the revolver shot from inside the house. He rushed upstairs and found Malley crying, still tied to the chair and covered with blood.

***

January 2018

THE MATOSKES

Sharon Novak Matoske hung up her office phone, sitting back in her black leather chair with a pleased grin across her face. She just received an offere to be the head volleyball coach at the University of North Mississippi! All her hard work as an assistant coach, along with her family's sacrifice, was finally paying off. Her impressive resume included a high school state championship, one Final Four and two Elite Eight appearances as a player in college, and sixteen straight tournament appearances as an assistant coach. Her determination and focus set her apart from most of her colleagues. She had been offered many head coaching jobs through the years, but was waiting for an offer from an administration serious about winning. The University of North Mississippi had for reputation of funding women's sports as aggressively as the men's teams, which was rare in college athletics.

The young university was created by the Mississippi Legislature in 1973 to replace the community college operating in Coffeeville. The contiguous campus area included rolling hills, gardens, and green space, and a nature walk. It was built of mostly early modern architecture with a southern antebellum mix. In the middle of the campus stood a thirty-foot aluminum Knight trimmed in red and black, holding a shield in one hand and a sword in the other. "Red Knights" was engraved across the shield. Just outside the campus was a vibrant bar and music scene known for blues and BBQ. Sharon believed the university's volleyball program was a sleeping giant ready to be woken by the right coach. She was confident that her grit and grind mentality would be the perfect fit for the young program.

Sharon grew up poor among the rich and famous of South Florida, living in a run-down, roach-infested house with an old VW van as transportation, trying to survive in a world of luxury cars and mansions. As a teen, Sharon searched secondhand stores for clothes to help hide her low-income reality. She lived with her mentally ill mom, Sofia, and out of the closet gay older brother, Mikey. Her mom was a great mother before the mental illness disrupted their happy life. They lived off the disability check her mom received from the government and child support. Her father, Fred, was a good father when he had time to spend with his kids. The constant fighting with Sofia kept him away most weekends. Sofia was quick to use her kids to hurt Fred, and was vicious when it came to the child support payments. Once he remarried and started a new family, his visits became rare.

By middle school, Sharon found herself taking care of her sick mom. Cooking and cleaning kept her busy and unable to hang out with friends. She was introduced to volleyball as a freshman in high school, and fell in love with the sport. She was able to focus on volleyball, escaping the problems of her home life. Her mom was not a fan of her playing volleyball, and demanded she continue her chores around the house in order to play. The dream of a normal life pushed her to excel in the classroom and on the court, earning an athletic scholarship to Ferg University in Jefferson, GA. Support from her parents was rare, but her gay brother Mikey and his life partner Rocky were always in the stands cheering for her through high school. Not wanting to be 12 hours away from her brother, Sharon considered staying closer to home. Mikey insisted she accept the scholarship to leave home, getting away from the family dysfunction. Taking her brother's advice, Sharon left home on the life-changing adventure.

Life in the hills of northern Georgia was a culture shock for Sharon. She struggled to understand the southern accents and culture. Northern Georgia was a foreign country compared to the upscale society life of South Florida. The historic campus was distinguished by its shaded brick walkways, fountains, sculptures, and historic clock tower, all tucked away in the rolling foothills of the Smokey Mountains. The colorful fall foliage magnified the campus's beauty. Sharon had never seen such bright red, yellow, and orange colors covering trees. She focused on volleyball and school as she learned to live away from home. She mostly hung out at teammates' houses, but occasionally went out, experiencing the dull nightlife in small town Georgia. One night while out with her teammates, she was hit on by an okay looking fellow student who bravely asked her to marry him. Laughing with pity, she politely told him no as she deflected the weak line before walking away. A few years later, the same guy asked her the question again.

Henry Matoske stood 6'2", skinny with broad shoulders, brown eyes, and a crooked nose from it being broken as a child.

He grew up in Memphis with his mom Bebbie, stepfather Warren, and two half-sisters, Rose and Nancy. Henry's father died when he was young. The family lived in a lower middle-class neighborhood on the Mississippi and Tennessee border. Bebbie remarried within a year of Henry's father's death, causing a wedge between her and her mother-in-law Agnes. Henry's mom, scared of being a single mother at such a young age, latched on to the first man to come her way. Warren was an in-and-out-of-work construction worker who enjoyed the comfort of the insurance money Bebbie received from Henry's father death. Bebbie was able to work her way through nursing school while Warren watched the kids in between bottles of whiskey.

Henry's mom Bebbie and birth dad, John Cross Matoske, were excited when they were told she was having twins. The high-risk pregnancy began having problems at week thirty-two when she began losing weight. At week thirty-six, the doctors could only hear one heartbeat. After Henry was delivered, his fraternal twin brother was stillborn. Due to the cramped uterus, Henry was born with clubfeet. At two years old, the doctor had to perform the painful surgery to lengthen the too-tight ligaments and tendons that held the muscles to the bones. After spending three months in a cast, then two years wearing braces, Henry's legs were normal except for the small ankles, under-sized calves, and the six-inch scars on both ankles. The strong willed little boy worked hard to overcome the painful surgery and rehab. The doctors were amazed that Henry only needed two years in braces, being able to start kindergarten brace free.

Henry and his half-sisters enjoyed a Catholic education provided by the insurance money and sacrifices made by Bebbie. Once Henry was in his teens, Warren and Bebbie would leave him home to babysit his two younger sisters while the couple would go out drinking at the local bar. Any given weekend, Henry would have to take $500.00 from his mom's top drawer and walk two miles to bail his parents out of jail for fighting or public drunkenness. Henry always found himself on the short side of everything. While his half-sisters wore new clothes and new shoes, Henry wore mostly secondhand stuff from the thrift store. In high school, the parish priest, Father O'Shea, noticed Henry wearing his dead father's clothes to school. The priest began taking Henry shopping for new clothes. In return, Henry would have to take young ladies from the Catholic orphanage to school dances. Father O'Shea would pick out the young ladies, always the ones no one else wanted to take out. Henry, always grateful, just smiled and enjoyed the dance.

Growing up, Henry spent the summers with his maternal grandmother Boba. She owned the family rice farm just across the Mississippi River from Memphis. The farm was run by Henry's uncle Sylvester. His uncle Bill also lived on the farm, but had a job at the rail yard in Memphis. Henry always looked forward to the summers away from Warren. The two uncles did their best to be good father figures. Both realized the mistreatment Henry endured from Warren. Uncle Sylvester took time to hunt and fish with Henry, while uncle Bill took him to sporting events at the local university and to see professional teams in Memphis. Uncle Bill was a former College football player and realized Henry's talent for football at an early age. His uncle made sure Henry attended football camps and any regional scouting camps offered to build his recruiting stock. Uncle Bill always reminded Henry that he may not be the biggest, fastest, or most talented, but he could always out-work the other guy. Once Henry realized his love for football, he began working hard and focused on his dream to play in college. Uncle Bill pushed Henry to excel, keeping him focused on the dream. Henry was too small to play Division 1 football, but after receiving all-state honors and multiple awards, he was offered a Division 2 football scholarship to play at Ferg University.

In high school and college, Henry spent the summers working with his uncle Bill at the rail yard in Memphis to earn extra money. The money was good and the work was hard, which kept him in great shape for football. Removing old cross ties and replacing them with new ones was a workout he could not get from a gym. A couple of weeks before training camp his sophomore year, Henry was headed to the break room when he spotted a four foot long section of cross tie half laying on the track, with an engine creeping toward it. Realizing he had forgotten to remove the cross tie, Henry sprinted over to snatch it. His left foot slid down between the track as his body turned. The weight of the cross tie with the force of his turn destroyed his left knee. He was able to remove his foot before the engine overtook his position. Blocked by the engine, his uncle Bill raced over, not knowing if he had cleared the track in time. As the engine passed, Henry lay clear of the track holding his destroyed knee in agony. The sound of the engine drowned out his moans of pain. Uncle Bill comforted Henry until the paramedics arrived. The paramedics placed his leg in an air cast before they loaded him into the ambulance. Henry was transported to the newly built Saint Ann's hospital where his mom worked as a nurse. He was taken straight into emergency surgery to reconstruct his knee. Henry laid in the hospital for a couple of days, praying to return to the football field. He was itching to start rehab in his attempt to get cleared to play. After being released from the hospital, Henry began rehab at the local sports complex.

Late that summer, Henry returned to the University to continue his rehab on campus. Due to the severe destruction of the knee, he was advised to end his playing career. Not having a choice, Henry accepted a medical hardship that paid for his tuition but ended his football career. Not being able to play football took a toll on Henry. Over the next three years, he began partying, drinking too much beer, and barely keeping up with his grades. Not only was he dealing with the loss of football, but life without his father had always haunted him. Henry jumped from girl to girl, never letting himself get attached.

One night at a club while playing pool with his roommates, he noticed an athletic girl slowly walk across the dance floor. Her dark hair hung straight just below her shoulders and she had a hoop earring at the top of her left ear. He stared for a moment, admiring the jeans she wore so perfectly, before returning to his game. Every so often, he looked across the club hoping to catch a glimpse of the beautiful athletic girl. After too many drinks, he stumbled up to her and asked if she would marry him.

A few weeks later, Henry and Sharon met at a friend's house. They laughed at the weak, unsuccessful marriage proposal.

Over the course of a few months, they became friends, then began dating. Henry stopped partying, becoming a regular at all her volleyball matches. The two spent their free time together doing outside activities and hanging out with friends. Henry tried to fight becoming close to Sharon, not wanting to give someone control of his heart. Before he knew what was happening, he fell deeply in love. After Sharon's playing career ended, the two continued dating. Henry took Sharon out for dinner in downtown Memphis to celebrate the three-year anniversary of their first date. After the nice dinner, they walked down to a famous hotel where Henry paid for a carriage ride. The two snuggled up tight under a blanket to protect them from the cold wind blowing between the tall buildings. The carriage driver maneuvered through the city, arriving at a park with a beautiful stone fountain and clear lights draped from tree to tree, lighting up the whole park. The driver stopped in front of the fountain as Henry exited the carriage. Helping Sharon down, the couple walked to the other side of the fountain as Henry dropped to one knee, pulling out Sharon's great-grandmother's wedding ring. Henry again proposed, and this time she said yes! After their South Florida storybook wedding on the beach, the happy couple moved to Iowa, where Sharon was hired as an Assistant Volleyball coach at a small Division 2 university.

In 2007, they were blessed with the birth of their son, Tyler. Sharon was then hired as an assistant coach at a large Division 1 school just outside of Denver, CO. In 2011, they were again blessed with the birth of their second son Will. The two boys were athletic like their parents, and began playing football, basketball, and baseball. While Sharon crossed the country recruiting and coaching volleyball matches, Henry enjoyed chasing their boys around, watching their various sporting events. Life was great. Sharon always dreamed of life with a happy home, happy husband, and happy kids. God had truly blessed her, making up for her rough childhood. Now she would be able to prove herself as a Division 1 head coach.

***

NEW ADVENTURE

The excited family packed up their house to set off on their next adventure in northern Mississippi.

They moved into a university-owned house on campus until they could find their own house. Their boys would attend Coffeeville Prep School, the K-12 school located on campus, built for students working toward a teaching degree. Henry talked Sharon into buying land to build a house. He would be able to teach the boys to hunt and fish. Considering the sacrifices her family made for her career, she agreed to purchase the land. They found a nice spread in Skuna Valley with a creek running through the middle. The boys would be able to hunt, fish, and run around being boys. The land was purchased, and they got blueprints drawn up for their dream house.

While their house was being built, Henry and the boys spent weekends exploring the land when they were free from athletic activities. Down from the house construction, Henry began building a small barn. With his newly purchased green tractor, he cleared enough land to begin his project. After all the materials were delivered, Henry and his boys began building the barn. To save money, Henry purchased a used saw mill to cut some wood for himself. After putting his mill together, Henry drove his tractor down the hill to the hardwoods to mark ideally sized trees for cutting. While tying a pink ribbon onto a tree, Henry noticed six black crows watching him from an oak tree across the small spring-fed creek. Henry followed the creek in search of the correct size trees. He became spooked as the crows began squawking at him. Feeling that he was being watched by the crows, Henry walked deeper into the hardwoods, hoping to escape the crows' view. One by one, the noisy crows flew ahead of Henry, squawking like a heckler at a sporting event. Out of the blue, Henry felt a sudden, sharp pain on the top of his head as he was thrown forward, fighting to retain his footing. He turned quickly to see an angry crow flying back to a tree. Panic set in as each crow took turns dive-bombing Henry, pushing him deeper into the hardwoods, with a couple landing painful pecks on top of his head. Plowing through spider webs, thorns, and dodging tree branches, Henry fought off the crow attacks as he ran into an old abandoned shack.

Catching his breath, Henry bent over and put his hands on his knees. "What the freak was that?" he said to the empty shack. Rubbing the top of his head, Henry felt blood from the fresh wounds caused by the aggressive crows. *They must be protecting a nest*, Henry decided as he peeked out the shack's broken window while he pondered his plan for escape. The old, two-room shack was constructed with plank wood and covered with vines and other vegetation. The mushy wooden floor was doing its best to hold Henry's weight as he waited out the crows. Looking around the rickety shack, Henry found an old copper still crushed in on one side and a couple of broken wooden barrels. Pieces of copper tubing were scattered between the two rooms. *How cool, moonshine!* Henry thought to himself. He inspected the discovery for a few minutes before turning his attention back to the angry crows holding him captive. He again peeked out the broken window. With no sign of the crows, Henry inched his way out looking into the trees for verification the birds had left. Convinced he was out of harm's way, he began the hike out of the woods, staying away from the creek. Hair on the back of his neck stood from the feeling of being watched. He carefully scanned the trees while following the compass on his phone. Henry stopped to listen, trying to hear the construction of his house. Stillness had overtaken the tract of woods holding Henry. His compass began spinning erratically, not providing the direction out. Kneeling down, he scanned the sky looking for the sun. Making an educated guess, he focused on one tree, walked to it, and tied a pink ribbon for a marker. From one tree to the next, he continued keeping his direction straight. A streak of a black silhouette, stirring leaves up into a funnel, darted across his path with a roar and disappeared, leaving Henry in a frozen state of sweaty panic. Refusing the urge to run, he took two steps back in disbelief. "What the hell was that?"

he said out loud. A quick scan of the forest gave him no clues of what he had just witnessed. A bit jittery, he continued his hike, focusing only on the next tree ahead. The years of hunting paid off, allowing him to escape the woods' grasp. He made the way to his tractor, then up to the house construction, still trying to make sense of his experience. Having enough for the day, Henry gathered the boys up and headed home.

The next day, Henry and his boys returned to continue working on their barn. An unknown blue truck was parked next to the barn construction. A short, stocky white man with a 90s "boy band" haircut with frosted tips was walking around looking over the barn's frame and drinking a beer.

The man saw Henry and approached, introducing himself with a strong southern accent. "My name is Kyle Leland," he said, sticking out his hand. After introductions, Kyle explained that he and his partner Roy lived down the road and he was just stopping by to be neighborly. The two exchanged background stories for a moment before Kyle offered Henry a beer.

"Ah, no thanks, its 8 a.m." Henry declined. Kyle laughed, "It is never too early for a beer!"

Still disturbed from his experience in the woods the day before, but trying to not sound totally crazy to his newly met neighbor, Henry shared with Kyle his battle with the crows, the moonshine shack, and the dark shadow that crossed his path.

Not able to control his smart-ass mouth, Kyle asked if Henry had seen a polar bear as well. Henry laughed off the reference to the early 2000s TV show with an invisible monster. "Nicely played," Henry said back with a laugh. The two instantly liked each other. They chatted a bit longer before Kyle asked to see where the crow attack occurred. Kyle grabbed his shotgun and they drove down the hill to the woods. The woods were alive with birds chirping and squirrels leaping from tree to tree. Henry lead Kyle to the spot of the attack, pointing to the tree across the creek. They both looked and listened for a moment and decided the crows were gone.

"I must have really pissed them off somehow while I was marking the trees." Henry said. Kyle again followed as they walked to find the moonshine shack. They located the ribbon trail Henry made on his way out, and began following it toward the shack. Henry stopped, telling Kyle to be quiet. "Do you feel that?" Henry asked.

"The 'being watched' feeling?" Kyle returned the question.

"Yes," Henry confirmed. The neighbors stood frozen, looking for an explanation.

The sound of a locomotive turned their attention deep into the hardwoods, seeing leaves, branches, and dust flying with the straight-line winds rapidly approaching. They dove into a nearby ditch to escape the windstorm. The dry ditch sheltered them from the wind, dust, and most of the falling debris. As quickly as the wind came, it was gone. Standing up, they brushed the dust off as they discussed what they just witnessed.

"Did the wind follow the ground down the hollow, then back up and over?" Kyle asked for assurance.

"You saw that too?" Henry answered.

"In all my life, I have never seen anything like that," Kyle confessed.

Henry realized he had left the boys up by the barn playing. "We need to get back to check on my boys," Henry explained. The neighbors followed the pink markers as they walked back to the truck to drive to the build site.

Both boys were playing around and the construction workers were busy doing their jobs. Looking back down the hill, Henry realized there was no sign of the windstorm. He asked his boys if the wind blew them around. "What wind?" they both asked.

Realizing the odd windstorm did not leave the woods, Henry smiled at Kyle, "Looks like we saw your polar bear." Kyle laughed as he admitted something weird was happening in the woods.

"You know, this area has a long history of ghosts, dating back to the Civil War and slavery," Kyle informed Henry. "I have heard stories but had never witnessed anything," Kyle confessed.

"Yeah, I have heard stories from all across the south, but assumed it was all a bunch of bull," Henry added. The two men laughed for a moment as they soaked in their experience.

Kyle had to head home, but invited Henry to stop by when he had time for a beer. Eager to use his newly assembled saw mill, Henry selected a tree on the outer line of woods, not ready to venture back into the woods alone. He dropped a tree with his chain saw, then began stripping the branches off. Tyler and Will helped remove the limbs and stacked them in a pile. Henry used his chainsaw to cut the logs into ten-foot sections and hauled them up to his small mill. One by one, Henry used the tractor to place the logs onto the mill, sawing each to his desired size.

Off in the distance, Henry heard a faint drumming. He stopped working to listen, asking the boys to be silent. The boys confirmed the drum beat as they listened quietly. The boys followed Henry as he walked toward the beating drum. Approaching the creek, the faint drum beat stopped.

"I wonder what that was." Henry said to his boys. The boys explored the creek banks as Henry looked around. Once the boys had enough time to explore the creek, they returned with Henry to continue building the barn. Irritated from the boys' complaints about helping, Henry yelled for them to take their dog Drake to go play. Back working on the barn, Henry again heard a faint drum beat. The beat was coming from a different direction. Henry cautiously followed a game trail into a kudzu covered tree line. Focusing on the beat, Henry walked into the ruins of an old plantation house.

Staring up at the kudzu covered old columns, Henry did not realize the drum beat had stopped. *This place was massive,* Henry thought to himself. He walked around inspecting his discovery. Henry tried to imagine how the house looked in its heyday, before its destruction. In awe, he squatted down and picked up an old brick to inspect. A crack sound just inside the tree line caused him to turn his attention away from the house. Looking into the tree line, Henry noticed a group of whitetail deer staring at him. After a few moments, the deer turned to retreat deeper into the woods. Henry walked around looking through the old rubble, inspecting the columns and fireplace. Lodged into the base of a column looked to be a softball-size rusted cannon ball. *This house was probably destroyed during the Civil War*, he thought to himself. The hidden thorns in the waist-high overgrowth made the expedition through the rubble tough. After looking around a bit longer, Henry made his way back to the unfinished barn.

Progress on the barn moved along nicely as Henry worked uninterrupted most of the day. Up on a rafter attaching brackets, Henry heard the faint drum beat again coming from the direction of the creek. Standing up on the rafter for a better view, Henry balanced himself and looked towards the sound. A gust of wind caught him off guard, causing a missed step. Slipping off, Henry's shoulder crashed into another rafter on his way down. He dangled a few feet from the ground by the safety harness he had attached to the oak rafter above. "That is going to leave a bad mark," Henry said to himself. He reached up, pulled on the orange strap to unhook the safety harness, and eased to the ground. The pain in his shoulder felt more like a deep bruise than a break. With his pride hurt, Henry rounded up Tyler and Will and headed to the university to have his shoulder checked out by the volleyball trainer.

The university's head trainer Eliana confirmed the deep shoulder bruise. "How did you hurt yourself?" Eliana asked.

"Ah, Sharron hits me at home for not having dinner cooked and the house cleaned," Henry answered with a smile. Not believing Henry's story about Sharon hitting him, Eliana asked again how Henry had hurt his shoulder. He explained the drum beating in the distance, the crow attack, and the straight-line wind.

"How many crows did you say?" she inquired. "Six," he answered. With Eliana's interest in folk magic, she knew six crows meant death was near, but decided to keep the information to herself. She instructed Henry to ice his shoulder for a few days.

A few weeks passed and Henry returned to work on the barn. He left the boys at home with Sharon so he could get a good start before she dropped them off later in the day. Arriving before dawn, he sat in the truck finishing his coffee with the windows down, enjoying the cool morning air and peaceful silence. A scream and screech, followed by hoot, broke the silence, startling Henry. *An owl at dawn, that is weird,* Henry thought to himself. Unknown to Henry an owl screech at dawn means danger is near. He watched the sun rise over the hardwoods before starting his saw mill. Working uninterrupted, Henry was able to finish the barn's roof before the boys arrived.

Henry and Sharon sat eating lunch, enjoying the view of their house construction and land. Caught up in the moment, Henry asked Sharon if she ever thought they would be so lucky to have such a great life. Tears formed in her eye as she said, "Yes! I always knew if I worked hard, God would make my adult life great to make up for my childhood." The two sat together absorbing their success. The couple walked around, inspecting their almost completed house before Sharon left for work.

***

SHADOW PEOPLE

Late in the afternoon, Kyle stopped by to visit and to share the research he had done on the black silhouette Henry saw in the woods. The new friends looked around, inspecting the almost completed barn as Kyle pointed out all the little mistakes the novice builder made in hopes of playfully irritating Henry.

After a few laughs, Kyle brought up the experience they had in the woods. "From what I have read, you encountered a shadow person."

"A what?" Henry asked in amused disbelief.

"Shadow people are spirits who do not have enough energy to reveal themselves," Kyle went on, "The good news is that there is no evidence to show that shadow people can be dangerous. Now, the straight-line winds, well I have not found anything to explain that. They are usually associated with storms. We both know there was not a storm cloud in sight when that happened."

"Ok, so I have shadow people and some strange weather phenomena going on in my woods?" Henry asked with a sigh and a smile.

"Yep, I told you that this area is full of spirits from the Civil War and slavery era," Kyle said with a smile, slapping Henry on the back. The new friends sat on the back of Kyle's truck drinking beer while watching Tyler and Will run around being boys.

A few minutes into their conversation, Kyle suggested the two venture down to the moonshine shack in the woods after dark to see if they could conjure up some shadow people. Henry didn't like the idea of going to the shack after dark, but went against his gut and agreed to accompany Kyle on his quest. Henry drove the boys to Sharon as Kyle went home to gather supplies for the conjure session. The two men met back at the barn, both armed with guns, flashlights, and a small cooler of beer. They drove down to the tree line and followed the pink ribbon markers to the rickety shack. Henry walked around the outside, inspecting the shack as Kyle set up the candles, creating a circle inside the back room. The two men sat inside the lit candle circle with a white candle between them. Kyle followed the steps he read online. He placed a white paper that read YES on one side of the candle and NO on the other side. He poured wax then salt, connecting the candle to both pages.

"I feel like a teenage girl performing some ritual to get back at an old boyfriend," Henry expressed with a laugh. Laughing, Kyle agreed with Henry's observation.

Kyle told Henry, "Shut up and think about the shadow people. After a few eerie, quiet moments, Kyle asked the first question, "Do we have shadow people in this shack with us?" The flame tilted toward YES. The two men smiled with excitement, not believing their eyes. Henry let out a slight giggle.

"Did you die in the Civil War?" Kyle asked. The flame tilted to NO. Kyle looked up at Henry whispering with a big grin, "I told you there are spirits around here."

"Did you live on this land?" Kyle asked. The flame tilted to the YES.

"Did you die of natural causes?" Kyle asked another question. The flame tilted to the NO. "Murdered?" The flame tilted towards, NO. "Accident?" The flame tilted, YES! The two men smiled at each other, enjoying the session.

Henry tried a question, "Are there other spirits here?" YES, the flame tilted. "Do you want us to leave you alone?" Henry asked with his second question. The flame tilted YES. The two friends looked at each other before Kyle asked, "If you want us to leave you alone, give us a sign." They sat in silence waiting for a sign.

A shadow moved across the candle circle and the shack wall before something crashed into the side of the shack, causing both men to jump with brief fear. They both laughed at each other once the rush of adrenaline had left their bodies. "I am buying a Ouija Board and we are coming back out here," Kyle said with excitement.

Henry left the shack to investigate what crashed into it. He found a tree branch dangling next to the shack, still attached to a higher branch by vines. After closer inspection, Henry could see the break was fresh. Henry slowly dropped the tree branch as he heard something walking just out of sight. Wishing he had not left his gun in the shack, Henry cautiously raised his flashlight, hoping to identify the source of the footsteps. Henry quietly told Kyle, "Stop! Do not make a sound," as Kyle made his way out of the shack. The two men stood still, listening to the slow, creepy steps just out of sight. An overpowering, gagging, dead odor overtook the friends as they tried to stay quiet. The thick fumes caused both to hide their noses deep down in their shirts, trying to escape the nasty odor. A scream of what seemed to be an elderly woman wailing in distress paralyzed the men with fear. They wanted to run, but were not sure which direction to go. Kyle raised his gun for protection as the two scared men cautiously stepped back into the old moonshine shack.

Facing the door with his gun still pulled, Kyle watched for the creature. In a shaken voice he asked, "What the hell was that scream, not to mention that awful freaking smell?"

"Seems to be a panther that has rolled around on a rotten corpse," Henry said, trying to convince Kyle and himself in his steady voice. The paralyzing scream again echoed through the woods, causing the scared men to turn their attention to the shack's unprotected entrance. Kyle stepped to the door and shot his shotgun twice into the ground. "That will scare off the panther," Kyle said to Henry. Feeling confident the panther left after hearing the gunshot, the friends cleaned up their mess and packed up for their hike. As they hiked back towards the truck, they searched the area along the marked trees with flashlights and careful alertness, not sure of the mindset of the panther prowling around. Once again, the overpowering, gagging, dead odor overtook them, causing the hike to stop.

"Stand with your back to my back. Panthers only attack from behind." Henry quickly commanded Kyle. They stood still in overmastering terror, listening for any movement to finger the beast's position. Both men could feel their hearts beating in their chests as they tried to control their breathing. The hike had made them vulnerable to an attack by the stalking panther.

"Now, as I walk forward, you walk backwards keeping your back against mine. Keep your flashlight scanning and gun ready to fire." Henry took charge of the dangerous situation. The friends slowly inched their way towards the truck. The moonless sky kept the forest black, not helping the situation. Another hair-raising scream, this time from up above, echoed around them from the treetops, causing heart-stopping panic. "Cover your ears," Kyle warned before firing off three rounds of buck shots in different directions, hoping to scare off the unseen beast. Picking up the pace, the scared friends moved closer to the exit of the woods, expecting an attack from behind each passing tree. A shuffling out in front of Henry caused the two nervous men to stop. They listened carefully, trying to locate the position of the beast stalking them. With a full clip, Henry had eight shots in his .45. Kyle was down to three buck shot shells left in his shotgun. Henry held his gun up with one hand and held the flashlight down the barrel like a policeman on a house raid. They slowly moved forward, ready to shoot anything moving in their direction.

Henry's flashlight reflected a single round red eye just far enough away that he could not tell what was staring at him. All he could tell was that it stood over eight feet tall, and was wide. "What is that Henry?" asked Kyle to confirm the massive beast. "Good lord!" Kyle expressed as the butt-clinching fear overtook him. The large, reddish-white eye stood without blinking. "Shoot it!" Kyle whispered to Henry. "Shoot that damn thing," he forcefully repeated. Going against the teaching of his uncle Sylvester about not shooting anything unless you are 100% sure what it is, Henry pulled the trigger two times. The beast stood, not budging, still casting its terrifying stare. Two more pulls of the trigger left the same results. A loud, unexpectedly shrill scream came from the old shack's direction, catching the two friends off guard and causing them to abandon the slow moving, plan. Full of uncontrollable panic, with bodies full of adrenaline, the two terrified men ran toward the truck, not concerned with the thorns and sharp, skin-tearing branches they ran through. Arriving to the truck unharmed, the two friends quickly opened the doors and secured their safety from the beast.

After a few moments, Henry broke the silence. "Great idea, Kyle, let's go conjure some shadow people. Let's conjure shadow people in the dark woods in the creepy moonshine shack! What could go wrong?" Henry said full of sarcasm and laughter.

"Yeah, what the freak was I thinking? Better yet, what the hell were you thinking to listen to me?" Kyle agreed laughing.

"Boy, I thought I was going to die. Especially when we started to run. I just knew my slow fat ass was fixing to be eaten by a panther. The only thing that could have made the experience scarier is if the crazy guy ran by in his boxers and flip flops!" Kyle laughed out loud, making fun of the man from down the street who liked to run in boxers and flip flops for exercise.

The two friends laughed as they sat in the truck, still looking for the beast to exit the woods. Kyle opened two beers for the friends to drink and tried to calm down. "You clearly missed that big ass beast," Kyle pointed out the obvious.

"I do not miss," Henry corrected Kyle. The two friends made their way home with plans of meeting at sunrise to reassess the night's events. The next morning, Henry picked up Kyle to investigate. The two friends carefully entered the woods where they had exited a few hours earlier. They searched the area, looking for any signs from their horrific encounter. Finding no signs of a panther or a beast, they did find an old tree with four holes nicely placed around a knothole full of water. "Told you, I do not miss," Henry held his chest high as they left the woods.

***

THE NEW HOUSE

The happy family moved from the university-owned house into their newly built dream home. Henry kept the creepy experiences away from Sharon, not wanting to worry her or make himself sound stupid. Sharon had an annoying knack for rolling her eyes about things she felt to be impossible. The first few days, Henry had to occasionally shake off the feeling of being watched as he took care of work around the land. He jokingly blamed his neighbor Kyle for introducing the shadow people into his life. After settling into their new home, the family hosted a housewarming gathering for Sharon's coaching staff, trainer, and their neighbors Kyle and Roy. The proud couple showed everyone around the house before sitting down to enjoy Henry's famous smoked ribs.

After Roy went home to check on the dog and the coaches began their volleyball talk, Henry and Kyle made their way out to the back porch to enjoy their beer. The two friends again laughed about their encounters in the woods.

Once henry had enough beer, he asked Kyle the hard personal

question he had been wondering. "So, ah, when did you realize, ah, when did you know you were gay? I mean, how did you know?" Fumbling his words, Henry became flustered, rethinking the question. Laughing at Henry's discomfort, Kyle responded, "Well, I really do not remember when I knew. I just kind of went down the gay road not realizing where I was headed."

Kyle stood, asking Henry if he wanted another beer. After a few moments, Kyle returned with the cooler of beer and tossed one to Henry. Sitting back down on the bench, Kyle continued to answer Henry's question. "My older brother Wick was an elite athlete, well liked and good with the ladies in high school. Wick was so good with ladies, he had been through four divorces by age 30. My older sister Beth was a popular cheerleader who ended up marrying her college boyfriend. I focused on football and baseball in High School, not dating anyone until college. I never had interest in women or men. I hooked up here and there with women, but never dated. I made the baseball team as a walk-on at North Mississippi, where I met Roy." Henry interrupted Kyle and pointed to the flock of turkeys feeding in the pasture. After a brief conversation about the wild turkeys, Kyle continued. "I met Roy in the training room, where we were both rehabbing from MCL tears. He wasn't the little bitch then that he is now." Kyle joked. "We began hanging out playing video games and drinking beer. When my brother Wick died, Roy was there through the process, keeping me from getting too depressed, making me get up out of bed every day. I do not believe I would have made it through Wick's death without Roy."

"How did your brother die?" Henry carefully asked.

"Well, the dumbass fell over twenty feet from his old climbing stand while deer hunting down in Wilmer, Alabama. His cheap ass did not want to spend the money for a new one. He broke six or seven ribs that punctured his lungs. He was able to make his way back to his truck. While driving himself to the hospital, he lost consciousness and crashed into an oak tree. Not buckled up, he went through the windshield. He was dead by the time he arrived to the hospital.

If he would have just bought a new damn climbing stand, he would still be alive." Kyle said with a hollow laugh, shaking his head. "Roy helped me through the whole episode. Apparently, he knew I was gay before I did. Everything with him just felt right."

"Roy was an athlete in college?" Henry asked in disbelief.

"Yep, he was a stud, All-Conference tight end." Kyle proudly spoke of his partner with a sparkle in his eyes. Still watching the turkeys feed, Kyle stood up in disbelief! "Who is that?" Kyle pointed down past the turkeys just before the creek. Henry looked, not yet seeing the tall old man dressed in black pants, with a white long sleeve shirt under a black vest and black gambler hat.

"Who's what? I don't see anyone." Henry stood, walking over to Kyle for a better view. "I still see nothing." Henry said, starting to think Kyle was messing with him.

"Look bro, past the flock of turkeys almost to the creek, on the edge of the tree line. It is an old white dude dressed in black," Kyle pointed.

"Oh crap," Henry said as he finally saw the man. "I do not know who the hell that is." Henry stood with Kyle, watching the old man.

The old man walked toward Turkey Creek and faded away. "Where did he go?" Henry asked as he started down the stairs toward the creek to investigate. Not answering, Kyle followed. The two friends made their way through the pasture, scaring off the wild turkeys. They both left a muddy trail as they walked through the grassy field, water-soaked from the hard rain earlier in the day. The area where the old man vanished showed no signs of the trespasser. The path the old man took across the pasture was undisturbed, unlike the muck the two friends created on their way across the pasture. "Damn it, Kyle! You and your shadow people!" Henry laughed. By the time the two friends returned, Roy was waiting on the porch, insisting for Kyle to call it a night.

***

TYLER MEETS SHAK

Henry was up early, shaking off the too many beers he enjoyed at their small gathering of friends. He knew the baseball field he had promised Will and Tyler was long past due. After three cups of black coffee sweetened with local honey, Henry and his eager boys were off to the barn to begin their project. The three worked together, erecting a ten-foot backstop made from chicken wire and 2x4s. The bases were cut out of the leftover plywood from the barn construction and painted white. Once they finished cutting the grass, Henry carefully marked off and painted the foul lines, completing the little ball field just after lunch.

After a shower and a well-deserved nap, Henry prepared his grill to cook the hot dogs Sharon had set out for dinner. The happy family sat down for dinner and discussed the newly built ball field.

Later in the evening, Tyler laid in his bed watching his new flat screen TV. The room temperature dropped suddenly, causing him to pull his comforter up over his legs for extra warmth. The TV reception began flickering in and out with static. Tyler looked out his window to see if a storm or wind was the cause for the poor satellite reception. Not seeing any issues outside, Tyler turned his attention back to the TV. Irritated, Tyler was staring at the fuzzy screen flickering a 70s sitcom when he noticed a shadow overtake his room. Frightened, Tyler sat up and pulled his comforter up to his chin as he watched the shadow slowly form into a silhouette. A friendly, dark blue-eyed face appeared surrounded with yellow hair.

"Hello!" a young African voice came from the silhouette's friendly face. "My name is Shak, what is your name?" the friendly voice asked.

"Ah, I am, ah Tyler?" Tyler answered, questioning what he was seeing.

"Can I play your game?" Shak pointed to the gaming console setting under the TV.

"Yeah, sure," Tyler got up to turn his console on, not taking his eyes off Shak. A good feeling of belonging overtook Tyler as he stood looking at Shak. Tyler grabbed both cordless controllers and tossed one on the ground at Shak's feet. Still standing across the room, Shak slowly picked up the controller.

"You like baseball?" Tyler asked.

"Yes, I am very fond of baseball."

Tyler was surprised how good Shak became after only a few innings of playing. The two played a full nine inning game, laughing and talking until Shak had to go back into the shadow.

"I will be back in a few days. Is that ok with you?" Shak asked his new friend.

"Sure, come back and I will give you a chance to beat me," Tyler laughed. Turning off the game, Tyler saw the TV reception was back to normal. Shak disappeared back into the shadow.

The next day, Tyler decided not to speak of his new friend to his parents, not sure if Shak was real or only a dream. Three nights later, Tyler's TV again flickered in and out as the room temperature dropped. Tyler sat up looking for Shak. Again, the silhouette stepped from the shadow and asked to play Tyler's game. Tyler jumped off the bed, eager to play with his new friend.

"You wanna play baseball, football, or basketball?" Tyler asked Shak, being a good host.

"I like baseball," Shak answered. The two friends played another nine inning game of baseball. Tyler won. "Thank you, my friend. I enjoyed your game," Shak expressed.

"What are you?" Tyler asked Shak.

"I am one of God's angels!" Shak answered proudly. "I will be back in a few days." Shak again disappeared into the shadow.

Tyler laid in bed wondering if Shak was really an angel. *Why would an angel want to play video games with me?* Tyler thought to himself.

Tyler went about the next few days without sharing his experience with his family. A little worried about his friendship, Tyler decided to ask detailed questions the next time Shak appeared. He wrote down a few questions to ask his new friend. On the third night, Tyler's TV began to flicker as the room temperature dropped. Excited to play baseball with Shak, Tyler sat up looking for his friend. The silhouette stepped out from the shadow.

"Hello Tyler," the friendly voice said as its dark blue eyes and yellow hair appeared. "Are you ready to play baseball?"

"Yep," Tyler jumped out of bed to turn his game on. During the third inning, Tyler decided it was time to find out more information about Shak.

"Can I ask you some questions?" Tyler looked at Shak for approval.

"Why sure, ask me anything." Shak nodded yes as he struck out for the third out of the inning.

"Where are you from?" Tyler asked the first question.

"Heaven," Shak answered as it threw a nasty pitch.

"Do you know God?" Tyler asked his second question.

"Yes, God sends me to do his work." Shak threw a knuckleball to Tyler's batter.

"What kind of work do you do for God?" Tyler asked a follow up question.

"Well, after the great war against the fallen angels in heaven, God sent me to Africa to track down the fallen angels that turned against him and rip their wings off."

"Rip their wings off?" Tyler asked in disbelief as he laid down a sacrifice bunt to move his runner from second to third.

"Yes, when an angel's wings are ripped off, the angel becomes human. The wingless angels live as humans until death. After death, they become demons. These demons will walk the earth for all eternity unless they repent."

"What happens to the demons who repent?" Tyler asked as he hits a double up the middle to score the runner on third.

"Well, I destroy the demons and take their souls back to heaven," Shak answered his curious friend.

"Do they all repent?" Tyler asked.

"No, unfortunately most feel more comfortable with evil, so they wander the earth creating evil," Shak again answered his new friend.

Not wanting to annoy Shak, Tyler stopped the questions for the time being. Tyler focused on his third straight victory against his new friend. After their game ended, Shak again disappeared into the shadow.

Three nights passed before the room temperature dropped and the TV flickered in and out. Before Shak could fully appear, Tyler had the game ready to play. During the third inning, Tyler began his questions for Shak.

"Are you able to go anywhere you want on earth?"

"No, God sent me to Africa to protect his African people against evil."

"How are you able to be in Mississippi?" Tyler followed up.

"Long ago, an African woman brought here for slavery prayed to God, asking for help against the evil here on this land. God gave me this land to rid it of the evil," Shak answered proudly.

Tyler hit a solo homerun off a nasty curve thrown by Shak. After his homerun dance, Tyler focused on their game. The two friends battled as Shak forced extra innings with a two out homerun in the ninth.

After Shak's celebration dance, Tyler asked the question Shak was waiting for, "What is it like being an angel?"

Shak looked deep into Tyler's eyes as it responded. "Take my hand, open your heart, and see the world through my eyes." Tyler dropped his controller before placing his young hand into the silhouette's hand. An explosion of extraordinary joy overtook the young boy's soul as Tyler saw a radiant black and white mosaic entwine into a solid geometric figure of brilliant color that engulfed him. Tyler felt a fearless, unfamiliar world, free of stress, free of death, free of evil, a calmness that humans live their lives in search of. The overload of ecstasy brought Tyler to his knees as he let loose of Shak and fell down on his hands.

Shaking his head to refocus his eyes back to mortality, Tyler exclaimed, "Wow! That was awesome! Can I go again?"

Shak laughed as he shook his head "No! That is enough for to-day." Returning to their game, Shak hit a walk off home run in the tenth to win his first game. "I win!" Shak exclaimed.

"Good job," Tyler proved to be graceful in defeat.

"I must go," Shak informed his friend. "Thank you for letting me into your soul," Shak added as he stepped back into the shadow.

Shak continued to visit Tyler every three nights, using baseball to strengthen their relationship while distancing Tyler from his family. Unknown to Tyler, Shak was taking over his body and causing havoc around the house.

***

SHAK ATTACK

Henry woke gasping for air as heavy pressure around his neck restricted his airway. He sat up in bed as much needed air filled his lungs and gagged for his next breath. After he sucked in enough life-providing oxygen, Henry looked around the room for the in-truder that had ahold of his throat. Satisfied no one was there in his room, he sat on the side of his bed looking at the clock. 2:19 a.m. Henry made his way into the bathroom to relieve the built up fluid in his bladder. A quick glance into the mirror reflected the red hand-print still visible across his neck. "What the freak?" Henry whis-pered, still relieving himself. He continued to stare into the mirror as he washed his hands, not believing what he was seeing. The prints faded away as he inspected his neck. Wide awake, Henry made his way into the kitchen for a drink of water. He stood at the sink look-ing out into the dark night when a thought entered his head. *Did I choke myself in my sleep?* Henry picked up his phone to Google "sleep strangle yourself."

"Okay, it seems to be a common occurrence," he said to himself after reading a few entries. "Apparently, I am in need of a better quality of rest."

Still looking out the window into the dark, hair rose on Henry's neck as the old man in the black vest and black poker hat stood off to the side of Turkey Creek. Caught off guard but not scared, Henry stood watching the old man. After a moment, the old man pointed over toward the woods before returning back into the darkness. Henry grabbed chips and Poncho cheese dip and sat at the kitchen table for a snack. He enjoyed the early morning snack until a strange sound started by the laundry room, zizizizizizizi zizizizizizizi zizizizizizizi. *What the hell is that?* Henry froze listening to the strange sound. Zizizizizizizi, zizizizizizizi, zizizizizizizi. Carefully, he walked towards the sound, looking for a reasonable explanation. Stopping, he listened again, zizizizizizizi zizizizizizizi zizizizizizizi. *That sounds like someone spinning a socket wrench,* Henry thought to himself.

Opening the laundry room door, Henry realized the sound was coming from the attic. Looking up, he saw the A/C filter housing. "Crap, it must be the A/C unit making the noise. I hope it is not going out, but it is still under warranty," Henry whispered. Grabbing a flashlight from over the dryer, Henry quietly opened the attic door and let down the stairs, trying not to wake the house. He quietly went up into the attic to inspect the A/C unit. As he crept along the plywood path laid across the beams, he noticed the noise had stopped. Reaching the A/C unit, he found it running correctly with no signs of malfunctioning. *Hmm, the noise stopped as soon as I got up here, I will call someone tomorrow to inspect the A/c unit just in case.* As he turned toward the attic door his left foot kicked a socket wrench. "Huh, you're not serious," Henry said in disbelief as chills ran up his spine. He picked up the socket wrench and spun it to confirm the noise, zizizizizizizi zizizizizizizi zizizizizizizi. *Crap, that is the same sound.* Shining the flashlight around the dark attic, Henry knew he was the only person there.

He quickly exited the attic and locked the door behind him. Knowing sleep was not an option for his rattled nerves, Henry turned on the TV as he flopped down into his recliner. Flipping through the guide he settled on a comedy sitcom about friends hanging out in New York City. The once popular sitcom took his mind away from the night's events and allowed him to slip off into sleep.

A loud thud followed by a hair-raising scream had Henry up, racing toward the stairs and up to Will's room. He found his son's mattress and box spring in the middle of the room with Will underneath crying for help. "What the hell happened?" Henry pulled his youngest son out from under the upside down bed. "How the hell did you do this?" Henry yelled at his startled son.

Sharon and Tyler entered the room as Henry had begun interrogating Will. Still crying, Will tried to explain that he was only sleeping. "I don't know how I got on the floor," Will cried, still confused.

Sharon stepped in, taking Will into her room as she demanded Henry and Tyler place the bed back into the bed frame. After everyone calmed down, Will was able to convince his parents he had no idea what happened. Henry had a suspicion: the throat choking, socket wrench, and bed tossing were caused by shadow people, or maybe the old guy he kept seeing out by Turkey Creek. Knowing Sharon would roll her eyes in disbelief at any mention of spirits, Henry decided not to speak to her about his suspicion.

***

OUIJA BOARD

Late in the afternoon, Henry drove down to Roy and Kyle's house to discuss the events from the night before. He walked up to their prairie style ivory and white house. River stone columns held up the front porch and hipped metal covered the roof. Henry knocked on the aqua front door that matched the roof.

After a few moments, Kyle answered the door. "What's up, ya jackass?" Kyle smiled at Henry.

"We need to talk about your shadow people," Henry answered.

Noticing the uneasiness in his friend's face, Kyle closed the door and lead Henry to the chairs in the corner of the porch. The two friends sat down as Henry shared the past twenty-four hours.

"I don't know if our conjure séance caused these events to happen, but we need to figure out how to make them stop."

Before Henry could say anything else, Kyle stood up. "I will be right back." Kyle went into his house and returned with an antique wooden box. "I have been waiting for the right time to use this board. I bought it off the internet for 250.00. This board was produced in 1902." Burned into the old wooden case, old lettering read, OUIJA.

"Oh, Hell no! Hell no!" Henry stood up as he interrupted Kyle before he could finish about his online find. "No, no, no, I am not playing that scary ass game."

"It is not a game," Kyle insisted, "it is a way for us to talk to the shadow people about the events at your house. I have read that sometimes they can tell you what needs to be done for them to find peace."

"No! Every time I see a movie or read a book, bad things happen when the Ouija board is used. Your candle séance caused enough problems," Henry shook his head with disapproval of the Ouija board.

"Nothing bad happened with my séance," Kyle defended himself.

"We thought we were going to die, Kyle!" Henry reminded his friend.

"Yeah, well, there is no proof that had anything to do with my séance. Us almost dying had to do with being in the woods at night with a panther prowling," Kyle corrected Henry. The two friends started to laugh.

Kyle excused himself and returned with a small cooler with six beers inside. After taking a few drinks Henry looked over to Kyle, "I am really freaked out with what's going on over at my house. You said shadow people can't hurt anyone."

"No, I said there was not any proof shadow people have ever hurt anyone," Kyle again corrected Henry. The two friends sat in silence for a moment before Kyle said, "Hear me out before you say no. There is a full moon Saturday. We take the Ouija board out to the shack to see what we can find out. What could it hurt?"

Henry stared at Kyle for a bit. A big grin covered Henry's face. "Hell, no! I am not going back into that scary ass shack, especially with a Ouija board during a full moon. I came over here to see if anything odd was happening at your house."

Kyle looked at Henry, "I really think using the Ouija board in the shack will help us figure out what is happening at your house. Just think about it," Kyle ended the talk about the Ouija board as he set the wooden case on the ground beside his chair. The two friends finished the six pack before Henry headed back home.

Two nights went by without any new events. Henry was sitting with Tyler and Will watching their favorite football movie when he noticed Tyler sitting on the other end of their sectional, mumbling an unrecognizable language while blankly staring at the TV. "What are you saying, Tyler?" Henry asked. Will looked at his big brother to see what was going on. Tyler continued to stare at the TV not acknowledging his father. "Tyler!" Henry yelled. Tyler snapped out of his trance and looked at his father.

"Sir?" Tyler asked.

"What are you saying?" Henry asked again.

"Ah, I am, ah, not saying anything," Tyler quickly answered, confused.

"Yes, you were," Henry corrected his son.

"Oh, um, I guess I didn't realize I was talking," Tyler answered, still confused.

After the movie, both boys went to their rooms to get ready for bed as Henry continued to watch TV. A loud knock at the door caused Henry to jump. *Its 9:00 p.m. who could be at the door.* Henry opened the door.

"I figured it was you, ya sorry ass!"

"Well, hello to you," Kyle laughed. Henry invited his friend in, offering a cold beer as they sat at the kitchen table. "Tomorrow starts the full moon," Kyle reminded Henry.

Shaking his head no, Henry smiled as he agreed to use the Ouija board. "Well, Sharon is in Las Vegas recruiting until Sunday. I am willing to use the Ouija board Saturday night inside my barn."

"I knew you would come around!" Kyle smiled as he chugged the beer. "You think 11 p.m. we can meet in the barn."

"Yep," Henry agreed. "I'll bring the beer," Kyle volunteered as he walked to the door. Shutting the door behind Kyle, Henry let out a deep sigh, *I hope this doesn't backfire.*

After locking the doors and turning everything off, Henry went upstairs to check on his two boys. Standing outside Tyler's door Henry could hear his son talking to someone. Henry opened the door to find Tyler sitting in his gaming chair playing baseball on his gaming console.

"Who are you talking to?" Henry asked looking around the room.

"Ah," Tyler picked up his phone, "a friend from school."

"Oh! Okay, don't stay up too late." Henry left the room content with Tyler's explanation.

"Woo, that was close," Tyler smiled as he continued his game against Shak. "I am not sure dad would understand our friendship."

Henry checked on Will before heading downstairs to prepare for bed. After watching more TV, Henry slipped off asleep. *He! He! Ha! Ha!* Henry, laying on his side, opened one eye. *Did I just hear a laugh?* he thought to himself still bundled up, nice and warm under his blanket. After laying there listening for a few moments, he only heard the sound of his TV, still playing reruns from the 1990s and waiting for the sleep timer to turn it off, Henry closed his eye. *I must have been dreaming,* he thought while focusing on going back sleep. *He! He! Ha! Ha!* Henry opened both eyes with surprise, still bundled up under his blanket. *He! He! Ha! Ha!* Again, the laugh echoed behind Henry.

Reluctantly, Henry sat up in bed, not sure what he would encounter. As he expected, the room was empty. "Who is there?" Henry asked the empty room. A grayish, clear blob floated into the wall as he heard a faint, *He! He! Ha! Ha!* Uneasy, Henry turned his TV volume up and reset the sleep timer. *These shadow people are exhausting,* he thought to himself.

At 10:30 p.m. Saturday, Henry made his way down to the barn. He pulled out an old poker table and a couple of chairs. He grabbed a Midnight Magic beer he picked up in Memphis from the Ghost River Brewing Company. He kept his good beer in the old refrigerator in the barn. Henry enjoyed the beer as he sat waiting for Kyle to show up. *Why in the hell did I agree to try the Ouija Board?* he thought to himself. *I know something bad will come out of this.*

Halfway through Henry's third beer, Kyle pulled up in his old truck. The two friends greeted each other and Kyle began setting up the board. He set the Ouija board in the center of the table, then placed white pillar candles on either side. After lighting the candles, Henry turned the barn's lights off.

"Before we start, we must move the pointer around in a circle over the center to warm the board up. All questions must be serious, and if the spirits are rude or vulgar, we have to end the session," Kyle explained the rules. Henry took a deep breath before placing his fingers onto the pointer. The two friends slid the pointer around the center of the Ouija Board. Once Kyle felt the board was warm, he nodded to Henry to stop.

Taking a deep breath, Kyle asked the first question. "Is there a spirit here in this barn?" Henry and Kyle waited to see where the pointer would go. After a few moments, Kyle removed his fingers from the pointer. "Well, that was intense," he looked at Henry while reaching for two beers from the cooler. Henry laughed, "My butt was puckered the whole time."

"Maybe we should wait a bit before trying again." Kyle suggested as they drank the beer.

"Well, I am not sitting out here all night," Henry stopped talking and Kyle's mouth dropped opened as they watched the pointer move unassisted. **L E A V E**, the pointer spelled out.

"I can't believe that just happened," Kyle said without taking his eyes off the pointer.

"What do we . . .?" A clap of thunder interrupted Henry. Strong winds began outside, as large hail began pounding the barn. Henry jumped up to look outside, confirming the bad storm was moving in.

"Is it supposed to rain?" Kyle asked, not remembering seeing a chance of rain on the 10 p.m. forecast.

Henry closed the barn door and sat back down at the table. "I am done! I, ah, am done with the Ouija board," Henry said to Kyle as he flopped back down in his chair. Henry reached for another beer when the pointer again began moving unassisted. **S A V E C H I L D R E N**, the pointer spelled out. Another clap of thunder scared the two friends. Lost for words, Kyle sat speechless. Henry stood up and shut the Ouija board box. "I knew using the Ouija board would be bad," Henry said over and over between chugging two beers.

"Yeah me too," Kyle agreed, still staring at the closed Ouija board box.

Irritated, Henry looked at Kyle, "What do you mean, me too? What happened to 'what could it hurt' and 'I think it will help'?"

Kyle laughed. "Don't blame me! You are the one who keeps listening to me!"

"Yeah, yeah, yeah! What do we do now?" Henry smiled.

"I really would like to know what 'save children' means. I think we should ask the question to see what the board says." Kyle suggested.

"Damn it, Kyle!" Henry sat back down and opened the Ouija board box. "I really hate you!" Henry said as he smiled. The two friends moved the pointer around in a circle to warm the board. Again, Kyle nodded when he thought the board was warm. Kyle asked the question, "Is there a spirit here with us?" The two friends' fingertips followed the pointer to YES. Kyle looked up at Henry, who had a serious, scared look on his face.

Kyle asked the next question, "Are you the spirit that said 'save children'?" Again, the pointer moved to YES! Henry looked up at Kyle with the same serious, scared face, "Good. Same spirit."

"What is your name?" Kyle asked. **T A N Y I A**, the pointer spelled out under their fingertips. "Whose children need to be saved?" Kyle asked while Henry held his breath. **T A N Y I A**, the pointer spelled.

"Save Tanyia's children?" Henry asked the next question. The pointer moved to YES! Feeling good about the Ouija board, Henry asked another question, "Did you live here?"

The pointer pulled away from under their fingertips as it rapidly moved, spelling **S A V E C H I L D R E N , S A V E C H I L D R E N**, over and over. The two friends watched for a few minutes before Henry slammed the box, closing the Ouija board game.

"Holy crap!" Kyle expressed as they could hear the pointer flopping around inside the box. After a few moments, the pointer stopped. "Wow, that was crazy!" Kyle looked up at Henry. "I am now done with this Ouija board!"

Henry stood up from the table to grab another beer. "Well, I am glad to know Tanyia was not telling us to save my children," Henry took a big drink of his beer.

"I gotta go," Kyle looked at his phone. "Roy has been texting me to come home for fifteen minutes." The two friends shook hands and headed towards their homes.

***

SHAK CONTROLS TYLER

Sharon returned home from recruiting in Las Vegas and instantly noticed something different about Tyler.

"What is wrong with Tyler?" Sharon asked her husband.

"Ah, nothing?" Henry was not sure where she was going, but had a bad feeling he was going to get in trouble for something.

"Have you not noticed that Tyler has not come out of his room since I got home? He is not eating much, and every time I go into his room to see who he is talking too, all I get is that 'it is a friend from school.' I checked his phone usage today and he has not used his phone. Now, how long has this been going on, or have you not noticed? I feel like when I am out of town, you relax on parenting!"

Henry held his head down once he realized everything was headed back to being his fault. "I knew I was fixing to get in trouble," Henry smiled looking at his wife. "I figured he was at the age of wanting to be by himself," Henry tried to deflect the blame. "We need to sit Tyler down to find out what is going on with him."

The concerned parents sat Tyler down to talk. Sharon took charge by bluntly attacking Tyler with direct questions. The young teen deflected the best he could until he broke under the pressure.

"His name is Shak, and we play baseball on my gaming console," Tyler blurted out after he had enough of his mom's verbal attack.

"Shak?" Henry asked, not sure where Tyler was headed.

"Shak visits me in my room to play baseball with me. I am the only one who can see him." The shocked parents kept their cool as they listened to their oldest son describe the dark silhouette with yellow hair and dark blue eyes. Needing time to let the new information sink in, Sharon asked Tyler to try to spend more time with the family.

Tyler was excused as the parents went into their room to talk privately. Henry sat in the yellow club chair next to the window.

"What the hell was that? Our young teen has an imaginary friend?" he said to his wife.

Sharon sat on the edge of their bed, staring at the ground. "He is too old for an imaginary friend. Right?"

"Yes, he is too old." Henry answered.

Sharon stood up and looked over at Henry, "I will ask my friend in the psychology department his opinion tomorrow."

The next day, Sharon called Henry to let him know what she found out. "We need to take Tyler to see a pediatric psychologist. I have already scheduled an appointment with Dr. Capps, the only pediatric psychologist in Coffeeville."

Another day later, Henry and Tyler met Sharon at Dr. Capp's office in Coffeeville. The family sat in the waiting room until the doctor greeted them at his office door. The mostly bald, blonde haired doctor wore glasses and a small hearing aid. His round belly, sticking out like a pregnant woman entering her third trimester, was enhanced by his small frame. The high-pitched voice pushing out his southern accent surprised the family. "Come on in," the friendly doctor stepped aside as the family walked into the office and found their seats. The olive walls were decorated with pictures of Razorbacks from the university the doctor proudly attended in Arkansas, along with his degree and certificates.

After introductions, Tyler left the room as his parents explained their situation to the doctor. Once Dr. Capps heard enough information, he sent the parents out in order to speak with Tyler one on one. The friendly doctor talked to Tyler enough to get a feel for the teen's side of the situation. The doctor scheduled the family to return the next week at the same time.

The next morning, Sharon stuck her head into Tyler's room to check on him. She rushed over to his bed after seeing a large amount of blood dried on his sheet. Looking over her son in a panic, she discovered he had gashed skin from deep bites up and down his forearm.

"What happened?" Sharon yelled at her barely awake son.

"I don't know," Tyler answered his mom, still not fully aware of his gnawed up, swollen, forearm.

"Have you been biting you forearm?" Sharon yelled at her frightened son. Tyler began crying once he noticed the gashes. Sharon yelled for Henry to bring the first aid kit so she could wrap Tyler's arm for the trip to the clinic on campus.

Dr. Lafferty, the head doctor at the campus clinic, was a volleyball booster, and sent Tyler straight back into a room without waiting. Tyler continued to tell his parents he had no idea how his forearm had gotten gnawed up. The experienced doctor gave Tyler a few shots to numb the pain and cleaned the torn flesh. After careful inspection of the forearm and teeth prints, Dr. Lafferty was able to confirm the bite marks were from Tyler's mouth.

Irritated with Tyler's lies, Sharon grabbed her son by the shoulders to express her anger. She looked him straight into his eyes. "Why are you biting yourself?"

Tyler, eyes full of huge tears, softly responded, "I'm not!"

Realizing his wife was losing her cool, Henry stepped in to take control of the situation. He took Sharon out into the hall while Dr. Lafferty stitched up the torn flesh on their son's forearm. Henry whispered into Sharon's ear, "Could these bites be from Shak? Could Shak be some kind of spirit or demon?"

Sharon shoved Henry away, "Don't be stupid, this is serious! Our son is hurting himself and you are trying to be funny." Henry knew from experience that Sharon did not believe in the paranormal.

After Dr. Lafferty finished attending to Tyler, he joined the parents in the hall. "I fear for your son's safety. He sincerely seems to have no memory of biting himself. Tyler must be going into some state of unconsciousness where he doesn't remember what he is doing."

Sharon looked at Henry, then back at Dr. Lafferty, "I will get him an appointment with the pediatric psychologist for this afternoon or first thing tomorrow morning." Later that night, Sharon went to check on Tyler before bed. She entered the room unannounced, finding Tyler with a pocketknife sketching a symbol into his thigh. Tyler ignored her when she yelled at him to stop. He continued running the point of the knife down into his skin. Sharon snatched the knife from his hand and he looked up at her with unfamiliar eyes. Sharon stepped back, surprised by the strange look of her son. Tyler's eyebrows were a little bowed and his head tilted to the left. "Why did you take my knife?" Tyler asked with a deep pitched, slightly gargled voice.

Unable to speak, Sharon left the room to find Henry. As the parents returned to Tyler's room, he was lying on his bed, panicked from the blood leaking from his thigh. "What happened?" Tyler looked up at his parents with frightened eyes. Henry grabbed the first aid kit still sitting on the dresser, and began to clean the messy thigh. "What is happening to me?" Tyler again cried to his parents. Sharon sat down to comfort her scared son as Henry inspected the symbol on Tyler's thigh. "It looks like a ladder or train tracks," Henry reported. The six-inch symbol took up most of Tyler's thigh. Henry covered the symbol with the medical cream they were given for the boy's forearm and wrapped his thigh with cloth. Henry helped Tyler downstairs to the sectional.

"You sleep here tonight, and I will stay to watch over you," Henry assured his son. Sharon fetched blankets and pillows to make her frightened son comfortable.

The worried parents stepped into the kitchen to speak while Tyler was fixing his bed for the night. Sharon looked at Henry, holding back tears. "When I walked into Tyler's room, he had a different look in his eyes. I mean, it was not him. He looked like something evil was in him." Henry held his wife and told her everything would be okay. Deep in Henry's gut, he knew the shadow people were responsible, but knew Sharon would not listen to his belief. Henry assured Sharon that he would keep Tyler safe through the night, and told her to get a good night's sleep.

Once Tyler was sleeping, Henry stepped into the kitchen for a beer to calm his nerves. He sat at the table, keeping Tyler in sight. Looking at the clock, he wondered if Kyle was up 11:30 p.m. Henry sent a text to his friend, "You up?"

"Yep, sitting on the couch drinking a sixer," Kyle responded with mugs of beer on each side of a smiley face. "What's up?" Kyle finished his text.

"Tyler is cutting and biting himself. I believe a shadow person has caused Tyler to hurt himself. What do you think?" Henry asked.

Taking a minute to respond, Kyle agreed. "Yeah, I guess it is possible. What are ya'll gonna do?"

"I do not know. We are taking him back to see the pediatric psychologist tomorrow." Henry answered. Kyle, not knowing what to say, offered prayers and support. Henry finished his beer and sat next to Tyler on the sectional. The concerned father slept with one hand on his son's chest.

The next morning, the family arrived for their appointment with Dr. Capps. After an hour with Tyler, Dr. Capps called the worried parents into his office. "After the events of the past two nights, and after talking with Tyler, I believe he needs to be evaluated by the Catholic Church."

"The Catholic Church?" Sharon asked, not sure why the church needed to be involved.

"Well, the Catholic Church has the resources to handle this type of condition," Dr. Capps answered.

Still not following the doctor, Sharon asked, "What condition?"

Henry leaned over to his confused wife, "The good doctor believes there is a spirit messing with Tyler." Sharon, unable to control herself, rolled her eyes in disbelief. The family left the doctor's office headed for home.

After arriving home, Sharon and Henry stepped out onto the back porch for a private conversation. "Clearly, Dr. Capps is an idiot. I will call the medical clinic in Memphis for a more qualified pediatric psychologist," Sharon bluntly informed Henry.

Already convinced before the doctor confirmed his suspicion, Henry put his foot down, "No, we will take Tyler up to Saint Paul Catholic Church after we eat lunch. If they can't help, then we will look in Memphis for a new pediatric psychologist." Sharon, realized Henry was serious and backed down, agreeing to take Tyler to the Saint Paul church in Coffeeville. After lunch, the family again loaded up for the drive to town.

Henry opened the door to the church rectory for his family. The old iron storm door sounded a bell, letting the nun at the desk know someone was entering. The orange brick building sat off to the side of the church. A nice middle-aged nun greeted the family. The plaque on the desk read Sister Robert Ann. "How may I help you?" the polite nun asked.

"We would like to speak with Father Patrick McGill, please," Henry said.

"One moment," the nun stepped into an office. She returned with Father Patrick. "What can I do for y'all?" The priest showed the family into his office. After introductions, Sharon asked Tyler and Will to wait in the lobby with Sister Robert Ann.

The office had two orange brick walls and two cinder block walls, all painted light blue. A picture of the Archbishop hung next to a picture of the Pope. Behind the old walnut desk hung the Father's degree from the University of Memphis. Henry and Sharon sat in the two walnut chairs that matched the desk. Father Patrick asked the stressed out parents how he could help. Henry took charge, explaining the events of the past 48 hours. Father Patrick took notes and contact information. "In situations like yours, all I am legally able to do is contact the Archbishop. I will call the Archbishop in Memphis to explain your case. Someone will be contacting y'all in the next few days."

"You can't offer any advice?" Henry asked.

"Sorry!" Father Patrick apologized as he led the family out of the rectory.

Sharon, not happy with the cold attitude from the priest, bluntly asked, "What is your deal? Why can't you give us any information to help our son?"

Caught off guard, Father Patrick calmly explained, "I am sorry, but I am not allowed by the church or by law to discuss anything regarding cases like yours. Someone from the Archbishop's office will contact you. I wish I could help." Sharon stormed to the car as Henry apologized to the priest. "She is stressed by our situation."

"I understand," Father Patrick assured Henry.

Sharon stayed silent on the way home, with huge tears filling her eyes. Henry noticed she was upset, but did not want to bring attention to her in front of the boys. Once home, the parents again stepped out back to the porch for a private conversation.

"I do not understand why Father Patrick was so rude. He just sat there like he did not care. I do not trust he will do anything to help Tyler. I'm going to call the medical group in Memphis tomorrow," Sharon insisted.

"Calm down, Sharon. Possessions are a taboo subject in the Catholic Church. If we do not hear from the Archbishop in 24 hours, you can call the medical clinic in Memphis. Right now, we need to act normal around both of our boys." Henry hugged Sharon to comfort her before heading back into the house. Again, Henry slept on the sectional with one hand on Tyler's chest.

***

FATHER BYRNE INVESTIGATES

At 8 a.m., the phone rung, waking Henry. "Hello?" Henry answered.

"Mr. Matoske, this is Sister Ashley Waugh from the Archbishop's office in Memphis, do you have a minute to talk?"

"Ah, yes ma'am, Sister."

"The Archbishop has reviewed the information he received from Father Patrick McGill of Saint Paul parish in Coffeeville. The Archbishop would like to send his senior priest down to meet Tyler tomorrow morning, if it is okay with you."

"Yes, sister, of course," Henry agreed to the meeting.

"Father Byrne will arrive between 10 a.m. and 2 p.m., if that time works for you."

"Yes ma'am, Sister," Henry agreed to the time.

"Father Byrne will want to meet with you and your wife. The meeting should only take an hour." Sister Ashley Waugh said goodbye.

Henry hung up the phone and turned to Sharon, "The Archbishop is sending his senior priest to meet with us tomorrow." Sharon smiled with relief, although she still did not understand what a priest would be able to do for Tyler.

At 10:05 a.m. Henry heard a car pull up. He yelled upstairs for the boys to join their mom downstairs on the sectional. Opening the door Henry, introduced himself to Father Byrne as he ushered the priest into the house. "This is my family, wife Sharon, sons Tyler and Will." After introductions, Father Byrne asked to speak with Henry and Sharon. Henry sent the boys upstairs for a bit. Father Byrne asked for an explanation of their situation. Henry explained the past 48 hours as Sharon sat quietly on the couch, still not sure how a priest could help their situation.

After listening to their explanation, Father Byrne stood to explain his thoughts. "I will have to assess Tyler to decide if he has a psychological issue or is a candidate for exorcism."

"A candidate for what?" Sharon interrupted Father Byrne.

Confused, Father Byrne looked at Henry, then back at Sharon. "A candidate for exorcism. That is why y'all went to see Father Patrick? From what Father Patrick explained to the Archbishop, Tyler might be dealing with a demon possession."

Sharon, not sure what to say, looked over at Henry, "You think Tyler is possessed?"

"I do believe Tyler is fighting some kind of shadow person. I do not think it is a demon," Henry answered his wife. With a roll of her eyes, Sharon sat back into the sectional.

Father Byrne continued, "If I feel he qualifies for an exorcism, I will go to the Archbishop for approval."

"Very well. What do we need to do to get started?" Henry asked. Father Byrne pulled out paperwork from his briefcase, allowing him permission to examine Tyler. After the parents signed the release form, Father Byrne asked for Tyler to be called downstairs. Tyler came down the stairs and took a seat in a chair from the kitchen table placed in front of the sectional.

"Okay, Tyler we are going to pray together. Is that ok with you?"

"Yes, Father," Tyler agreed.

Father Byrne looked over to the parents, "Y'all are encouraged to join in with our prayers." Father Byrne began the Our Father. "Our Father, Who art in heaven, hallowed be Thy name; Thy Kingdom come, Thy will be done on earth as it is in heaven." Father Byrne placed his right hand on Tyler's forehead making the sign of the cross with his thumb, using blessed oil. "Give us this day our daily bread; and forgive us our trespasses as we forgive those who trespass ..." Tyler stopped saying the prayer as his body began to tremble.

Tyler shook his head, trying to fight the irritation from deep in his soul. Losing the inner battle, his eyes rolled back into his head as his body went limp. Sitting off to the side, Sharon stood up, suspicious of the scene. Tyler opened his eyes, speaking in an unfamiliar language, "Vernietig wortel omdat hulle vrot is. Moet God se siele kry. Vernietig wortel omdat hulle vrot is. Moet God se siele kry."

Sharon collapsed in horror onto Henry, who was still sitting on the sectional in shock. The horrified parents could only stare in disbelief, unable to help their demon-controlled son.

Father Byrne recited the Athanasian Creed until the demon-controlled Tyler spat a green, bile-filled wad onto Father Byrne's face. The Father stopped the Creed and wiped his face before continuing. Finishing the Creed, Father Byrne stood up and shouted with authority, "What is your name, demon?"

With an African accent, the demon spoke in broken English, "You are not welcome here, you are not welcome here, priest! This is my land. God sends me for his souls!"

Father Byrne went up on his toes, yelling down at the demon, "Leave this boy's body, in the name of The Father, The Son, and The Holy Spirit!" Father Byrne then splashed holy water on Tyler's head.

"I am not a demon, priest," the demon yelled. Father Byrne made the sign of the cross over Tyler as the demon let out a loud, boisterous laugh and Tyler's body went limp. Father Byrne continued to pray for God to remove the demon from Tyler's body.

Sharon and Henry still sat in horror, not able to speak. Tyler came to, looking around at his parents as Father Byrne pretended Tyler had passed out, not telling the confused boy about the evil deep within. After Father Byrne felt Tyler was back to himself, he excused the young teen in order to speak with Sharon and Henry in private.

The parents were still horror-stricken, sitting on the sectional, as Father Byrne began to talk. "There is no doubt in my mind that Tyler is possessed by a demon. Sometimes these demons will leave after a few sessions, and sometimes it takes multiple sessions. Be assured that my years of experience will guide us through this journey. Moving forward, I will conduct these sessions out of family view, in order to keep Tyler's stress level down. I will have to follow procedure and submit my plan to the Archbishop. Once he signs off on my plan, I will contact y'all to schedule the next session. For Tyler, y'all will have to treat him no different than normal. Prayer will be the best defense in fighting this beast. Keep all sharp items locked up, away from Tyler. Any questions?"

"Ah, no?" Henry, still shaken up, answered.

"If you need anything or have questions, you can call." Father Byrne set his card on the table before letting himself out.

Henry walked over to the door to lock it behind the priest. "I can't believe what we just witnessed," he looked over to Sharon as she poured herself a scotch and tonic. "Wow, drinking before noon?" Henry pointed out, looking at his watch. Sharon took a big gulp of her drink, looking for some mental relief. "I am so mad!" Sharon shot a mean look at Henry.

"Mad, really?" Henry asked, confused.

"Yes, mad! Why is this demon targeting Tyler?" Sharon took another gulp of her drink.

"I do not know why this demon has targeted Tyler, but I have had several encounters with unexplained events since we began building this house. Not only have I witnessed these events, but Kyle has seen them too. Now, I know you do not believe in the paranormal, but at this point, you need to start," Henry said with attitude.

Sharon, now open to the idea of the paranormal, did not want to argue or admit Henry might be right, rolled her eyes as she took another gulp of her drink. "What do we do now?" Sharon asked her husband.

"We do what Father Byrne said to do. We treat Tyler the same and pray."

Henry continued to sleep on the sectional each night with his hand on Tyler's chest, fearing that his son would hurt himself. The third day went by without any signs of the demon. The house sounded like a normal Saturday, with the boys outside playing baseball on the field they built with their father.

A loud, screaming cry moving toward the house caused Henry to jump up from the sectional, where he was watching his Redbirds play on TV. At once, he knew Will was on his way to the house in pain. Henry met his son at the back door. Will had his hand on his head with blood running through his fingers and down his arm. "What happened?" Henry asked, inspecting the gash at the top of Will's head.

"Tyler hit me with a rock." Henry looked down to the baseball field where Tyler was laying on his back looking up at the sky. Henry grabbed a towel for Will to apply pressure and went down to confront Tyler. Walking up, Henry noticed Tyler was speaking in a strange language. He was lying perfectly still, mumbling, "*My God stuur my om sy siele in te samel. Ek moet al die siele vind wat my God soek.*" Henry could tell his face was off center, and voice was gargling a deep tone. Not sure what to do, he backed away slowly.

Returning to the porch, Henry grabbed his phone to call Kyle. "I need you here now, right now!" Henry yelled into the phone as Kyle was saying hello. Without asking any questions, Kyle hung up his phone and headed toward his truck. Henry opened the front door without taking his eyes off Tyler, who was still laying out on the baseball field grass. "What is going on?" Kyle asked as he entered the house, holding his .45 in his right hand.

Kyle followed Henry through the house and out to the back porch, where they could both see Tyler still lying on his back. "Why is Will bleeding? Why is Tyler laying in the grass? What is going on over here?" Kyle asked as he holstered his pistol.

"Tyler is possessed with a demon, and I think he hit Will in the head," Henry answered, still looking out at Tyler.

"Possessed by a demon? Are you sure?" Kyle asked, looking confused.

"Yes, we are quite sure. We had the first attempt at exorcism with a priest from Memphis the other day. Now, can you stay here watching Tyler while I take Will to the clinic?"

Still confused, absorbing the unexpected information, Kyle stared down at Tyler. "Ah, what do I do if he comes after me?"

Looking down at Kyle's holstered pistol, Henry smiled, "Shooting him is not an option. Just sit here watching him. If he comes to the porch, I am sure he will be normal. If he wanders off toward the woods, follow him. If he comes after you as the demon, there is no evidence that he will hurt you!" Henry said with a laugh. Still not taking his eyes off Tyler, Kyle agreed to watch him so Henry could take Will to the clinic.

Returning from the clinic, Henry found Tyler and Kyle sitting on the back porch talking. Henry walked out and excused Tyler to his room so he could talk to Kyle in private.

"Will received one staple to close the gash. How did things go with Tyler?"

"Well, after about 30 minutes, Tyler sat up, looking around like he was confused. He sat there for a few minutes before walking up to me to ask where y'all were? I told him Will had cut his head and was at the doctor. So, he sat down and we small talked until now."

Henry shook his head.

"Now, what the hell did you mean earlier that Tyler was possessed by a demon?" Kyle asked, still confused from the earlier conversation. Henry started the explanation, "Tyler began spending more time in his room, I figured he was discovering himself." Both men laughed. "Then we found out he had an imaginary friend. We took him to a kids' shrink. The shrink said Tyler needed help from the Catholic Church. When the priest from Memphis came by to determine if Tyler needed an exorcism, Tyler began talking in an unfamiliar language with evil eyes. The priest began praying and Tyler passed out, not remembering anything. The priest is supposed to return for a second session."

"Oh shit," Kyle sat in disbelief. "Do you think it is one of the spirits we have seen?"

"That is what I was thinking, and wondering if it is that old man we saw out by the wild turkeys," Henry added. "Sharon did not believe in demons until the demon began speaking through Tyler. Her ass puckered up quickly!" Henry laughed.

"Damn man, that sucks!" Kyle expressed.

"The priest says the exorcism could take a couple of sessions, up to a couple of years, but he will be successful. It has been very stressful." Henry finished explaining. Kyle, not knowing how to help his friend, just said, "Let me know if I can do anything." After a few moments, Kyle left, leaving Henry to watch over his boys alone.

Henry, still sleeping each night on the sectional with his hand on Tyler's chest, woke to the house phone ringing. When he answered, he heard Father Byrne's voice, "Good morning, is this Henry?"

"Yes, Father," Henry mumbled, still groggy.

"The Archbishop has approved my request to begin the exorcism process. If it is okay, I will be down tomorrow morning around 10 a.m."

"Sure, that sounds great. Sharon returns home this afternoon," Henry confirmed. The two men hung up. Henry sent Sharon a text to tell her to clear her schedule for the next morning.

At 10:15 the next morning, Sharon and Tyler sat on the sectional as Henry opened the door for Father Byrne. Will was out spending the day with a friend. After they exchanged greetings, Father Byrne took Tyler back to Sharon's office. The priest sat Tyler down in the antique cedar chair in the middle of her office. Because Tyler did not fully understanding why he was having a prayer session alone with the priest, Father Byrne spoke to him about the power of prayer. He explained how he wanted Tyler to focus on the meaning of each word. The two began the Our Father. Midway through the prayer, Tyler's body began to quiver and convulse as sweat formed on his nose and forehead. Realizing the demon was taking over Tyler's body, Father Byrne quickly restrained his wrists to the chair arms. Looking down on the demon fighting to overtake the innocent boy, Father Byrne started the Athanasian Creed. Tyler's eyes rolled back into his head, then protruded back out as the demon successfully overtook the body.

"Why you here, priest? This is my land." The demon spoke in its deep, gargling voice.

Finishing the Athanasian Creed, Father Byrne took his crucifix in one hand and his prayer book in the other. He yelled down at the demon. "What is your name, demon?" The demon laughed from deep within its stomach as green, slimy bile leaked from its mouth.

Father Byrne again yelled, "Give me your name, demon!" The priest, full of adrenaline, bullishly shoved the crucifix into the beast's chest and yelled, "I expel you, demon, in the name of God the Almighty."

The demon controlling Tyler's body again laughed, "I am no demon, priest," causing the green bile and saliva saturating its face to splatter on the priest. The demon's hands rolled back, bending against its natural movement, as its morbid breath caused a nauseous feeling deep within the priest, who still held the crucifix firmly against its chest. "Priest, you have no power against me!" The demon again yelled.

Sharon and Henry stood in silent horror against the other side of the door as they heard the demon fight the religious power of Father Byrne. "God sends me to collect the souls he needs," the demon continued, spraying green bile on the priest. "This is my land, priest. You must leave my land," the demon fought its restraints. Father Byrne placed his prayer book and crucifix down on the table before removing his holy water container from the supply pack. The priest splashed holy water down on Tyler's body, making the sign of the cross above his head. The demon let out another animated laugh, saying, "You have no power over me. God sends me to collect his souls. My God protects me, priest." A dark silhouette engulfed Tyler's body, revealing its dark blue eyes and yellow hair. A painful sensation ran from Father Byrne's anus, up his spine, and into the base of his skull as he stood, surprised at what he was witnessing. The demon returned into Tyler's body, laughing aloud as the body went limp. Father Byrne continued mumbling prayers, still not sure what he witnessed. For the first time in his career, a demon showed itself.

Tyler slowly woke, still restrained to the antique cedar chair. "Wha… what is going on?" Tyler asked the Father, breaking his silent prayer. Realizing the demon was gone, the Father removed the restraints holding Tyler. Henry and Sharon, who were still on the other side of the door, quickly entered the office after hearing Tyler's voice. "What is happening?" the frightened young teen asked his parents. Father Byrne nodded approval as Henry began explaining, "Tyler, buddy, your friend Shak is a demon that is controlling your body from time to time." Tyler sat, still staring at his father with a confused look. "Father Byrne has been sent by the Archbishop in Memphis to rid your body of this demon." Still confused, Tyler looked over to his mother for confirmation. Sharon teared up as she gently shook her head in agreement with Henry.

Still dazed, Tyler looked down at his feet trying to absorb the news. "I don't understand," Tyler looked over to Father Byrne for a better explanation.

The experienced exorcist was ready with a more detailed explanation. "Tyler, this demon you call Shak has attached itself to your soul. There is no reason to be afraid. I will use the power of the church to remove this demon from your soul."

Still trying to understand, Tyler asked, "How did the demon get inside me? Am I a bad person?"

"No, you are not a bad person!" Sharon quickly answered her son, trying not to tear up.

"That is a good question," Father Byrne told the young teen. "Your mom is correct, you are not a bad person. Actually, demons go after people who are close to God. At any time, when you and Shak were playing your games, did you agree to let him into you or you into him?" the priest asked.

"Ah, one night I asked Shak what it was like being an angel. Shak told me to take his hand and open my heart to see." Tyler shared.

"Did you take his hand?" the Father asked.

"Yes," Tyler confessed, looking down ashamed.

"It is okay, I would have taken his hand also," the priest tried to help. "What did you see?" Father Byrne was truly curious.

"I do not know how to explain what I saw, but it was awesome. I asked to do it again, but Shak said once was enough." Father Byrne tried to think if any of his past patients experienced anything similar, but had no luck. The two parents listened quietly as the priest probed Tyler for information.

After digesting the information, Father Byrne shared his thoughts, "Shak gained access to Tyler's soul through Tyler taking the demon's hand. I need to figure out its name to expel it quicker."

"Shak is its name," Tyler spoke up.

"No son, Shak is the name it has given you. It will not voluntarily give its real name," the priest corrected the young teen. Father Byrne excused Tyler to talk to Henry and Sharon in private. "Expect this demon to continue to act out through Tyler. Do not try and engage the demon. Many times, multiple demons inhabit one person, which allows them to jump to other souls. Do not touch Tyler if you believe he is under this demon's control." Henry and Sharon agreed to be careful. Father Byrne cleaned up his supplies and headed back to Memphis, leaving the dumbfounded parents to care for their demon-controlled son.

Early the next morning, Henry woke to the sound of deep, gargling screams upstairs. He jumped up from the bed and headed for the door, not realizing his feet were tangled up in the covers. Still half asleep, Henry face planted onto the floor with his feet still up on the bed. Sharon, who also heard the commotion, was able to exit the bed cleanly, and moved toward the screaming upstairs as henry gathered himself to join her. Reaching the top of the stairs, Sharon paused as she realized Tyler was inside his room screaming. Thankful Will was staying the night with a friend, she waited for Henry to reach the top. "What do we do?" Sharon looked to Henry for leadership.

"I am not sure." Henry stood, staring at the door. "I guess you go back down to bed while I sit outside the door," Henry told his wife. Sharon returned to bed, but couldn't sleep listening to her oldest son scream and yell with an unfamiliar voice. Henry grabbed Will's beanbag to sit in and watched the door. The screams stopped after twenty minutes. Wide awake, Henry took a deep breath and enjoyed the quiet. After a few minutes of silence, Henry passed out from the mental exhaustion.

Henry woke the next morning curled up, half hanging off Will's beanbag. His neck had a lump from the awkward position. He opened Tyler's door to find the young teen passed out on the floor. Focusing on Tyler's chest, Henry made sure he was breathing and closed the door. He stumbled downstairs, fighting a non-drinking hangover, and spotted a black silhouette streaking across the kitchen, through the wall, and head out across the back field. Henry rubbed his eyes, still fighting the exhaustion. Shaking off the silhouette, Henry collapsed onto the sectional to watch the morning news. A little before noon, Tyler stumbled down the stairs and plopped onto the sectional next to his father. "How do you feel?" Henry asked, wanting to see if Tyler remembered the screaming.

"My body is sore. I woke up on the floor, must have fallen off. My throat is also sore," Tyler shared. Henry was relieved his son had no memory of the previous night.

Three nights went by without incident. Henry and Sharon were enjoying each other's company, watching TV in their bedroom. Up through the center of the mattress came a burst of energy, throwing both to the ground on either side of the bed. The mattress continued up, falling just shy of the ceiling. Sharon landed on her shoulder and rolled out of the impact while Henry landed flat, with his head catching the front of the nightstand. Both quickly bounced up on their feet, surprised by what they had just witnessed. "What was that?" Sharon looked over to Henry for an explanation.

"Just a guess, I would say Shak is trying to piss us off, but that is just a guess!" Henry answered, clearly irritated. Outside their bedroom door, they heard a bang as their cat screeched from being slammed into the wall. Still rubbing the knot on his head, Henry ran out of the room to look for their orange tabby cat, Pouncer. The normally energetic, social cat was curled up under the coffee table with his hair standing up. Henry picked up the frightened cat to console it and looked around the room for an explanation. Pouncer's hair again stood on end. The cat hissed as the black silhouette streaked across the room. The startled cat left deep scratches across Henry's chest as it raced away from the streaking silhouette. Henry yelled as the cat's claws dug deep into his chest. Sharon appeared in their bedroom doorway to check on her irritated husband. "What is going on?" She asked.

"That damn silhouette we have been seeing streaked across the room, causing Pouncer to tear my chest up," Henry answered as he went to the bathroom to pour rubbing alcohol over the fresh wound.

Father Byrne arrived at 11 a.m. the next morning for his third attempt to remove the demon from Tyler. Henry updated the Father on the events since his last visit. After the update, the Father took Tyler back into Sharon's office, leaving the parents to listen from the other side of the door. As with the other two attempts, Father Byrne strapped Tyler's wrists to the chair. The nervous boy stared into the Father's eyes for a word of encouragement. Before he began the Our Father, the priest told Tyler to relax and focus on the prayer. Midway through the prayer, the demon mumbled in its gargled voice, "Why are you here priest?" Ignoring the beast, Father Byrne finished the prayer and began the next.

The demon fought its restraints and yelled its demands. "Leave my land, priest! You are not welcome here!" The priest irritated the demon by ignoring its babble. Finishing the prayer, Father Byrne yelled down at the beast, "What is your name, demon?"

Henry and Sharon, still standing outside the door listening, prayed for this attempt to be successful. A faint drum beat started off in the distance as Father Byrne battled the terrible beast. The experienced exorcist's clothes were saturated with sweat as his heart pumped blood full of adrenaline. He stood looking down over the powerful demon inhabiting Tyler's body. Following the textbook procedure he had memorized decades earlier, the Father continued yelling at the beast to reveal its name. Calmness had escaped the normally cool-headed priest as the demon began digging its long sharp fingernails deep into the soft skin of Tyler's palms. Thick, red blood began dripping onto the floor from the chair's arm.

Again, Father Byrne yelled down at the demon, "Give me your name. In the name of God the Father, God the Son, and God the Holy Ghost, I demand you relinquish your name." Greenish foam goo that circled the demon's mouth splattered the priest with each deep breath, as the demon panted and fought the straps holding it to the chair. "Why do you keep bothering me priest? Don't you know God sends me to collect the souls?" the demon growled in its African accent from Tyler's mouth.

"Leave this boy's body and return to the pits of hell!" the priest commanded. Struggling to free itself, the demon broke the wooden arm away from the chair, instantly swinging it as a weapon towards the priest's head. The twenty-plus years of Jujutsu training paid off as Father Byrne, hearing the wood break, anticipated the unsuccessful swat of the chair's arm toward his head. The well-trained priest quickly grabbed the demon's wrist, twisting it before positioning the arm behind its back. Father Byrne's quick reflex helped overcome the abnormal strength the possessed body received from its inhabitant. Grabbing a zip tie from his supply bag attached to his belt, the Father tied the demon's wrist to the back of the chair, in the same manner a cop restrains a suspect. "Why do you keep bothering me priest?" the demon again grunted, splattering green goo as it spoke. Standing outside the door, Sharon began crying, unable to handle the fight inside her office. "Your power will not stop God's will." The demon continued to fight the strap and zip tie holding it to the back of the chair. Ignoring the demon's babble, Father Byrne placed his knees against its chest to help hold the demon-controlled body steady.

Reaching again for his supply bag, Father Byrne removed the crimson tin container of holy oil and plastic bottle full of holy water. He rubbed holy oil across the boy's forehead while mumbling the Our Father as he sprinkled holy water over the boy's head. He began the Glory Be in Latin, "Gloria Patri, et Filio, et Spiritui Sancto. Sicut erat in principio, et nunc, et semper, et in saecula saeculorum. Amen."

The demon laughed out loud as its black silhouette engulfed the boy's body, revealing its deep blue eyes. "You have no power over me," the demon again laughed before leaving the boy's body. Tyler's exhausted body went limp, temporarily released from the demon's control. He opened his eyes confused, not remembering the fierce battle between Father Byrne and the demon. A rush of unexpected emotion overcame Tyler as he struggled against the restraints that held the demon. "I need help," Father Byrne whispered as he looked down at the exhausted boy, who was unloading raw emotions as his torn flesh leaked dark red blood from his palms. As Tyler began to weep, Sharon opened the door and saw the blood covering the floor. She quickly yelled for Henry to grab the first aid kit. Tyler began crying as he noticed the amount of blood and size of his wounds. Sharon carefully cleaned and wrapped Tyler's palms as she tried to calm her frightened son. Father Byrne and Henry stepped out into the living area as the Father explained how the exorcism process takes time, encouraging Henry not to give up.

Still irritated from the previous day's failed exorcism, Henry woke up in a foul mood. Having taken a leave of absence from work to be home with Tyler, he decided to lay on the sectional all day relaxing. After his early afternoon nap, Henry lay groggy and half awake, still on the sectional. A banging from upstairs caused him to sit up. The muffled sound of a yell for help prompted Henry to head upstairs to investigate. Almost to the top of the stairs, he clearly heard banging and yelling coming from Will's bedroom. As he opened the bedroom door, Henry found Tyler trying to light a towel stuffed under the closet door with Will inside screaming for help. Anger flashed through Henry as he grabbed Tyler and threw him onto the bed. Henry opened the closet door. As Will ran out and wrapped his arm around his dad, Tyler lay on Will's bed, staring blankly at the ceiling mumbling foreign words. Henry took Will downstairs to comfort him. Not wanting Will around the house for a few days, Henry called Mr. Loeffler, the father of Will's friend Brian to see if they could keep their son for a few days. After a brief explanation of Tyler's sickness, Mr. Loeffler, who was known as being a standup, trustworthy guy, agreed to help out with Will.

Once Sharon returned home from work, Henry shared his horrible day with her, as well as his decision to send Will off for a few days. Pacing back and forth, Henry broke down as he told his wife, "I think we need to turn Tyler over to the Mississippi State insane asylum." Sharon began to cry, as she knew, deep down, that Henry was right. Unable to control his emotions any longer, Henry rushed from the house out into his barn. He found a spot in the corner and began crying uncontrollably. Overcome with emotions, Henry cried loud, long, and hard, losing control of his breathing, gasping for air, suffocated by his own emotions.

Sharon opened the barn door to find her husband unleashing raw emotion. She quickly rushed over to hold him tightly in her arms. With the help of his loving wife, Henry was finally able to regain control. "I can't do this, I just can't!" Henry shook his head. Sharon looked into his eyes with a loving smile. "You can't, but we will together!" The emotional couple sat there in the barn holding each other, not sure what to expect next. As they walked back to the house, Sharon reminded Henry, "Father Byrne will be here tomorrow for another attempt. I think we should wait to see how tomorrow's session goes." Henry agreed as they sat in silence, still confused how they had reached their current situation.

The next morning, Father Byrne knocked on the Matoskes' door. Sharon greeted him and with another priest. Father Byrne introduced Father Cashin to the exhausted couple. "Father Cashin just returned from Rome, where he was trained to be an exorcist. He will be assisting me as we continue to treat Tyler."

Henry, still at the end of his rope, looked up at the priest with eyes full of heartbreak. "Tyler locked Will in his closet and tried to set it on fire. If I had not heard Will screaming," Henry paused, "we can't trust Tyler being here any longer." Seeing Henry struggle with his words, Sharon, with eyes full of tears, finished his thought. "We think it is time to put Tyler in the Mississippi State insane asylum."

Father Byrne stood up, startling Father Cashin, "Oh no! No! No! No! You can't send him to the state insane asylum!" Father Byrne firmly blurted out. "They do not have the resources or experience to treat a possession. I can assure you that Tyler is possessed and needs the help of the Catholic Church. We would like to take Tyler to St. Treasea's hospital psych ward to continue the exorcism process," Father Byrne suggested. "The asylum will not get rid of the demon. They will only keep him drugged up and locked away. Tyler will spend the rest of his life fighting the demon alone," Father Byrne finished. Henry and Sharon, both emotional, did not take long to agree. St. Treasea's sounded much better than the state's insane asylum.

With the exorcism back on track, Father Byrne excused himself to check on Tyler. As he walked up the stairs, he noticed all the pictures were off center or broken. Halfway up, his nose began to burn from the rotten stench. The Father fought back the urge to throw up. A nervousness caught him off guard as he stood outside Tyler's door listening to the demon chant, "Uba uba uba yah yah yah." Father Byrne said a quick prayer for strength. Knocking to announce himself, the priest opened the door to enter. A flash of red and black preceded the sound of crushing bone that echoed in Father Byrne's head as his cheek bones and nose were shattered by Tyler's Louisville Slugger bat. Father Byrne's blood splattered the wall and door as his eyes rolled back into his head from the unbearable pain that felt like a thousand needles shoved into his face at once. Blood soaked the tan carpet dark red as he laid on the bedroom floor.

Tyler stood over Father Byrne chanting, "Uba uba uba yah yah, uba uba uba yah yah," still tightly holding the Louisville Slugger. Hearing the commotion, Henry raced upstairs leaving Sharon and Father Cashin behind. He found Tyler standing over Father Byrne with blood spattered on the wall and door and took a moment to absorb the situation. Henry calmly asked Tyler to drop the bat and back away from Father Byrne. Tyler looked up at Henry with unfamiliar dark blue eyes. Again, Henry asked his son to drop the bat and back up. Losing his balance, Tyler fell backwards onto the floor. Dazed and confused he sat up to look at Father Byrne lying unconscious on his floor. Henry moved toward Tyler and took the bat. Tyler asked, "What happened?"

"The evil spirit hit the Father with your bat." Checking Father Byrne's pulse, Henry yelled for Sharon to call 911. Father Cashin joined Henry upstairs and tended to the unconscious priest, using a towel to stop the blood flow from Father Byrne's nose. Sharon removed Tyler from the room as Henry and Father Cashin worked to stop the bleeding.

Father Byrne came to as the ambulance arrived to shuttle him to the local hospital. The police, after investigating the awful scene, sat down with Father Cashin and the Matoskes to discuss what to do with Tyler. The Archbishop suggested, through Father Cashin, to admit Tyler to the Saint Treasea Catholic Hospital psych ward in Whitehaven, Tennessee, a suburb of Memphis. The police officer got an approval from a judge and had Tyler transferred to St. Treasea's.

***

SAINT TREASEA HOSPITAL

Father Byrne was in stable condition with a broken nose and fractured cheekbone. He was expected to be out of hospital the next day. Henry rode with the police officer to admit Tyler into Saint Treasea Catholic Hospital while Sharon and Will packed clothes for their stay in Memphis with Henry's mom, Bebbie.

The old hospital was located in a rough neighborhood of Whitehaven, just down the street from Graceland, a dead famous singer's mansion. Built in 1921, the Mediterranean architecture, four floor, rectangular floorplan hospital was built by the Catholic Church with white stucco walls and a red tiled roof. A tall, whitewashed brick barrier surrounded the hospital to help keep patients from wandering off. Every window was in the shape of arches with iron grilles covering the glass. There were over twenty rooms on each floor, except the basement. The basement had a living quarter, a small chapel, and three exorcism rooms. Connected by an underground tunnel was the Saint Treasea Catholic Church. Under the church was another exorcism room with more of an old fashion exorcism technique. On the back lot was a convent that housed the Dominican sisters who worked for the hospital.

Tyler was admitted, then taken to his room in the psych ward of the hospital. His room had a two-way window for observation, a bed, and a caged TV.

Sharon arrived to the hospital after dropping Will off at Nana Bebbie's house. Sharon had explained everything to Nana Bebbie on the way up from Skuna Valley. The Matoskes met with Father Cashin to sign papers and receive instructions. The Father informed the parents that the Archbishop requested for them to wait for Father Byrne to proceed with the exorcism. Father Byrne should be back on his feet in two or three days. They would start the new patient interview process, then therapy with Sister Elizabeth. Due to Tyler's age, one parent would be able to stay nightly, but would not be able to stay in same room.

Two days passed with Sister Elizabeth, and showed no signs of a demon possession. Tyler seemed like a normal thirteen-year-old kid. Everything about him had returned to normal.

Father Byrne arrived on the third day ready to begin the exorcism. The bruised priest entered Tyler's room with a purple and yellow swollen eye and tape across his nose. Tyler apologized for hitting him with the Louisville Slugger. Shaking off his apology, Father Byrne assured him it was the malicious demon. Father Byrne and Father Cashin took Tyler down to the exorcism room in the basement to begin his treatment. The cold room was twelve by twelve, walled with cinder blocks painted a rainbow of colors. The ceiling and floor were covered with 70s shag carpet to help absorb sound. A lone bed sat with three stained cedar chairs against the wall under a two-way mirror.

Tyler laid down on the hard, uncomfortable bed, and had his ankles and wrists strapped to the bed frame for protection. Sister Elizabeth joined the two priests for prayer support. Father Byrne began the exorcism with the sign of the cross, then began the Our Father. With holy oil, he made the sign of the cross on Tyler's forehead using his thumb. With no abnormal response from Tyler, he began The Athanasian Creed. The session continued until it was finished. Although nervous at the beginning, Tyler remained himself throughout the process. Once finished, the Father praised Tyler for the manner in which he handled the session.

Afterwards, Tyler was returned to his room while Father Byrne asked to meet with the concerned parents in the priest's office. The large office was located on the ground level, just inside the hospital's entrance. The red, oak-paneled walls created richness and warmth in the old office, and at the same time, infused it with charm and sophistication. At the rear of the office sat an antique 19th century French desk and chairs that matched the walls. The rear wall hid a private bathroom with a shower and a dressing room. The large, arched windows allowed the priest to look out onto the large grassy buffer that lead to the parking lot. The walls were decorated with pictures of past popes and bishops. The secretary escorted Henry and Sharon into the office and motioned for the couple to have a seat. Father Byrne offered drinks while pouring himself a stiff one from the wet bar hidden in the wall. Everything went well. There were no signs of the demon. Father Byrne informed the parents how sometimes a demon will hide and not show itself. "We will continue daily therapy with Sister Elizabeth and the prayer sessions until the beast shows himself." With approval of the plan, Sharon went up to Tyler's room while Henry walked over to the church to pray.

The Saint Treasea Catholic Church was opened October 1,

1867. The two-story structure was originally built with a school on the ground level and the church on the second level. Two concrete stairways formed an arch over the school entrance for access to the church, and served to protect the school's entrance from the weather. The four-story bell tower, built into the back corner of the school, had arches on each side of every level. The school closed on May 26, 1966, due to the Catholic population moving east. The church was then moved to the lower level, making access for the older members easier. The church was decidedly Romanesque design, featuring ten large interior arches. The stained glass windows that lined the sides of the church depicted Jesus's miracles. The plain altar was a huge slab of Calacatta marble, supported by two smaller slabs of marble for legs, with a life-size crucifix hanging on the back wall. Henry walked over to the side of the altar to drop a few dollars into the donation box before lighting a candle in front of a statue of Jesus. He knelt to pray. Henry said the Our Father and asked God to give Tyler and his family the strength to beat the demon. After a quick, emotional moment Henry exited the church.

***

HENRY MEETS SHAK

Henry returned to Skuna Valley to check on things and refresh their cloths. At home, Henry checked on the house and land, then called to let Sharon know he would stay the night before returning to Whitehaven in the morning. He hated being away from his family, but looked forward to his time alone. After eating the food he picked up in town, Henry kicked back to watch some TV and drink a few beers.

A banging on his front door caused Henry to jump to his feet. Not expecting company, Henry quietly walked over to peek out the window. *Oh great,* Henry thought as he opened the door. It was Kyle and he was with Roy. He was okay with Kyle, but Roy's snarkiness irritated him. "What can I help you all with?" Henry politely asked.

"Oh, we lost our poodle Skippy. We were wondering if you had seen him." Roy said.

"Nope, I have not seen Skippy. I will let you all know if I do." Before Henry could close the door, bluntly Kyle asked, "What the hell was going on over here the other day?"

"I do not know what you mean," Henry answered with sarcasm. After a brief smile, Henry said, "Oh, you mean the ambulance and police car!"

"Yep, we want to make sure everything is okay," Kyle replied.

Henry went on to give a short explanation, knowing Roy did not believe in spirits. Roy rolled his eyes and walked off the porch when he heard that Tyler might be possessed. "He does not believe in possessions, demons, or even a God," Kyle reminded Henry. "He completely blew me off when I told him about the shadow people you saw in the woods. Roy can be such a prissy bitch," Kyle stated the obvious. The two friends went inside to have a few beers and conversation as Roy marched home, not wanting to listen to their nonsense. After a text from Roy, Kyle expressed his concern, and wished Henry luck with Tyler before leaving.

Henry went back inside to his beer. Watching a documentary about a Bigfoot trolling a community off the White River in Arkansas, Henry felt a creepy feeling come over him. *This show is getting the best of me,* he thought to himself. A distant rumble outside startled him. *Must be a storm moving in,* he thought. Checking the radar on his phone, Henry saw that the severe storm moving his way was prompting tornado watches and warnings across the area. The wind and heavy rain knocked out his satellite reception, so Henry sat listening to the storm while finishing his beer. He thought back to when Tyler was a baby, enjoying the memories. The power blinked, then went out completely. A sudden adrenaline pop caused Henry to stand and look toward the front porch. Slow and heavy footsteps moved across the porch. Henry quietly moved into his bedroom, opened the safe, and removed his .45 and flashlight. Against every instinct in his body, he slowly opened the front door to confront the trespasser. To Henry's delight, no one was around. Feeling confident he stepped out, holding his breath. A sweep of the porch proved all was clear. The intense storm shook the house as lightning pounded the area. Laughing at himself, he returned to his beer. "Damn Bigfoot show," Henry said to himself. Finished with his last beer and still a little jumpy, Henry checked all the windows and doors before he moved off to bed. The storm's intensity continued to shake the house with wind and thunder. The lightning lit up his room with every loud crack.

Watching an old sitcom on his phone propped up on Sharon's pillow, Henry heard a faint voice whisper as another clap of thunder shook the house. Henry sat up in bed and muted his phone. "What the hell?" he said to himself. He listened intensely, only hearing the wind and rain. "Cassius, Cassius," the faint voice softly whispered again, "Die, Cassius, die." Adrenaline burst through his body as he jumped out of bed and grabbed his .45. Henry tried to turn the lights on, forgetting the storm had knocked them out. He struggled to dress, falling down twice trying to pull up his pants too quickly. "Die, Cassis, die," the voice softly whispered. "Who's there?" Henry yelled, turning around in panic, not finding anyone. "Who the freak is there?" Henry yelled out. A dark silhouette stepped out from the shadows. Dark blue eyes met Henry's eyes, and again Henry heard, "Cassius, Cassius." After the dark silhouette revealed it had yellow hair, it darted left, then right, then disappeared.

Wasting no time getting out of the house, Henry mumbled, "Shadow people, my ass," as he jumped into his car and headed toward town. Once in town, Henry pulled over to get control of himself. "What the hell was that?" He said to no one. "Cassius? Who the hell is Cassius?" After calming down, he decided to drive to Memphis. On the way to his mom's house, he kept asking himself, "Who is Cassius, and what did I see. The shadow people? Maybe a Civil War ghost?" Nothing made sense.

Henry's mom Bebbie was surprised when Henry showed up at

10:30 p.m. and let himself into her house. Henry explained what happened and his decision to drive back. Still spooked, he stayed up talking to his mom.

Henry was at St. Treasea's first thing the next morning, explaining his unpleasant experience to Father Byrne. After listening to the story, the Father admitted he had not considered the house being possessed. "Tyler has all the signs. Could there be a ghost?" Henry asked.

"I guess there could be a spirit lingering around," the Father answered, "but what I experienced with Tyler was not a ghost. I am sure of that," Father Byrne insisted. "You heard the name Cassius?" the Father asked.

"Yes, Cassius," Henry confirmed. "Die, Cassius, die," Henry corrected. "The dark blue-eyed silhouette with yellow hair showed itself, then disappeared," Henry explained, trying not to seem insane.

In deep thought, the Father sat back into his chair and rubbed his chin as he absorbed Henry's experience. "There might be something going on at your house or land," he admitted. Father Byrne asked to work with Tyler a couple more days before moving to the next step.

After a few more sessions with no signs of the demon, Father Byrne called for Henry and Sharon to meet. "I have not had any luck getting the demon to reveal itself. I am starting to believe it has something to do with your house or land," the Father confessed. He suggested that the parents get their house checked by a paranormal researcher. Not fully convinced, Sharon wanted to know how this would help. Father Byrne explained, "The paranormal researcher would perform a channeling session to gather information. She will speak to the spirits."

"You believe in the paranormal?" Sharon probed.

"It is not important what I believe. What is important is that we figure out what is going on so you can continue with your life. Although, if you believe in God, you believe in spirits, good and bad," the Father answered. Henry inquired about who to contact. "Momma Jeanne LaOpal is a local lady who I have used in the past," the Father suggested. "She is the best in the area, if she accepts your request," the priest continued. The Father gave Henry the address on South Lauderdale and Mallory. "It is an abandoned shack on the northwest corner. In chalk, write Father Byrne/Matoske on the south side wall tomorrow before 10 a.m. Go back the next day to see if she accepted your meeting. A circle around the name means she accepted. An X over the name means she did not accept. If she accepts, there will be an envelope under the stone with a map to her house." Understanding their hesitation, Father Byrne assured the apprehensive parents they had nothing to worry about.

***

MOMMA JEANNE

The next morning, the cautious couple arrived at the address. Henry knew the area, and carefully checked his surroundings before exiting the car. Two homeless men, one in a wheelchair with no legs holding a Chihuahua, were talking at the edge of the lot, making the nervous couple more nervous. The old shack was supported with white cinder blocks, tilting a little to the back. Fading red paint was peeling off, exposing rotted wood. Black painted plywood covered the windows, keeping out unwanted intruders. They walked across the rutted parking lot around to the south side of the old shack. Sharon neatly wrote, FATHER BYRNE/MATOSKE on the wall as instructed. A barking dog came running up from behind a fence that was hidden by a thick, overgrown row of canebrake, scaring the already nervous couple. "Damn dog!" Henry grunted as they hurried back to their car. The two homeless men laughed as they watched the couple rush away from the barking dog.

Later that evening, Momma Jeanne arrived at the shack. She stopped to speak to Brad and Paul, the two homeless guys still talking at the edge of the lot. She slipped both a fifty, thanking the watchers for their protection. She removed the padlock from the door and entered the old shack, locking the door behind her. The four walls inside the shack were painted a flowing pattern of red, black, and white. The ceiling was painted light blue with big white clouds to simulate the sky. The old floor was unfinished cedar wood, marked up from old sessions. Two shelves were filled with different types of oils, powders, and spices. The other shelf had figure candles, statues, and water containers. Pictures of African tribal rituals and symbols covered the walls, along with pictures of the Holy Trinity. Four cedar chairs were aligned against a wall with a cedar table pushed into a corner.

Momma Jeanne walked around the shack, lighting seven candles and incense. Kneeling down, she drew a circle around herself with white chalk. Looking up at the crucifix on the wall, she began a prayer of meditation:

"O Lord our God, accept, we beseech Thee, the prayer which we, Thy servants, now make unto thee. Shine into our hearts, O loving Master, by the pure light of the knowledge of Thyself, and open the eyes of our minds to the contemplation of Thy teaching, and put into us the awareness of Thy blessed commandments, that by trampling down all that is worldly, we may follow a spiritual life, thinking and doing all things according to Thy good pleasure. Help us now to be aware of Thy nearness as we are of the material things of every day. Help us to recognize Thy voice with as much assurance as we recognize the sounds of the world around us. Oh God, we beseech thee to purify our hearts from all vain and worldly and sinful thoughts, and so prepare our souls to worship and speak to Thee. Scatter our darkness with Thy source of light and wisdom. Stretch forth Thy hand to help us, who cannot without Thee come to Thee. Give unto us, O Lord, that quietness of mind in which we can hear Thee speaking to us, for thou art our illumination, and to Thee we render glory, Father, Son, and Holy Spirit, now and ever, and unto all ages. Amen."

Finishing her prayer, she sat back on her heels with her back straight and her hands folded in front of her chest. Momma Jeanne began her meditation, focusing on the case Father Byrne discussed with her over the phone. She hummed a soft tune she learned as a child from her grandmother. Her stomach turned as the light from all seven candles flickered and went out. Momma Jeanne felt a strong pull to investigate, even though she did not have a good vibe. Finished with her meditation, she sat back collecting her thoughts. Realizing her decision, Momma Jeanne cleaned up and left the shack.

The next morning, the Matoskes returned to the shack. The two homeless guys were across the street watching their every move. The nervous couple quickly checked the shack and found a circle around their name. A car backfiring from around the corner made the nervous couple jump with fear before realizing there was not any danger. Henry picked up the stone and looked up at Sharon with a smile, "I can't tell if I am happy or scared of the approval." They raced back to their car and opened the envelope to read the instructions. *After 10 p.m., follow West Shelby Drive until it ends. Look toward the railroad tracks for a red light. Follow the light through woods to the back of the house.*

At 10:20 p.m., the nervous couple arrived at the end of West Shelby Drive as directed. Henry pulled his .45 from the glove box and placed it into his belt holster. Normally against guns, Sharon was glad Henry brought protection tonight. They both got out of the car and scanned for the red light. Across the railroad tracks, Sharon spotted the target. "I will follow you," Sharon requested.

"Okay, but panthers always attack from behind." Henry said with a sarcastic giggle.

"Panthers?" she asked, looking around.

"You will be fine. We have not had panthers around here in years." Sharon tightly held onto Henry's shirt as they began their hike. Over the tracks and down into the tall buck brush, the jumpy couple hiked toward the red light. A frightened deer jumped up and ran out in front of them. The couple froze in horror before realizing it was just a deer. "I think I just peed myself a little," Henry joked. They came across a game trail that opened up to make the hike easier. Arriving to the back of a modest brick home with well-manicured yard at the end of a lower middle-class neighborhood, the Matoskes knocked on the back door next to the red light. The couple held their breath until the door opened.

"Welcome," said a nicely dressed white woman who looked to be in her 70s.

"Are you Momma Jeanne LaOpal?" asked Henry.

"No sir," the lady replied. "Momma Jeanne will be out in a moment." She motioned the couple into the house, then to have a seat at the kitchen table. She asked if they wanted anything to drink. The nervous couple passed on the drink and sat down. The kitchen walls were covered in 70s wallpaper, white with small red and yellow flowers. The old table was painted white, and each of the four chairs was painted a different pastel color. The cabinets were stained a walnut color. Laminate countertops posed as wood. A dark brown, hard plastic sliding door separated the kitchen from the other room, keeping visitors guessing how the rest of the house was decorated. As the old woman left the room, Henry whispered, "I expected an old shack on stilts in the middle of a swamp."

Henry stood as Momma Jeanne stepped into the kitchen and introduced herself. Tall and fit, she looked to be in her early to mid-70s and of mixed race. Her soft, wrinkled face was light brown, highlighted by her sharp green eyes. She had old school grey bouffant hair with black streaks and teacher glasses hanging around her neck from a silver chain. The old woman's Chanel perfume filled the kitchen, making it hard for Henry to breathe.

She sat down and looked over the concerned parents before explaining her background. "My grandma on my dad's side was a Voodoo Queen in New Orleans, and my granny on my mom's side practiced Hoodoo magic," Momma Jeanne shared. She went on to tell them she was a practicing Catholic, attending St. Treasea's every Sunday. My relationship with Father Byrne goes back almost fifty years, and he is the only reason I accepted your unique case," Momma Jeanne explained with a serious look.

"Father Byrne tells me your son Tyler showed signs of being possessed at your house, but the demon has not shown itself since he arrived at St. Treasea's?"

"Yes, ma'am," Henry answered. Henry tried to tell Momma Jeanne about his experience at the house a few nights earlier but she refused, wanting a clear head for her investigation. Momma Jeanne reached out both her arms and grabbed their hands, holding them together. She closed her eyes to pray in silence. Once finished, she turned their hands loose and looked deep into their eyes for a moment. "I will take your case," she said to the couple. "A thousand dollars cash upfront for me to inspect your house. I will have my partner's son drive me down. No one should be home or anywhere near the house. Usually I spend three to five hours listening and talking to the restless spirits. After I have completed the investigation, I will send for you all," Momma Jeanne finished.

"How do we pay if we decide to hire you?" Henry asked.

"You have 24 hours to decide. If you hire me, leave an envelope with the cash, a key, and directions to your house with Father Byrne. He knows how to contact me. Any more questions before you go?" Momma Jeanne asked.

"Yes, why did we have to walk through the woods when you live in a neighborhood?" Henry asked.

Smiling, Momma Jeanne explained, "Because my easily spooked neighbors call the Memphis police if cars pull in after dark. They get all scared, thinking I am a wicked witch," she answered with a chuckle.

The couple left the same way they arrived. After a long discussion, Henry convinced the skeptical Sharon to hire Momma Jeanne. The next morning, Henry dropped off the envelope to Father Byrne as instructed.

***

MOMMA JEANNE'S INVESTIGATION

Butterflies started to form in Momma Jeanne's stomach as they approached the Matoskes' residence. Momma Jeanne's partner's son Wilbur, a six-foot-six, golden-brown skinned, big boned man with black curly hair and hoop earrings in both ears, noticed her uneasiness, asking if she was okay. "Yes, it's just been a few years since I have been involved in an investigation," Momma Jeanne answered.

The once confident paranormal researcher became jittery during investigations after her mother was murdered, her body found mutilated. She was killed by a spiritual Satanist group performing an orientation ritual. Her remains were scattered on the banks of the Wolf River, north of Memphis. Momma Jeanne became angry with God and questioned her faith. How could God allow her mom to be mutilated? She could not forgive her God. The night after her mom's death, she woke to a freezing room. Sitting up in her bed, she saw the tail of the serpent slide in through the bedroom door. Her alarm clock sounded, turning her attention away from the serpent. She reached to turn the alarm off. She had not set it. The clock read 3:33 a.m. Looking back to the serpent, she came face to face with Lucifer. Frozen with fear, she stared into its eyes, realizing at once that the devil stood before her. Lucifer's monstrous, unbalanced face had horned bumps above its large forehead, with yellow eyes surrounding red pupils. Burnt wings protruded from its shoulders. Blackish red bile oozed from its peeling skin, dripping off the pitchfork it held with its left hand. Long black fingernails dripped dark red blood from doomed souls it had collected. Just below the chest, its body remained in serpent form, with the tail flopping back and forth, pounding the floor with a death beat. The purplish black, cowlike tongue slithered foul goo from its mouth as it began to speak in a deep, dead voice. "Renounce the God that mutilated your mother, renounce the God that murdered your mother, renounce the God that has abandoned you," Lucifer commanded. Unable to breath, she stared in horrified disbelief. Reaching into her nightstand drawer,

Momma Jeanne nervously grabbed the white plastic bottle of holy water, not taking her eyes off Lucifer. She began pouring the holy water over her head and heart. Emptying the little bottle, she turned her back to Lucifer, kneeling down on her bed under the crucifix hanging on the wall. Momma Jeanne prayed the Our Father then the Hail Mary, followed by a prayer of contrition with all of her heart blocking out the word from the devil. Lucifer continued his quest. "Renounce your God, follow my angels to the truth. Renounce your God who has forsaken you!" it yelled. Momma Jeanne continued to pray, ignoring the foolish demands from Lucifer. A bright light flashed in the room, knocking Momma Jeanne against the wall, then down onto the floor between her bed and the wall. Peaking up over the bed, she saw the devil had vanished. She laid back on the floor, catching her breath for a moment before carefully getting up. The bottom of her bed was blood-soaked from where Lucifer stood. Momma Jeanne looked around the room and found a trail of blood drops and splatter from the path the serpent traveled through her house. She eased downstairs, not sure what she would find. Searching over the house, she found the back door open. *This must be the devil's entry*, she thought, the only door without a cross hanging above it. After making a pot of coffee, she called Father Byrne, who immediately drove over to comfort her and bless her house. The Father explained how the devil was trying to trick her into giving up her soul during her moment of weakness. The Father shared with Momma Jeanne how God sends our souls here to experience emotions and situations that he has chosen. God does not want to be worshiped. God wants only to be loved in good times and bad. The Bible says God made man in his own image, meaning man only wants to be loved, as God only wants to be loved. The experience with Lucifer caused Momma Jeanne to reduce the amount of time she committed to paranormal researching.

Momma Jeanne took a deep breath as they pulled into the Matoskes' driveway. The two admired the house from the car. "You want me to stay or go?" Wilbur asked.

"Stay here in the car until I need you." Not understanding her nerves, Momma Jeanne continued to sit in silence. *Something bad happened here,* she thought to herself. Gathering herself, she stepped out of the car. Before she could take a step, a hurricane of emotions knocked her down to her knees. Wilbur jumped out of the car to help but she waved him away. "Leave, boy. Leave," she said. "Go away. I will be fine." Wilbur got back into the car and pulled into the street where he could still keep an eye on her. Momma Jeanne rolled over onto her back and started to cry. Heartbreaking sadness, rage, fear, horror, sickness, and evil all overtook her while lying there on the thick Bermuda grass lawn. Not understanding her wide range of emotions, she began praying for control, pulling a rosary from her pocket. Hate and love boiled up from her stomach together. For over an hour, she laid there in a deep, sobbing prayer, trying to fight the conflicting emotions. Never before had she encountered such a spiritual battle. Breaking the emotions, she rolled over onto her stomach and covered her face with her hands. In the vision of darkness, she saw a woman running, chased by a dark silhouette. The fearful woman kept looking back as the silhouette closed in on her. A soft drum beat sounded as the silhouette captured the woman. Taking a silver dagger, the silhouette stabbed the woman and gutted her from the navel, cutting left then right. The woman let out a silent scream as she dropped to the ground. Having enough, the fatigued Momma Jeanne motioned for Wilbur's help. He pulled back into the driveway and assisted her limp body into the car. She waved for him to drive, unable to talk. A couple of miles away, Momma Jeanne regained control and cound finally speak. "What happened?" Wilbur asked. Not sure how to answer, she just shook her head, trying to make sense for herself.

"I do not know," she finally replied. "I did not see much, just a bunch of different emotions and a silhouette stabbing a woman. I was unable to get up to investigate," Momma Jeanne shared.

Pulling into Coffeeville, they stopped to eat at Little Johnny's

Catfish House and discuss their next move. The restaurant was an old log cabin home, used to demo for potential buyers looking for a log cabin to purchase. The inside was decorated with old fishing equipment hanging from the walls and ceiling. The old country cooking aroma filled the room made their stomachs turn with anticipation of the upcoming meal. Wilbur could tell Momma Jeanne was dumbfounded by what she felt during the investigation. "Do we need to come back tomorrow to try again?" he suggested. Looking down and fidgeting with a pack of sugar, Momma Jeanne did not answer, still thinking about the botched investigation. Wilbur reached out and touched her hand to get her attention. "What? I am sorry Wilbur, what did you say?" Wilbur repeated the question with concern. "Do we need to come back tomorrow?" "No, I just need to regroup and clear my head. It is my fault. I did not prepare myself like I used to." She continued, "Back in the day, I had a routine I followed to prepare myself."

"Did it involve smoking a fatty?" Wilbur laughed out loud at the notion of Momma Jeanne smoking a joint.

"Actually, we used to smoke all kinds of different natural things to help connect with the spirit world. Marijuana opens our mind to a different dimension, allowing us to hear and see things around us that we normally miss." Wilbur's smile turned to disbelief as Momma Jeanne admitted to smoking fatties back in her day. The waitress refilled their drinks and let them know their food would be right out. Wilbur thanked the waitress for the update. Momma Jeanne got on her soapbox about the differences of smoking marijuana for recreational use and spiritual use while they ate their lunch. Finishing their lunch, Momma Jeanne shared her plan to continue the investigation. To avoid the hurricane of emotions, she decided to return, but would be dropped off away from the house and walk up slowly. Wilbur drove Momma Jeanne back toward the Matoskes' house. A little under a mile from the house, Momma Jeanne got out of the car. She slowly walked as Wilbur followed in the car. Around fifty yards into her walk. she stopped and closed her eyes. She saw a beautiful plantation from the Civil War era, a massive house full of happiness and life. After a moment, she continued her walk. Stopping again, she closed her eyes and saw a slave community with dogtrot houses and white fields being worked. A melody was being sung by the hardworking slaves. The community seemed to have good spirits.

She continued walking cautiously slow. With a sudden stop, she backed up to the front of the car. Momma Jeanne leaned back for balance. Spirits of murdered slaves flew past as she witnessed their torturous deaths on the whipping poles. Out of respect to each spirit, she watched with sadness as each was murdered. The story of the land was revealing itself. Momma Jeanne continued walking toward the Matoskes' house until an unseen force knocked her back against the car. She caught herself with her hands on the hood and closed her eyes. She watched as a little slave girl was raped by a tall white man. Paralyzed, she then watched as a young slave man was hung from his ankle. The same tall white man shoved a spike into the young slave's anal canal. She watched as the spike moved into his body and took his life. The horror caused her to begin crying. She looked over to see a slave man's throat sliced open as blood pumped out onto the dirt with each beat of his heart. The tall white man held the slave's head up so all could see. Pushing through the emotional pain, Momma Jeanne noticed a slave woman inside the Seal of Solomon chanting her magic spell. "WOO-WAY-AH, WOO-WAY-AH, WOO-WAY-AH. Lay waste this evil, Shankpana. Lay waste this evil, unleash Shankpana wrath upon this blood and this seed. Curse this man and his branches for this be rotten. WOO-WAY-AH, WOO-WAY-AH, WOO-WAY-AH, SHANKPANA, SHANKPANA, SHANKPANA!" Black smoke bellowed as the demon rose from the seal. The demon killed the white man before turning toward Momma Jeanne. "DIE, CASSIUS. DIE," Shankpana said. An inner fight to break the trance began as Momma Jean stood eye-locked with the demon. "DIE, CASSIUS. DIE," the demon continued to say. Moving toward Momma Jeanne, the demon began to chant, "Uba, uba, uba, yah, yah, uba, uba, uba, yah, yah!

Uba, uba, uba, yah, yah!" Closer and closer, the demon moved toward Momma Jeanne. Still paralyzed, Momma Jeanne stood helpless, trying to run, trying to scream for help. She began to pray, hoping to regain control. She knew her soul was the target as she began fidgeting to control her body. Tears formed in her eyes as she began to cry. Her body began trembling and twitching. "DIE, CASSIUS. DIE," the demon kept saying.

Noticing Momma Jeanne in distress, Wilbur pulled her into the car and sped off back toward town. He was surprised how clammy and saturated she was in sweat. Her body was trembling and slumped over, like an addict breaking the grasp of drugs. Slowly, Momma Jeanne shook the trance and steadied herself. Unable to talk, she continued the silent prayer.

For the safety of Momma Jeanne, Wilbur decided to drive back to Memphis without giving her the option to continue the investigation. She slowly regained control and started to speak. "Thank you, Wilbur," she said with a soft voice.

"What happened back there?" Wilbur asked. Momma Jeanne explained everything she saw. She paused, still not understanding what happened. Visually intimidated, she continued, "The demon, it came up out of the seal and locked eyes with me. Chanting, it moved toward me, coming after my soul."

"Did you recognize the demon?" Wilbur asked. There was a long pause before Momma Jeanne answered. "Yes, it's a Hoodoo angel commanded by God. Just saying its name can cause you harm. It is a ferocious angel that inflicts insanity, disease, and death on mankind. This angel, Shankpana, fought under the archangel Michael during the war in heaven between the angels and dragons. After the dragons or fallen angels were defeated, they were thrown down to the earth. Shankpana was sent down by the archangel Michael to remove their wings and make them human. Since then, God has used Shankpana to rid the world of evil through insanity, disease, and death." Hair stood up all over Wilbur's body as he continued to drive. "The slave woman cast the Hoodoo curse, so why was the demon after you?"

"I do not know. The demon's name flashed through my head when I saw its face. I guess I was surprised to see the demon, or maybe scared, causing it to turn toward me," Momma Jeanne confessed, shaking her head. They drove in silence until Wilbur asked, "How do we stop this demon?"

"I am not sure it can be stopped," Momma Jeanne sighed. "If I am right, this angel can only stop when it has completed the curse or God commands it to stop."

Confused, Wilbur asked, "Why would God allow such an evil curse?"

"We often forget how God punished people in the Old Testament. Not knowing God's plan makes it hard for us to understand why he would allow such a curse," Momma Jeanne answered. "We must trust his plan."

Sitting down with Father Byrne, Momma Jeanne returned the envelope of cash and the key.

"I can't help these people or take their money. I am too old, and do not have the strength for this kind of investigation."

Looking at his dear friend, the Father asked, "What did you see?"

Her eyes watered as she tried to control her raw emotions. Looking down at the floor, Momma Jeanne was quiet before describing the demon. "It is a powerful demon, Father. A nasty, nasty powerful angel." She went through the story, but left out her battle with the demon.

"Is it a demon or an angel?" the Father asked.

"It is both. It is an angel but acts like a demon. I am talking Old Testament type. This angel fought under the archangel Michael during the war in heaven, then was sent down to destroy evil. I am not experienced with this angel, but have read that it is sent by God to do God's work. It can only enter a body when it is welcomed. This angel can only stop when it has completed the curse or God commands it to stop," she said, frustrated, not sure how to explain. Looking away from the Father's confused look, she regathered her thoughts. "This is God's hitman!" She went on to explain the words she heard, "*Curse this man and his branches for this be rotten. Die, Cassius. Die.*"

"Somehow, this family has upset this angel. Normally, when a curse plays out, the angel will leave, taking all the souls with it to the afterlife. For some reason, this angel has not left. The curse was cast during the slavery time period. I have never witnessed a curse this old," Momma Jeanne explained. "They need to figure out how, or if, they are connected to the curse before they can get peace. They need to carry a little bag of garlic and brimstone with them at all times for protection, and they need to stay away from that area. Henry heard 'Cassius' the other night when he was at his house."

"Could the land be cursed?" the Father asked.

"Yes, but angels do not normally attach themselves to land. Maybe they disturbed a burial site or sacred ground, but I do not see that being the reason they are having problems," Momma Jeanne said, shaking her head. "I just, I can't commit the time or energy for this investigation." Momma Jeanne stood to leave.

"Why are you so emotional?" the Father asked.

"I witnessed pure evil in the way those poor spirits were murdered. I just can't help these people," Momma Jeanne answered.

Noticing the fear in his friend's eyes, Father Byrne asked, "You can't or won't?" Not looking back, she answered, "Both."

In the parking lot, Wilbur opened the car door for her and he asked, "Why are we going to New Orleans?"

The car ride was eerily quiet as Henry and Sharon made their way over to meet with Father Byrne. Both were deep in thought, wondering about the outcome of the investigation. Exiting the interstate, the uncomfortable silence was broken. Henry asked, "How in the hell did we get here?"

"Get here?" Sharon questioned his comment.

"Yes, get here! We are headed to find out if our son, our house, or maybe both are possessed by demons. How the hell did we get to this point in our life?" Henry again asked.

"I do not know," Sharon said with a sigh, shaking her head. They pulled into the hospital parking lot. "Positive thoughts," Henry requested as the uneasy couple exited the car. Father Byrne greeted them in the lobby and escorted the couple to his office. Starting with small talk, the Father tried to calm the tense room. He slid the envelope filled with money over to Henry. "What is this?" Henry asked.

"Momma Jeanne has decided not to continue the investigation." With hesitation, the Father continued, "She feels that she can't be any more help. She no longer has the time or energy for long investigations." Father Byrne began relating what Momma Jeanne had seen and heard during the investigation. The couple sat in horror as they absorbed the disturbing details. Father Byrne's secretary buzzed his office phone and asked if he could speak with the Archbishop. After a quick conversation with the Archbishop, Father Byrne continued his meeting with the Matoskes. Taking a deep breath, Henry asked, "Momma Jeanne believes there is a connection between the murdered slaves and one of us?"

"Well, the land could be possessed, but she believes there is a deeper connection," the Father answered. "The curse was cast back during slavery. She also heard the name Cassius. Do either of you have someone named Cassius in your family ancestry?" Quiet filled the room as they sat in deep thought. Breaking the silence, Sharon shared that her mom's family immigrated from Czechoslovakia in 1905, well after slavery, and her dad's family all lived in upstate New York until the 1960s. "I have never heard the name Cassius. We can exclude my family," she said, turning her attention to Henry. Henry, having an interest in genealogy, had a good grasp on his family history, but knew he would have to do a lot of research. "I had never heard the name Cassius until the other night at our house, and have never heard it mentioned with my family. I will have to do some research to know for sure." The Father assured the stressed couple that Tyler would be safe at the hospital while continuing therapy with Sister Elizabeth.

Sharon excused herself to be with Tyler. After Sharon left the office, the Father stared at Henry for a moment flicking his pen and thinking. Father Byrne finally broke the silence with a sigh and shared the fear he saw in Momma Jeanne's eyes as she explained the power and nastiness the angel possesses. Looking directly into Henry's eyes, he spoke with utmost seriousness, "Do not take this situation lightly," the Father warned. "This is a dangerous angel we are dealing with. We need to know all the facts to be able to ask God to stop the curse."

Sitting back in his chair, Henry took a deep breath and wondered how he was going to keep his family safe. Seeing defeat on Henry's face, the Father reminded Henry of his faith and the power of God. The Father quoted scripture:

"Finally, be strong in the Lord and in his mighty power. Put on the full armor of God, so that you can take your stand against the devil's schemes. For our struggle is not against flesh and blood, but against the rulers, against the authorities, against the powers of this dark world and against the spiritual forces of evil in the heavenly realms. Ephesians 6: 10-12."

Henry thanked Father Byrne and exited the office.

***

THE BIG EASY

Driving south down I-55, Wilbur again asked, "Why are we headed to New Orleans?"

"To see my little sister," Momma Jeanne answered.

"Little sister? I thought you were an only child?"

"Well, I am not. My grandmother Quassy Booker on my mom's side moved up to Memphis from Vicksburg, Mississippi. Her husband Lou Booker was hired to play the saxophone in a black-owned club on Beale Street. Quassy worked at a fancy downtown hotel a few blocks from Beale Street. She also performed Hoodoo magic that was passed down through her family from the Mississippi delta. My mom was born and raised in Memphis." Momma Jeanne went on to explain how her mom Jennevea Booker had gotten pregnant by a half black, half American Indian guy, Oscar LaOpal, who played for a New Orleans professional baseball team in the Negro Southern League. He was up playing against the Memphis team when they met. They would see each other every time he came to town. "When mom became pregnant, he did not want to marry or quit baseball, so she raised me herself, although Oscar stopped by to check on us from time to time. Most summers, momma sent me to stay with my grandparents in New Orleans. Oscar finally settled down and married."

"So, she is your half-sister," Wilbur interrupted.

"That is correct. She is a highly regarded Voodoo Queen and psychic. She is able to look deep into your soul just by touching your hand."

"Okay, I see. You are worried about that demon," Wilbur chuckled.

"Yes, Wilbur, I am worried. In all my years, I have never had a demon come after me," Momma Jeanne snapped. "I have to find out why before I can get it out of my head!" Realizing the stress Momma Jeanne was under, Wilbur turned up the radio and put the car on cruise control. Momma Jeanne replayed her encounter with the demon over and over, trying to make sense of it. She knew she needed help from her little sister.

Driving through the Quarter, Momma Jeanne rolled down her window to take in the dirty, musky, mud smell provided by the constant flow of Mississippi River water pumped out from under the city. The distinct smell took her back to her happy childhood. Looking out the window, she enjoyed the newly refurbished cottages with a variety of painted pastel colors mixed in with old rundown cottages. The housing in New Orleans was just as diverse as its people and culture. The roar of the busy city, mixed with jazzy music that filled the air, created an excitement she only felt in the Big Easy.

Momma Jeanne began thinking back to the summers of her

youth. She much enjoyed the time with her grandmother. Her grandmother, Carla Jill LaOpal, practiced Hoodoo and Voodoo. She taught her granddaughters the foundation of both. Momma Jeanne favored Hoodoo, and her half-sister favored Voodoo. Carla saw the power both girls drew from the spirits. She encouraged both to explore and master their craft. The proud grandmother pushed both toward their gifts. Momma Jeanne loved being in New Orleans. She could feel the spirits welcoming her back each time she visited. Although New Orleans shares the same racial tension as Memphis, Momma Jeanne felt a sense of belonging. Unlike Memphis, New Orleans never judged her because of her sexual beliefs. Momma Jeanne realized she was gay by age fourteen. While her friends were becoming interested in boys, she was becoming interested in her friends. Knowing she would be outcast, she kept her secret from everybody except her mom. Jennevea did not like the news about her only child being gay. She took her to their parish priest after a long conversation about spending eternity in hell. Not only was she worried about her daughter's soul, but also the embarrassment she would cause for herself and her family. After a few sessions with the priest, Momma Jeanne decided to hide her sexual preference. To please her mother, she began dating men.

In an attempt to please her mom, she began attending Christian Youth Organization functions. While involved with the CYO, she met a man named Tom who shared her interests in God, spirits, saints, angels and demons. The two spent hours together discussing different theories and challenging each other's beliefs, even arguing over if Jesus could be considered an alien. The courtship lasted a couple of years before Tom asked for her hand in marriage. Momma Jeanne decided Tom was the only man she could spend her life with, and agreed to marry him. Eight months into their engagement, the couple became distant, feeling pulled in different directions. Momma Jeanne finally told Tom she was sexually interested in women, and Tom confessed he wanted to become a priest. The two remained close, supporting each other through life. Once Tom was ordained a priest, Momma Jeanne was the first to call him Father Byrne. When Momma Jeanne began dating women, Father Byrne stood by her side, never questioning or judging her decision.

Momma Jeanne studied the Bible, focusing on Hoodoo stories and the Psalms. She performed Hoodoo spells for luck, love, money, or any positive requests. She always turned down requests for revenge, curses, or to cause pain. Father Byrne occasionally asked for her help identifying demons during exorcisms. Momma Jeanne volunteered weekly at Saint Treasea Church, making and handing out peanut butter and jelly sandwiches to the homeless.

Momma Jeanne's sister lived in the northeast side of the Quarter, not far from their grandmother's old house.

They pulled up to an old, one-and-a-half story Creole cottage with orange stucco on the front and brick on the sides. All of the windows and doors were arched with green shutters for protection against the wind. The red, slate tile roof protected the house from the severe storms that constantly rolled through New Orleans. The orange front door opened right onto the sidewalk under a balcony, but with no porch. Momma Jeanne firmly knocked on the arched door. A moment later, they heard multiple locks and dead bolts click open. The door opened with a jerk and a head peaked out.

"Oh Lordy," a loud, friendly voice yelled as the two ladies embraced, passing greetings. "I was wondering who the hell be at my door unannounced," the lady happily said in her southern Creole accent. Momma Jeanne introduced her half-sister, Phyllis Ann Porre, to Wilbur as they were ushered into the warm cottage. "Call me PA," Phyllis Ann requested. The loud, humorous, full-figured lady was full of one-liner comments, never missing an opportunity to take fun jabs. She had much darker skin than Momma Jeanne, and her black hair with purple tips stood straight up like a porcupine. Wilbur immediately liked her. "I thought I might have to karate chop someone when you all knocked," PA said with a laugh and karate motioned her hands.

"My little sister thinks she is funny," Momma Jeanne said jokingly to Wilbur. The four-room cottage was well decorated with old French-style antiques and filled with the smell of fresh flowers. Each room was painted with a different pastel color. The fireplace sat in the middle of the cottage for all of the rooms to share. Wilbur noticed the odd red, orange, and yellow shag carpet on the ceiling and burnt orange trim in each room. A painting of a Voodoo Queen sat over the front room fireplace. The two ladies caught up over some seasoned rice, shrimp, and ice tea. Wilbur sat back, enjoying PA's fun personality.

PA was born with a limb anomaly called dysmelia. Her left hand had thick skin between her fingers, up to just below her nails. Her parents often explained that her hand was a special gift from God. PA never questioned the explanation. On her first day of grade school, PA came home crying, not wanting to return to school. She told her mom about the mean kids telling her she had an ugly frog's hand. The kids laughed and called her frog-girl. PA's mom decided they would go down first thing in the morning to speak with the principal. Believing her mom could fix everything, PA calmed down and went about her afternoon as normal. The next morning, PA arrived at the breakfast table happy and ready for school. Surprised, her mom asked why she was in such a good mood. PA informed her mom that there was no need to speak with the principal, and that a man came into her room last night to tell her everything would be okay. Concerned with the news of a man in her daughter's room, PA's mom asked for more information.

"Well, I was sleeping and heard someone calling my name. I opened my eyes and saw a bearded man in my window surrounded by white puffy clouds. He was wearing a tan robe with the sun behind his head," PA explained. "The man told me he had given me my hand because I am special. Then he told me not to listen to the mean kids at school." Her mom smiled, agreeing with the man in the window, "You are special PA."

Over the next few years, PA enjoyed going off by herself to pray and speak with spirits. Occasionally, she would have visions and mystical experiences. As a teenager, she traveled with her father Oscar to visit Momma Jeanne in Memphis. They checked into an inn not far from Momma Jeanne's home. The first room they were given had an awful odor and was full of flies. The two gagged and closed the door. The second room seemed okay until Oscar flopped onto the bed and wetness soaked through his pants. After pulling the blankets back, he discovered the bed was urine soaked. The third room, after a close inspection, was good. It was clean but secluded toward the back of the old complex. PA prepared for her nightly shower, placing her towel and undergarments on the toilet lid as always. When she stepped out of the shower, they were stacked neatly on the counter. The bathroom door was still locked, ruling out Oscar rearranging them. Dismissing the neatly arranged items, PA got dressed and went on to bed. The next day, they reunited with Momma Jeanne and Jennevea. After returning to the inn, PA again prepared for her shower. This time, she made sure she placed her things on the toilet lid. When she finished the shower, she again found her clothes neatly stacked on the counter next to the folded towels. Figuring a spirit was messing with her, she went about her business and got ready for bed. The following night, she left her clothes next to the folded towels before getting into the shower.

While washing her hair, she felt an eerie presence behind her. She stood still, trying to feel for a spirit. Foul, dead, hot breath blew across her back, causing her to turn with a panic. She stood face to face with a demon. Caught off guard, PA ripped down the shower curtain as she exited the bathroom. Not stopping to tell her dad, she ran out of the inn and into the parking lot with only the white shower curtain for cover. Oscar followed his daughter out of the inn, wondering if she had lost her mind. The frantic PA explained her terrifying experience. Oscar returned to the room to inspect the shower and found nothing unusual. He returned to the parking lot with their belongings. They stayed the night with Jennevea and Momma Jeanne before returning to New Orleans the next day. After hearing about PA's experience, her grandmother Carla Jill explained how the devil will chase the souls of people who have been visited by God. Turning a soul visited by God made the devil more powerful. For PA's twenty-second birthday, Carla Jill sent her to Haiti to study under the Haitian Voodoo Queen. The experience elevated PA to Supreme Voodoo Queen status in New Orleans. Over the years, she was visited by politicians, musicians, actors, sports stars, and anyone looking for spiritual help. From time to time, she helped Father Byrne with exorcisms.

Finished catching up, the two ladies moved to the back room, leaving Wilbur to entertain himself. PA's back room was covered with unique looking skulls, handmade dolls, a bird cage with a stuffed raven, and a couple of saint statues. Black, pleated silk material covered the ceiling, walls, and stone pattern floor. A round cedar table was centered in the room. Above the table hung an old disco ball. Walking around the room, PA lit candles and incense. The flickering of the candles reflected off the disco ball, creating a tranquil setting. Momma Jeanne sat at the table prepared to discuss her encounter with the demon. PA began asking questions about the encounter. As Momma Jeanne answered, PA's tone got under Momma Jeanne's skin. Turning into more of an interrogation, the little sister began second-guessing her big sister. Realizing Momma Jeanne was becoming irritated with the interrogation, PA took control to pray. She reached across the table and grabbed Momma Jeanne by the wrist. Humming a song of prayer, she focused on her big sister's soul. She spoke with the spirits, asking to be guided safely and honestly into their realm. PA's body began to twitch and sweat as she dove into Momma Jeanne's soul. Flashes of the demon came in and out of PA's view as she focused on the intent of the monster. The table shook as PA let out an awkward yelp. Letting go of Momma Jeanne's wrist, PA pushed back from the table with a frightening expression across her face. Shaking her head with concern, she said, "Oh Jeanne, have you seen this beast?"

"Yes, the demon was after my soul. It was eye-locked with me until Wilbur pulled me into the car and sped off," Momma Jeanne answered with her head down.

"You been cursed girl. You been cursed by a mean, evil beast. Damn girl, you know better. I can't believe you let the demon into you. Did you say or think its name?"

"I did not say it aloud, but I did recognize the demon. The demon locked eyes with me as it rose from the Seal. I could not shake it on my own. It has been haunting me ever since," Momma Jeanne explained.

"Damn girl!" PA again exclaimed. The sisters sat in silence. Wilbur interrupted by knocking on the door. Peeking his head in, he told PA that a man was at the front door to see her. Jeanne overheard her sister at the front door giving the man the business for his unscheduled arrival. Slamming the front door, she returned to her big sister, still mumbling about the unscheduled visitor. Sitting back down at the table, she continued the session. "You thinking the beast's name might have been enough to turn it toward you. Sometimes there ain't no difference between recognizing and saying the name. We are going to attack this beast head on," PA decided. "Let me pack some items."

"No, no PA, I do not need you involved. It is too dangerous," Momma Jeanne demanded.

"You know I am the only one that can fight this beast," PA grinned. "Plus, you ain't got no say, and you ain't gonna stop me," PA laughed. "I ain't seen Father Byrne in years. Oh Lordy, he is gonna be surprised to see me." Before pulling away from her house, PA informed Wilbur, "We are gonna need to make a few stops for spiritual supplies. I know you all ain't got what I need up north. We gonna fix this nasty demon with a nice spell." Stopping at WC's Spice Hut, Wilbur escorted the two ladies as they gathered supplies to stop the curse. They then made a quick stop at the old number one cemetery to gather dirt from under their family crypt. Satisfied they had everything they needed, the three headed north to Whitehaven.

***

FAMILY ROOTS

After not getting any helpful information from his mom, Henry sat down with his 94-year-old grandmother on his father's side. Due to the early death of his father, Henry's knowledge about his father's family history was limited. John Cross Matoske died when Henry was a baby. His father fell from the new Memphis bridge over the Mississippi River during a safety inspection. Henry's Grandfather Andros Matoske died in WWII during the Guadalcanal Campaign fighting the Japanese. Andros's mother Bell Matoske died during his birth. Everyone else in his family came from Slovakia after 1880. For being 94 Agnes Konecny Matoske was in great shape and still mentally sharp. Living alone with her dog, Agnes resisted emotional attachment to people. The loss of her husband and son pushed her to live hermit-like, not relying on other humans. Showing up unannounced, Henry knocked on her door. The one bedroom cottage seemed lifeless until the door opened.

"Well hello, Henry!" Agnes acted pleased to see him in her steady tone. The pain of a broken heart rushed blood through her body at the sight of Henry. She didn't see Henry, but the past pain of her lost husband and son. Taking a moment to wander back in time, Agnes stood in silence. Finally opening the glassless iron storm door, she invited him into her house. Her front room walls were all painted flat white, decorated with old Christian pictures she had collected through the years. Little statues of saints, other trinkets, and old books were placed on every shelf. The old scratch cedar floor was partially covered by a blue, oval, braided, wool rug. Lemon lavender scented candles filled the house, covering the moist musty smell.

After a quick "how you been" conversation, Agnes became suspicious of his unannounced visit. She motioned for him to sit with her on the sofa as she wondered what his visit was about. Not wasting her time, Henry began asking questions about his grandfather's family history.

"Oh, you are here about your grandfather," Agnes sighed.

"Well, this visit, yes." Henry went into the dealings with the demon and his quest to figure out if they had a connection to the land. Taking a long deep breath, Agnes sat back in her hard plastic-covered sofa, thinking back seventy-plus years. As distant as she was, she could not handle the loss of Henry or his sons. "Well, let me see, my father-in-law, your great-grandfather John Matoske immigrated from Slovakia and his wife, your great-grandmother Bell, died giving birth to my husband Andros," Agnes explained. "He grew up without a mother, and wanted your father to grow up with both parents. When he left for war, he told me that he was not afraid of death, but was afraid of our son growing up without both parents." Agnes paused to regain her thoughts while fighting her repressed emotions. "Let's see now, Bell's father Malley, your second great-grandfather grew up in an orphanage in Pine Bluff, Arkansas, I believe. He committed suicide in his fifties. His wife Nora Hendrichovska immigrated from Slovakia. Malley and Nora met at a Knights of Columbus dance in Slovak, Arkansas, where all our families lived. Slovak is a little farming community outside of Stuttgart, AR. A few thousand acres were bought in the late 1800s for Slovakian immigrants to farm. The Catholic Church there was built by our family around 1915. My father, your great-grandfather, performed mass when the priest could not make it from Little Rock. Most of our family is buried there in the little cemetery. Nora was the first in the community to marry a non-Slovakian. My husband, your grandfather, did not speak much about his family history, saying it was no good looking back. People in the community talked that his family had a dark history."

Henry wrote down the family history from his grandmother. "So, Malley must be the link I need to follow?" Henry asked. Shaking her head yes, Agnes agreed. "What was Malley's last name?" Closing her eyes in deep thought, Agnes shook off the question. "I do not remember."

"The orphanage name?" Henry pushed his luck.

"No, I am not sure I ever knew the name of the orphanage." Finished with the questions, Agnes went out of the room and returned with a box of picture books. She gave him a crucifix, a couple of pictures, a written letter she received from her husband while he was off in the war, and three old journals. "These are a few items I would like for you to have. These three journals were delivered to me by Mr. Hall twelve years after your grandfather's death. He was with him when he died. I believe your grandfather called him Slugman. Anyway, the last journal before his death might help you on your quest. Mr. Hall informed me that your grandfather was not killed in action as the Army claimed. He was not even killed in the South Pacific as his records read. Mr. Hall could not elaborate on the cause of death, but mentioned abnormal behaviors by your grandfather leading up to his death. I tried to contact Andros's commander to get more information, but was unsuccessful. I dearly loved Andros, and I have been lonely every day since he left for the war."

Henry became emotional, seeing this part of his grandmother he had never experienced. She informed him she probably did not have much time left to live, and wanted him to have the items. Henry laughed, reminding Agnes she had been saying that for over thirty years. Henry excused himself to continue his quest, promising to bring the boys by as soon as he could. As Henry gave her a hug goodbye, Agnes grabbed his face with both hands, then paused and looked deep into, his eyes. For a moment, she was back in 1942 staring into the same brown eyes, remembering the face she fell in love with. Letting go, the cruel sadness of the unfair life she lived alone resurfaced. She insisted that Henry be careful as he walked out the door. Once in his car, Henry shook off the long, slightly awkward goodbye.

Refocused, he searched his phone for the orphanage in Pine Bluff, Arkansas, 1800s. Only one came up, Saint Cyril and Methodius Catholic Orphanage. Henry clicked on the address and followed the turn-by-turn directions from his phone. The two-and-a-half hour trip flew by as he thought about all the history his grandmother shared. Due to the fractured relationship between Agnes and Bebbie, Henry did not spend a lot of time with his grandmother. Agnes was not big on sports, but always had news clippings of Henry's accomplishments hanging from her refrigerator. She attended every Catholic sacrament he received, even making the long drive to South Florida for his wedding. He thought back to his favorite memory with his grandmother. One Thanksgiving, his mom and half-sisters went to Warren's parents and left Henry with Agnes. Coming down with the flu, Henry laid on Agnes's couch all weekend while she took care of him. When he was awake, she softly rubbed his head and told him old family stories about his dead father. It was the only time he could remember one-on-one time with her. Henry always admired her strength, and wondered how she managed to stay sane after losing the man of her dreams, followed by the death of her only child. His grandmother had walked the Slovak death march to the little family cemetery too many times in her long life.

Stopping at the local hotel, Henry got a room to stay the night and wait for the orphanage to open for visitors.

After checking in, Henry took a quick shower to knock off the accumulated road dirt before opening his grandfather's journal. The old room had a mix of seventies style and modern decoration. The dingy white ceilings were scattered with pee-colored stains from old roof leaks. The outdated lighting buzzed as a slight flicker lit up the room. Henry picked up the old journal and inspected it. The soft, worn, black leather cover protected the brittle pages that were dark yellow from the years of decay. He untied the twine wrapped around the flat knob that kept the journal closed. An emotional, excited feeling overtook Henry as he carefully opened the cover protecting his grandfather's words. Andros Matoske was written on the inside. He looked down at the words written some seventy-plus years ago to describe life through the eyes of his grandfather. Nervous, Henry took a deep breath before reading the first page of neatly written cursive, not seen much in today's society.

May 8, 1943 Tuesday

Oh boy, it is a boy! I received a letter today from my darling Agnes to inform me she had a healthy baby boy on April 21, 1943! I hope she named him John Cross as we discussed before I shipped out. I am so excited and can't wait to see him. I hope I make it back home to teach him to hunt, fish, and we can have a catch. I miss my darling Agnes more than ever now. I sent her a letter asking for a picture of her little boy. It is funny how I already love the little boy even if I have not seen him. I pray that God allows me to return home to take care of my family

May 16, 1943 Sunday

Tonight is our last night in Puerto Rico before leaving out toward the Panama Canal. Me and some of the boys are headed out for some entertainment.

May 22, 1943 Saturday

Our ship entered the Gulf of Guinea today. We are not sure where we are headed or why we have been redirected from our original destination. Someone said they thought we were off the African coast, but that does not make any sense. Last briefing, we were headed to the Panama Canal to join the fight in the South Pacific. I asked Slugman if he knew anything, but he claimed that information was above his pay grade. He can be a fathead from time to time. I began having pressure in my chest that keeps me from sleeping. The Doc says it's probably just butterflies, nothing that I should worry about. I lay here in my bunk wondering what my sweet Agnes is doing back home. Is she thinking about me also? Is she wanting me like I am wanting her? I look forward to seeing my sweetest girl, my darling Agnes. I pray to God to keep me safe so I can return home to her and my son.

W.S. HENDRICHOVSKY

May 25, 1943 Tuesday

*After two days of waiting off the coast of Cotonou Africa, we were fi-
nally briefed. They shared with us this morning why we were redirected.
Our platoon was selected to search for an underground base where the
Germans have hidden gold and silver after the First World War. Our
orders are to follow the Oueme River up to where it meets the Okpana
River. There, we will set up camp until new orders arrive. Slugman is
just as excited as I am to be avoiding the heart of the war. We will begin
moving ashore tomorrow. I sure hope the rain stops. The constant storms
have made life on the ship more miserable than normal. I am still having
pressure in my chest, and have begun to have horrible dreams that cause
me to wake in a panicked sweat. I keep having the same dream of being
chased by something I can't see. I miss the dreams about my darling Agnes.
I sure miss her body up against mine. I miss our long talks and our long
walks. I can't wait to hold her again. I am the luckiest man alive to have
such a beautiful wife!*

May 28, 1943 Friday

*Extreme exhaustion has overcome our tent city, due to the past days of
preparation for our journey up the Oueme River. The rain continues to
come down, for we arrived during the peak of their rainy season. Although we have been ordered not to interact with the local people, we have
played with some of the children who have been watching us work. Slugman gave a few boys some US lettuce. I can't believe he is giving away
his money to strangers. The children are very interested in everything we
do. They follow us, laughing and pointing as we work in the rain. The
countryside here is green and overgrown as far as I can see. Must be from
all the rain. I hope for the rain to stop and a good night of sleep.*

May 29, 1943 Saturday

At the morning briefing, we were told to be prepared to pull out at day-break tomorrow. We also received a list of wild animals we were expected to encounter. Lions, cheetah, buffalo, elephants, and monkeys to name a few. I am not too excited about all the deadly snakes. I hate snakes! The instructor made it clear that everything out here wants to kill and eat us. I am looking forward to seeing the wildlife. Slugman, being from Chicago, has not been around many animals other than at the circus. I think he is scared, although he will never tell anyone. I received a letter from my darling Agnes. Her letter makes me happy, followed by sadness. Her perfume on the letter was great! I wish she would write longer letters. I long to return home to her.

June 3, 1943 Thursday

The route up the river has been exhausting. The swamps and marshes keep trying to swallow us, our trucks, and our equipment. The snakes are everywhere. I hate snakes. I keep feeling that we are being watched. Seems like something or someone is watching from a distance. I think I see shadows moving across trees in the sunlight. Slugman says I am freaked out, due to the crappy conditions we are working around. It is taking us much longer to reach…

A loud knock at the door caused Henry to jump. He had forgotten about the pizza being delivered. He marked his spot before opening the door. After paying the delivery driver, Henry flipped the pizza box onto the table and took a slice. Sitting back down on the bed, he continued to read as he enjoyed the buffalo chicken pizza.

It is taking us much longer to reach our objective than expected. The local guide claims the ground will be much better the further away from the coast we get. When the rain stops, the heat becomes so intense, making this trek more difficult. I try to focus on my darling Agnes. Her beauty keeps me moving forward.

June, 7 1943 Monday

The guide was correct. Soon as we got away from the lagoons and swamps, the ground hardened up. The flat, green, grassy fields are much easier on the feet. We saw our first group of lions yesterday. We all stopped and stared as the pride of lions laid in the shade watching us. The local guide has built up a makeshift fence, circling the camp with thorn bushes to keep the wild animals away at night. Nighttime is the most dangerous, due to it being prime hunting time for the animals. The sounds of the animals surrounding us at night makes it hard to sleep. The yells and screams echo across the plains. I began to feel a strong pull from across the plains that is unexplainable. A pull of belonging, a feeling of being united. Slugman says it is from exhaustion. He might be right. This mission has taken a toll on most of us. My feet are blistered up pretty good. The medic has given me some salve to help.

June 11, 1943 Friday

We have finally made it to our destination. We have set up a more advanced camp while we wait for further instructions. A herd of hippos live just around the river's bend to the east of camp. We have been warned to stay far away. The wildlife has left us alone, but the sounds at night continue to be stressful. I keep seeing a man from a nearby tribe watching us work, but every time I try to point him out to Slugman, the guy seems to disappear. Slugman keeps telling me I am losing my mind. I spend most of my downtime daydreaming about my darling Agnes. I must be the luckiest man alive to have such a beautiful gal back home.

June 13, 1943 Sunday

G.I. Jesus came by today to perform mass. I was able to receive communion for the first time in weeks. Felt great! Made me grateful not to be in the middle of the combat. I could not keep from thinking of all my brothers on the front line. Tears kept forming while I prayed. Very emotional day!

June 16, 1943 Wednesday

A herd of elephants chased us off today while we were out on a run. The squad leader decided we would be okay venturing away from the approved area. Guess he was wrong. I thought Slugman was going to get trampled by the big bull elephants. That Yanko really needs to get in better shape. I keep seeing men from the local tribe watching me. I stopped trying to point them out to anyone. I seem to be the only person who sees the tribesmen. I dreamed of Agnes last night. I dreamed she found a civilian to replace me. Hope that is not the case.

Henry placed the journal onto the table to think. *Andros seemed to be on more of a fun African escape than off fighting in the war,* Henry thought to himself. *Wow, it's only 6:30. I need some beer.* He grabbed his keys and ran over to Sandy's Qwik Stop on the edge of the hotel's lot for beer and candy. Returning to the room, he removed the old, worn out comforter and made himself comfortable on the lumpy bed. The aged A/C unit buzzed as it circulated the stale, cigarette-laced air around the musty room. Fully engaged with his grandfather's words, he had not noticed the occasional cockroach crawling across the floor. Henry kicked off his shoes as he opened the brittle journal.

June 20, 1943 Sunday

I was off hitting the head this morning when a black silhouette moved across, just beyond the trees. At one point, it stopped as to look at me. It scared me to death.

What the freak! Henry jumped from the bed still holding the journal. He refocused before reading again.

A black silhouette moved across, just beyond the trees. At one point, it stopped as to look at me. It scared me to death.

Henry laid the book down onto the bed and began pacing around the room talking to himself. "Andros witnessed shadow people over in Africa? Can there be a connection? How can that be?"

Henry sat back down on the bed, picking up the journal to continue reading.

At one point, it stopped as to look at me. It scared me to death. I have not spoken of what I saw for fear of being laughed at. Slugman already gives me a hard time about seeing what he calls invisible tribesmen. Later in the afternoon, I heard a soft drum beat off in the distance.

Henry looked up from the journal, again not believing what he just read. Soft drum beats? A tingling feeling ran up Henry's spine. Chills engulfed his body after reading his grandfather had the same encounter in Africa he had experienced in Skuna Valley. *What the freak is going on?* Eager to know more, Henry returned to reading.

I looked around to see if anyone else was listening to the beat. Just as I expected, no one else was looking toward it. I am starting to believe I am going mad. I miss Arkansas, my family, and my wife.

June 21, 1943 Monday

I woke up last night to the soft drum beats. I laid there just listening. A foul smell encircled me as the temperature dropped and I saw a flash of black move across the room. I raised up to see who was moving about. Fear overcame me as something whispered, "Cassius! Cassius!"

"Oh, shit!" Henry said in disbelief as he dropped the journal onto the bed. He again stood up and stared down at the journal. In complete shock, he walked around the room trying to get his head around what he just read. "How could it be? How could he hear Cassius's name, in Africa?" Henry mumbled as he slowly sipped his beer. "I just do not understand!" Completely freaked out, he sat back down on the bed and stared at the journal. Finally, Henry picked it up and continued to read.

Fear overcame me as something whispered, "Cassius! Cassius!" I stood up quickly to inspect the room. Nothing! Nothing was around. I sat in my bed in a stressful state of fear, not able to move. "Cassius! Cassius! Die, Cassius. Die," the voice held me captive. Maybe I dozed off a few times, but not for long. The long night finally came to an end. Am I going mad? I just do not understand.

June 23, 1943 Wednesday

We have finally received our orders. Tomorrow, we began our search for the hidden base. About ten clicks north of our camp, we will search a large area of dense forest. We are to expect hostile resistance. I am nervous knowing we might experience our first combat tomorrow. Oh, I would do anything to be in my darling Agnes's arms one last time. I pray for God to protect me.

June 26, 1943 Saturday

We have searched a large portion of the forest and found no signs of the German base. We have found no more than game trails. The monkeys yell and scream at us as they move from tree to tree, following us throughout the forest. We found a sacred cave covered with paintings of the ancient history of the local Ewe tribe. Our guide has advised us to stay away from the sacred cave, although we had to search it for signs of the German's base. The inside walls were covered with paintings and symbols. We made our way through a narrow passage just big enough to crawl through. It opened up into a beautiful chamber with water running down the wall and mist floating down, wetting all the rock. The beauty made me think of my darling Agnes. I stared at the sunlight peeking through the cracks in the cave's ceiling. Off behind the mist, I saw a set of deep blue eyes staring at me. Chills ran up my spine, not sure what I was seeing. I could not decide if they were really eyes or just a reflection off the wet cave wall. A gentle, cold breeze blew from the back of the chamber. At once, we all believed there must be a passage to reach further into the cave. After a search of the back wall for another chamber came up empty, Slugman looked at me with disbelief. Everyone could tell the cold breeze was displaced there at the end of the chamber. After finishing our search of the cave, we returned back to camp, unsuccessful in our search for the Germans.

July 1, 1943 Thursday

I woke to the sound of soft drum beats again. I sat up in my cot and looked around the tent for the source. Across the tent, I saw the black silhouette move toward me. Great fear overtook my body and kept me from moving or speaking as I tried with all my strength to do so. Paralyzed in fear, I could only stare at the intruder. The dark silhouette stood at the foot of my cot and revealed its deep blue eyes and yellow hair. "Die, Cassius. Die," the dark silhouette said before disappearing. I am so scared about what has come of me. I feel like I am breaking. Even if I return to my darling Agnes and John Cross, will they want a broken man? I do not remember the last time I slept more than a few minutes. I am not able to shut my brain off to sleep. I do not know how much longer I can go. I pray to God to release me of this pain.

Henry finished the journal entries and sat in the cold bed, isolated in deep thought. His grandfather's last entry was of a scared, broken man just hours before death. Henry began crying softly, unable to get his mind around what was happening to his family, or what had happened to his grandfather. Henry sat up and turned up his beer to chug, trying to remove the creepy feeling from the shared experience with his grandfather. Henry's thoughts turned to his dead father. Could the black silhouette be responsible for my father falling off the bridge? Although the thought seemed reasonable, Henry knew there was no way to prove it one way or the other. Unable to leave his father's death alone, Henry called his mom for any evidence to connect the silhouette to his father's deadly accident. After a long conversation, Henry learned nothing helpful from Bebbie. Henry felt his mother had purposely forgotten that his father even existed.

Henry opened one of the letters written from Andros to Agnes:

May 8, 1943 Saturday

Dearest Honey,

Received your letter + was glad to get it after waiting so long. I'm still o.k. + hope you and your son are the same. You said you haven't heard from me in a long time. Well, I'm sorry but I wrote you a couple of letters in the past two weeks. I can't make the mail travel faster. There are a lot of times I don't get any mail for two weeks. I get mail from cousin Samantha the same day I get it from you. Hers was mailed March 26, + yours mailed April 6, + I got both on April 17. So, you can see how this mail travels. You said you guess Cousin Samantha and Aunt Trisha told me about the baby. Well, all they told me is you had a baby + was o.k. Well Hon, how does it feel to have a baby? Pretty tough or not? Say Honey, every letter I get from you, they are o.k. but couldn't you write just a little more? About the time I get started reading, I'm at the bottom + that's all. Say Honey, guess who I got a letter from today? Donna + Rose Price. I might write

214

them a letter if I stay here long enough. I haven't heard from Cousin Alyshia for months, but I guess she is waiting for an answer from me. I guess she will have to wait. I had been going to church every Sunday, but I'm just in a place now where I can't go. Say Honey, I would like to know what you named our son + how is he? A good boy, or is he like me, always into something? You want to know what I want for my birthday? I sure don't know what I would like. I don't care if you send me one or not, just suit yourself. Where is Cousin Allen's platoon at + what service is he in + is Cousin Steven Matoske still around home? Or is he in the army too? Well, the only worry I have is that the local tribe man in our squad is scared always. He sleeps with a bayonet always under his pillow. I haven't been sleeping good the past weeks. I think because of the workload. We sure got a great view. How would you like to say you could throw a rock into the ocean from your bunk? Well Honey, I guess I'll have to close til next time. So, bye, bye with lots of love to you and son.

Your Husband
P.F.C Andros Matoske
P.S. Tell the folks all hello

After finishing the last of the twelve beers, Henry fell asleep.

***

THE CONNECTION

The next morning, Henry pulled through the gate of the orphanage. He followed the long, winding driveway up to the building's entrance. The driveway was lined with tall hedges, keeping people from seeing across the campus. The pre-Civil War Italianate Victorian style building was well maintained, and looked nice from the outside. Oak trees were scattered across the campus to provide shade during the hot summers. Different colored crepe myrtles added beauty. In the center of the roundabout was a ten-foot plaster statue of Saint Cyril and Methodius.

Henry opened the frosted glass door, walked into the historic orphanage, and asked to see the headmaster. Looking around, Henry was impressed by the cleanliness of the inside as well. The plaster walls were painted tan with white trim. The offices were lined with different colors of Georgian marble. Pictures of past headmasters and notable alumni covered the wall. Henry was impressed, seeing pictures of eleven professional football players, seven professional baseball players, a professional basketball player, and a professional wrestler. *Not a bad alumni group*, he thought to himself. After a short wait, Sister Mary Phillips invited him into her office. Henry gave a short version of his story before asking to see records of Malley from the mid to late 1800s. "All record requests must be approved by the diocese office in Little Rock," the Sister quickly informed Henry.

After a quick phone call to Father Byrne and a thirty-minute wait, Henry was escorted by the assistant headmaster, Sister Jean Marie, to the basement in search of the file. Sister Jean Marie looked to be in her late 60s, about five feet tall, with glasses and a little overbite. She was dressed in the white robe and black habit, with a long rosary hanging from her waist. Stepping into the dark, musty basement Henry jumped back after a face-to-face encounter with a life size Saint Cyril statue stored against the wall. Sister giggled as she informed Henry the statue was harmless.

After some mathematical guessing, Henry decided Malley was there around the 1860s. Searching all morning, Sister Jean Marie and Henry continued their quest to find Malley from Skuna Valley, Mississippi. Not having any luck, Henry took Sister Jean Marie to the local burger shop, The Sportsman's Café, for lunch. Henry shared more details about the possession and having Tyler at St. Treasea's. "In Whitehaven?" Sister asked. "Yes," Henry answered.

"I used to be the principal at Saint Thomas High School in Whitehaven before it closed in 1998 due to low enrollment." She shared with Henry how much she enjoyed being a principal. After lunch, the two returned to the orphanage to continue their quest.

They continued to search into the late afternoon.

"Born 1851, Malley Stephen Shannon, Skuna Valley, Mississippi. Arrived November 15, 1861," Sister Jean Marie read aloud. "That's it!" Henry yelled as he rushed to Sister's side.

Reading the file ,Sister Jean Marie's face turned from happy to sad as she realized the horror Malley went through before he arrived to the orphanage. She handed the file over to Henry. "Father, Cassius Lue Shannon. That is the connection," Henry shared with Sister Jean Marie. Reading to himself, Henry discovered that Malley's twin brother Clifton killed his father, two sisters-in-law, a nephew, a niece, possibly his mother, and was trying to kill Malley when he was shot by their dying father. Malley was found still tied to a chair and covered with blood. All other family had died weeks before with no obvious connection to Clifton. Malley was sent to live with a half-sister in Florence, Alabama, who died a few weeks later from a heart attack. Malley was then shipped to Saint Cyril and Methodius Orphanage. Doctor Lamar Waters described Malley as being quiet, keeping to himself, not wanting to engage anyone or discuss the horror he witnessed back on the plantation. Nightly, Malley woke up from terror-filled dreams, covered in cold sweat. Dr. Waters began having understudies sit in Malley's room to observe him sleep. Over the course of a couple weeks, the understudy documented Malley crying out, "Cassius brought this punishment onto this land. Cassius and all his roots must be removed." The understudy also noted, "Shak is coming, Shak is coming for me." When Dr. Waters spoke to Malley during sessions, Malley claimed to have no memory of anything observed by the understudy. As the years went on, the night terrors slowly stopped. Malley was able to begin forming friendships with a few classmates. After years of therapy, Dr. Waters felt Malley should have a productive life. "Wow," Henry said aloud as the Sister stood in silence, waiting for his reaction. "No wonder he committed suicide," Henry revealed to the Sister. "Poor guy went through hell." Henry took pictures of the file with his phone before putting everything back. Walking to the exit, Henry thanked Sister Jean Marie as he left the orphanage. Driving the three-and-a-half hours to Coffeeville for further research at the county seat, Henry questioned his goodness against his family's past horrors. "All families have skeletons," he told himself.

***

STAY AWAY FROM SKUNA VALLEY

Henry pulled into his driveway not thinking about Momma Jeanne's warning to stay away from their possessed house. The county seat in Coffeeville had closed hours before he arrived. He walked into his house and grabbed a cold beer from the fridge to chug. Finishing it, he grabbed another beer and sat down to watch TV. As he kicked his shoes off, he remembered the warning to stay away from their house. *I will be okay for one night*, Henry thought to himself. A light caught Henry's eye down the hill. It was moving toward the house under the moonlit sky. A slight adrenaline rush popped through his veins. Moving behind a curtain, he peeked out the window. "Oh crap," he laughed, realizing his neighbor Kyle was walking toward the house carrying his dog Skippy and a flashlight. Henry stepped out on to the porch and yelled, "Get off my land, ya jackass," Kyle walked up to the porch covered in mud, thorns, and stickers. Laughing, Henry asked, "You taking Skippy for a walk?"

"No, ya asshole," Kyle grinned. "This damn dog keeps getting out, and Roy is too scared of the dark to chase Skippy around. Next time, I might shoot the damn thing."

"Awe, Skippy is just trying to get you some exercise," Henry laughed.

"So, how are things with Tyler?" Kyle asked.

"We believe this land is cursed by an evil angel sent by God to gather souls, I think that is right," Henry thought out loud. "Anyway, I read my grandfather's journal he kept during WWII. He experienced a silhouette with dark blue eyes and yellow hair in Africa before he was killed."

"Holy crap!" Kyle expressed. "Y'all have some jacked-up stuff going on!"

"Yeah, I know," Henry agreed. "This silhouette has caused problems in my family for years. We are in the process of trying to figure out why," Henry finished.

"Well, if we can do anything, let us know." After the brief conversation, Kyle went on his way.

Henry settled back down with another beer to watch his favorite TV series. Not long after relaxing, he fell deeply asleep in his recliner. The long road trip from Pine Bluff to Skuna Valley had worn him out. Drool leaked onto the leather as Henry lay dead to the world, sleeping.

A loud banging startled Henry out of his slumber. He stumbled to the front door, still half asleep. Opening the door, he found his neighbor Kyle in a panic.

"Roy is lost in the woods," Kyle yelled before Henry could ask.

"What? What do you mean lost in the woods?" Henry repeated, trying to shake the deep sleep.

"I mean he went out into the woods and has not returned. I made him chase after Skippy an hour ago, after thirty minutes, I got worried and started looking for him. I am not having any luck finding him. Can you help me search?" Kyle asked.

"Yeah sure, let me get my boots and flashlight." The two friends set out for the woods to look for Roy. The big, bright, full moon lit up the night and made it easier to maneuver. The two men spread out fifty yards apart, hollering Roy's name as they made their way deeper into the hardwoods. Off in the distance, Henry spotted a light flickering off and on. He yelled over to Kyle as they turned their direction toward the flickering light. They both realized it was coming from the old moonshine shack Henry hid in to escape the attacking crows. The two men approached cautiously, not knowing if Roy was the one flickering the light. They stepped into the front room and found a flashlight on emergency mode lying on the rotted wooden floor. Turning their flashlights toward the back room, they saw a puddle of blood leaking through the cracks in the floor. "Oh God!" Kyle cried out as he rushed into the back room. "Oh crap," Kyle turned, gagging, and left the back room as quickly as he entered. Looking into the room, Henry saw the freshly mutilated fawn lying in the corner. As an unfamiliar smell of fresh guts burned his nose, he gagged and turned his head away.

"Who would do such a thing to a baby deer?" Kyle asked with a disgusted look on his face.

"Well, at least it was not Roy," Henry looked back at Kyle, trying to lighten the anxious mood. "Roy probably freaked out when he saw the blood and dropped the flashlight." Seeing the worry on his friend's face, Henry grabbed each side of Kyle's shoulders him looked him in the eye, "We will find Roy. I bet he is back at your house right now, wondering where you are, pissed that you are not there."

Kyle smiled at Henry, "You are a pretty good friend for a jackass!" A soft drum beat started off in the distance as they exited the rickety shack.

The two stepped out of the shack and back into the hardwoods as a spatter of thick, red blood covered Henry's face. Shocked, Henry looked up with horror as he saw a silver machete lodged into Kyle's shoulder where it meets his neck. Kyle let out a hair-raising scream and stumbled, holding his wound as he went down to his knees and fell forward. Henry saw Roy standing before him, still holding the silver machete now covered with Kyle's blood.

"What the hell did you do, Roy?" Henry yelled, not sure what was happening. Roy turned his focus to Henry, "Die, Cassius. Die," Roy said as he slowly moved Henry's way. Henry tried to talk some sense into Roy before noticing the dark blue eyes protruding from Roy's head. The dark silhouette with yellow hair flashed, showing itself to Henry and confirming the serious situation.

"Die, Cassius. Die," Roy cried out and moved toward Henry. Not wanting to lay with Kyle, Henry turned to run, but fell face first into a shallow ditch full of thorns and vines. As he struggled to get up, he became tangled in the vines and could not free himself. Feeling Roy standing over him, he turned to face the killer.

Roy began mumbling, "Cassius and all his roots must be removed. Die, Cassius. Die." Still struggling to escape the grasp of the thorns and vines, Henry begged Roy to stop. Roy stood over him with the silver machete repeating, "Die, Cassius. Die!" Roy lifted the silver machete over his head and started hammering it down at Henry. In a fight for survival, Henry held his forearms up, trying to protect himself from the silver machete's rapid blows. Little by little, Roy chopped the flesh, exposing the bones and spattering blood all over his face. Roy kept yelling, "Die, Cassius. Die."

Henry screamed in excruciating pain as he fell off his recliner and onto the floor. He jumped up, checking his forearms for damage and not finding any. In uncontrollable fear, he looked around the room for Roy. Henry was still not aware he was in his living room. Taking repeated deep breaths and trying to calm down, Henry bent over and held his knees, still looking around the room. "What the freak was that?" Henry said to himself as he started to calm down. Not able to shake the anxiety from the dream, he paced the room, replaying it in his head. Henry walked around the house, checking the doors and windows to make sure they were all locked. Satisfied with his safety but still shaken up, he sat down at the kitchen table to enjoy a cold beer. He could not get over how real the dream seemed. Even the pain from the machete seemed real. Henry thought back to his and Sharon's talk with Tyler, when Tyler described his friend. Black as night, yellow hair and dark blue eyes. *Just like the silhouette that showed itself from Roy's body in my dream.* He finished his beer, and was grabbing another when he heard a soft drum beat start off in the distance. Henry listened for a moment before getting up and heading to his car, not in the mood to investigate.

Driving to town, Henry called Sharon to let her know where he was and tell her about his plan for the next day. Not wanting to stay at his house, Henry slept in his car in front of the courthouse. After breakfast and coffee, Henry entered the courthouse to request the recorded history of the land he owned.

The two-level, octagon brick building had two chimneys raised out of the roof. The newly stained brick gave the building a look much newer than its actual age. All of the windows shared the same arch as the front entrance. Inside, the receptionist directed Henry to the second level for land records. After making his request, he was escorted to a small office to wait for the file to be pulled. He looked over the wall-sized map of Yalobusha County as he waited.

Receiving the file from the lady, Henry read over the land history until he found the name he was looking for. *Just as I expected, the land was owned by Cassius Lou Shannon. Die, Cassius. Die,* Henry thought to himself. Henry confirmed what he already knew. Cassius was the tall white man in the vision Momma Jean saw during the investigation. Continuing to read, Henry learned that the plantation was destroyed in the battle of Coffeeville during the Civil War. With no surviving legal owner, the land was auctioned off during the reconstruction of the south after the Civil War ended. Henry could not help but think, *I bought land that I already owned. Just my luck,* he laughed and returned the file to the lady at the desk.

Leaving the courthouse, Henry called Kyle and asked him to meet for lunch at Chubby's Hotdog Hut. Chubby's was a hot spot for the college crowd from 11 p.m. to 2 a.m. Nothing tasted better than a fully loaded, foot-long hotdog after a night of partying. The two friends sat out under an oak tree on a picnic table watching the college students come and go with their meals. They enjoyed the famous hotdogs while Henry told Kyle how his family once owned all the land around their houses. Henry decided to share his upsetting dream with Kyle. Not leaving anything out, Henry told Kyle about the disturbing images of Roy possessed by the demon. After soaking in the morbid details, Kyle laughed, "Sounds just like that prissy bitch, trying to kill us." The two laughed before silence overtook the table. Realizing his friend's stress, Kyle changed the subject and began talking about his funny college drinking stories, trying to give Henry a break from the overwhelming situation his family was facing. After an hour of laughing, Henry needed to get back to his quest. He thanked Kyle for lunch before leaving.

Once in his car, Henry called Sharon to share his family's history and connection to Cassius and the land. After listening to Henry, Sharon asked him to pick up Will from Nana Bebbie and to meet at St. Treasea's. Father Byrne and Momma Jeanne were already discussing the next step.

"Momma Jeanne?" Henry asked.

"Yes, Momma Jeanne. She has decided to help."

During the drive back to Whitehaven, Henry thought back to Momma Jeanne's investigation. He became angry, developing a hate for Cassius and the horrible things he did to the slaves. Henry's stomach cramped from disgust as he realized his life was the result of evil decisions made by a white trash slave owner who had zero respect for human life. Still in deep thought, Henry decided to spend the rest of his life trying to spread goodness to make up for all of Cassius's evil actions. A big smile crossed his face and a warm feeling filled his heart as he realized that both his boys were being raised not to see color!

***

THE DREAM TEAM

As he walked into Father Byrne's office, Henry saw an unfamiliar black woman rubbing Father Byrne's bald head, saying "I love me a white man's bald head." Father Byrne jumped up and asked PA to stop. "Oh Lordy, Father, you know you can't resist me," PA laughed. Momma Jeanne and Henry laughed as PA chased the Father around the desk. Finally getting control of his office, Father Byrne introduced PA to Henry, informing him that she had come up from New Orleans to help him and Momma Jeanne get rid of the demon. The Father went on to explain how Momma Jeanne was pulled into the curse because of a mistake she made during their investigation.

Enjoying the mood, Henry asked "Is it good that she is helping, or bad that we need more help?" PA assured Henry that he was in good hand with this dream team. Henry informed the room of everything he learned about his family's past.

After a discussion, Father Byrne called for a nurse to take Tyler down to an exorcism room. The group went to join him. PA sat down with each member of the Matoske family. She grabbed Sharon by the wrist and closed her eyes, humming a song to help her search the soul.

Letting go, PA smiled, "You are curse free, my lady!"

PA then grabbed Henry, Tyler, and Will by the wrist one at a time. She saw the same demon as with Momma Jeanne. Leaving the boys with Sister Elizabeth to pray, the group went into the living quarters in the basement. Father Byrne started to talk when PA interrupted, "Excuse me Father, but we gonna have to go by my lead this time."

"That is what I was about to say," the Father grunted, shaking his head with a smile.

"Tomorrow morning, we will all meet at Momma Jeanne's Hoodoo shack at 10 a.m. so we can dig into this curse as a group. I need more information to be able to attack this curse with the correct spell," PA shared.

Later that evening, Father Byrne took his two old friends across the street to the famous Italian Rebel restaurant for pizza and beer. The family-owned pizzeria was a small, tan brick building that stood alone across from the church in a lot used for overflow parking during Sunday Mass. The freshly made Italian sausage aroma filled the plainly decorated pizzeria, which only had neon beer signs and too many Italian flags scattered around the walls, and an old shuffleboard table for entertainment. The windows were up high, letting in the sunlight but keeping the inside activity hidden from passersby. The three old friends finished off a pizza and a pitcher of beer while telling fun stories they shared from their youth. The multicolored jukebox was playing a mixture of country and pop songs as four men played a game of shuffleboard. Starting on the second pitcher, the conversation turned serious when Momma Jeanne shared her reoccurring dream since the unsuccessful Matoske home investigation.

After a long sigh, Momma Jeanne began describing her dream, looking down at her beer mug. "I am walking out behind my house in the woods after dark. Walking next to the little lake, I hear a faint drum beat off in the distance. As I look for the source of the drum beat, I come across an old moss-covered, wooden shack up on stilts above the lake's backwater. Through the cracks in the walls, I see a light flickering inside the shack. As I walk up the rotting, vine-covered ramp to the door, I see hundreds of black butterflies sitting on the porch, watching me approach. I push open the ajar door, surprised to see a little black boy standing on a wooden crate stuffing meat into an old, rusty meat grinder. Without turning around, the little boy says, 'Come in Jeanne, you are just in time for dinner.' He was dropping the ground meat into the big black iron pot he had boiling on the cast iron, wood-burning stove. A rancid smell gagged me as I moved through the shack. I walk up to see what he is cooking."

A loud Italian man entering the pizzeria interrupted her story, yelling with excitement, "Hey Padre!"

"Hey, Tony B.," Father Byrne stood up to embrace the loud man. Tony B. yelled to the guy behind the counter, "Hey Rocco, put the Padre's table on my tab." Before walking off, Tony B. slapped Father Byrne on the back and told Momma Jeanne and PA, "This guy, always trying to get a free meal out of me." They all laughed as Tony B. headed behind the counter. Father Byrne sat back down and told his two friends how Tony B. was a football legend back in the 90s at St. Thomas High School before it closed. His family owned the pizzeria and protected the area around the church. Momma Jeanne and PA understood what kind of protection he meant without asking.

"His nickname is Tony Bologna because he is full of crap," the priest laughed, taking a chug of beer.

Momma Jeanne continued her story, "I walk up to see what he is cooking, and see my mom's decapitated head staring at me from the sink full of blood. I reach down to pick her head up and she starts yelling over and over, 'Run Jeanne, run Jeanne, he is after you.' I look over at the little boy, and he is staring at me with his dark blue eyes and an evil look, holding a rusty, blood covered machete in one hand and a sawed up section of an arm in the other. I turn and run out of the shack into the woods to escape. Deep into the hardwoods, I run. I keep falling down, trying to escape in full state of panic. Once I believe I am far enough away, I drop down under a large fallen oak tree. I hide in the thick overgrowth surrounding the fallen tree. Off in the distance, I hear the little black boy laughing as he gets closer, 'he he he he, ha ha ha ha.' A swarm of mosquitos engulfs me as I lie still under the log and make me miserable. I begin to focus on my breathing, ignoring the mosquitoes. I again hear a soft drum beat from off in the distance. The closer he gets, the more nervous I become. I begin praying for him to walk past me. He stops beside the fallen tree. I see his bare feet are next to my head as he slams the machete down into my hip. I wake up screaming, grabbing my hip looking for damage. The dream seems so real, it takes me a long time to recover." Momma Jeanne finished her stressful story and chugged the rest of her beer. PA and Father Byrne sat quietly, soaking in the story and staring at Momma Jeanne.

"That demon really has screwed you up," PA blurted out, letting out a fun laugh and shaking her head. Father Byrne and Momma Jeanne joined in the laughter. "We gonna put a stop to this demon," PA assured Momma Jeanne. The three friends finished the second pitcher before leaving.

At 10 a.m. the next morning, Henry, Tyler, and Will sat inside the hoodoo shack around Momma Jeanne's cedar table. PA finished lighting the candles and incense and sat at the table with them. Soft African spiritual music played in the background. The boarded windows kept the sunlight out for the full candle flickering effect. The group sat with their eyes closed, holding hands around the table. Father Byrne, Wilbur, and Sharon stood in a corner watching.

After a short prayer, PA slipped off into a trance, softly mumbling unrecognizable words. Her eyes were moving erratically behind the lids as sweat formed across her forehead. The table began vibrating as a foul smell filled the room, causing Tyler and Will to cry with fear. Deep in PA's trance, she saw Shankpana dancing around, holding a broom in one hand and a silver machete in the other, "Uba uba uba yah yah, uba uba uba yah yah!" Shak danced up to Henry and took a swing with the machete, decapitating his head. Turning toward Will, Shak again took a swing with the machete at Will, then Tyler, both with the same results. Then Momma Jeanne knelt down on all fours, begging to have her head removed. "End the curse, please end the curse!" She cried out to Shak. Shak raised the machete to execute her when PA slammed both of her fists down on the table while standing and yelling, "Stop, just stop!"

Everyone in the room jumped with fear, not knowing what the outburst was about. PA opened her eyes with an angry look on her face. Everyone was staring up at her in surprise. She looked around the room before speaking. With a fake laugh, she apologized. "Sorry, ah, that damn ex-boyfriend of mine who died over thirty years ago still likes messing with me during these séances. He will not leave me alone, you know, can't get enough of old PA even in the afterlife," she again laughed. "I need to clear my head," PA said as she walked outside, slamming the door in irritation.

Momma Jeanne followed her out. "What was that?" she asked.

"I was being harassed by a crazy spirit," PA said unconvincingly.

"I do not believe you, PA," Momma Jeanne said.

"I got this, now go back inside while I clear my head," PA insisted, pointing her finger at the shack's entrance. Not happy with PA, Momma Jeanne reluctantly returned inside the shack.

After pacing back and forth, she walked over to the watchers. Brad and Paul could see PA was upset. "What's up PA?" Brad mumbled. "I just saw some terrible visions in there that shook me up. I saw Momma Jeanne being murdered."

"Oh, crap," Paul quietly sighed.

"I do not know what to do," PA confessed. The three sat in silence for a moment.

Brad looked firmly into the eyes of his old friend, "You are going to take you black ass back into the hoodoo shack and throw some mojo hojo crap on that table to cast a spell to stop whatever is happening! You are going to stop anything from hurting your sister!"

"Yeah, what he said," Paul echoed.

"Thanks guys," PA said with a smile and returned to the shack.

PA returned to begin another session. She sprinkled a mixture of spices across the table as she began humming. Again, she slipped off into a trance for a few moments, then pushed away from the table. "I got it," she exclaimed, "I know how to beat this evil beast!" The group looked up at her with relief. "We got to find the point of entry and reverse the curse."

"Me and my assistant, Father Byrne," PA said with a giggle, "will go down to your house this afternoon to stay the night together." She winked at the Father. Shaking his head with a smile, the Father remained silent. "We will figure out the best way to set up our battlefield. Once we set up, I will call Momma Jeanne, and we all will meet at the University in Mrs. Sharon's office," PA finished.

Insisting on clean souls, Father Byrne demanded the group meet Father Cashin in the morning at St. Treasea's for confession. PA and Father Byrne left for Skuna Valley. En route, while Wilbur was driving, PA confessed to Father Byrne. "I did not see no ex-boyfriend," she said shaking her head with concern. "The beast was toying with me. It needs these four souls to complete the curse."

"So, you faked the second session?" the Father asked.

"Yes, I did," PA admitted. "They need hope to have a chance against this beast."

"Why does this demon want these four souls?" the Father asked.

"I do not know," PA answered, shaking her head with concern.

"So, how do you plan to stop the curse?" the Father asked.

"I do not know that either," PA sighed. "I hope to figure that out during our investigation tonight." The two sat in silence for the remainder of the ride, preparing themselves.

***

PREPARING FOR BATTLE

Pulling into the Matoskes' driveway, PA threw a handful of garlic onto Father Byrne's head, "That is to give ya some extra protection," she laughed.

The two exited the car and ventured into the house. Wilbur unloaded the car while PA and the Father wandered around the house to get familiar with the setup. They both set up their supplies for the night's investigation. "Now, Father, if you see the demon, do not say or think its name be sure to not lock eyes. I do not need you getting sucked into this curse like Momma Jeanne," PA said with seriousness.

Starting the investigation, PA slowly walked throughout the house, room to room, stopping every so often to close her eyes and search for spirits. Following close behind, Father Byrne held his cross in one hand and prayer book in the other. He prayed in silence, keeping watch over PA. Wilbur followed the two, recording everything with a video camera. "The spirits are silent," PA shared. Not finding any abnormal activity in the house, the two moved the investigation outside with Wilbur in tow.

Behind the house, PA sensed an evil energy pulling her into the darkness. She continued with Father Byrne. They walked down past the barn, then followed a game trail through the kudzu-covered trees. The two investigators continued to focus on their task, with no worries about the environment as they maneuvered through the overgrowth. Stopping, PA whispered, "Something bad happened here." Looking around, she spotted old brick columns partly covered with crumbled stucco, still standing amidst other fallen columns. In the middle, a lone fireplace stood holding an iron staircase. Kudzu and brush had reclaimed the once proud plantation house. They carefully moved about the old ruins. "I see shadows moving, but the spirits are not talking," PA explained. "I feel the bad energy, but see nothing." A pile of old bricks fell over, turning their attention toward the back of the ruins. "Who is here? What do you want?" PA called out. PA caught a glimpse of a spirit streaking into the woods. A burst of energy knocked PA to her knees as she witnessed the brutal murders of Harriett and Lilly. Their souls screamed with pain as they were stabbed over and over with the dagger. She saw Little Lorre crying as the noose tightened around her little neck and turned her face blue. The beautiful baby girl struggled for her last breath. PA explained her visions to Father Byrne as he prayed silently. A chilly breeze blew a light fog across the old plantation ruins and caused a shiver down both investigators' spines. PA saw a vision of Clifton's body blown across the room as his father's body fell dead after the blast. A section of the old fireplace fell, causing the investigators to jump in fear. Father Byrne grabbed PA's arm, ready to protect his friend. Faces showing the plague suffered by the plantation's residents flashed in and out of her vision. PA watched the story that the spirits were telling her in hope of relieving their pain. After the spirits finished, Father Byrne blessed the area to help put the spirits at rest.

"We need to find the source of the curse, where the demon entered," PA whispered to Father Byrne as she led him down the hill away from the plantation ruins. As they approached the old whipping post area, the spirits came alive. She stopped to take in the cruel torture of the slaves. Wilbur filmed the session as PA began talking softly. She described the horror the wandering souls endured. Listening to PA, Father Byrne realized why Momma Jeanne was so upset talking about what she saw during her investigation. PA again asked the two questions, "Who is here? What do you want?" After a few moments, Father Byrne pulled out the holy water and began to bless the area while praying for the souls to find peace. A strong wind funneled dirt and debris upwards as the priest yelled his prayers over the noise. With her eyes closed, PA watched the spirits lift up into the funnel and enter their afterlife, released from their torturous pain. When the prayer was complete, Father Byrne wiped the sweat from his forehead and sat down on an old stump. "Wow, that was intense," he shared.

"You okay, old man?" PA asked with a smile. "We still have not found the source of the curse." Father Byrne laughed off the "old man" remark as he stood up to continue the quest. The two kept going in search of the demon's entry.

Further down the way, among the thick overgrowth of thorns, PA stopped. "I feel pain, agony, misery," PA shared with Father Byrne. She began shaking her head as chills ran down her spine. "We have found the entry. This is the entry," PA said as she stomped the hill into the ground. "I can see the spell being cast over the Seal of Solomon. Who is here? What do you want?" she again asked the two questions. PA marked a bigger spot where they stood. An inviolable force quickly moved between PA and Father Byrne, causing their clothes to move. They both stepped back, surprised by the encounter.

Father Byrne blessed the area while praying. After the prayer, PA looked around. "We gonna need to clear this area out." They looked over the layout, marking the amount of land that needed to be cleared. PA instructed Wilbur how she needed the area set up for the battle. The three made their way back to the house to prepare.

Sitting at the kitchen table, PA downloaded Wilbur's recording onto her laptop. Father Byrne stood behind PA as she played the high definition video and enhanced the sound. The two listened for sounds or voices they missed in real time. In the background of the plantation rubble, Father Byrne noticed the outline of a shadow person knocking over the pile of bricks. After hearing PA's two questions, they heard in a static-broken, woman's high-pitched voice, "Stop him!"

"Wow, did you hear that?" PA became excited. Continuing to listen, they heard the same woman's voice say, "Protect my family!"

"What does that mean?" the Father asked.

"I am not sure," PA answered, moving on with the video.

Not hearing anything from the whipping pole area was a disappointment.

After the two questions were asked at the point of entry, things got interesting. A different woman's voice clearly whispered, "Leave now!" A few moments later, "Let be done!" Followed by, "Finish the curse!" right before the two stepped back from the force moving between them.

"Wow, I can't believe how clear the voice was, and how we could not hear it in real time!" Father Byrne said, amazed. They replayed the video to make sure there was nothing missed. Turning off the video, PA decided there were two different female voices that wanted two different results. "It sounded to me like the first voice wants the curse to stop, and the second voice wants the curse finished."

Realizing she was stating the obvious, Father Byrne looked at PA with a sarcastic smile, "You have no idea, do you?"

"Nope," PA laughed as she left the table.

Relaxing in the living room, Father Byrne asked PA her opinion about the odds of a successful ending to the curse. "I do not know," PA paused with concern. "This demon or angel we are battling was unleashed by God to rid this land of the evil. We both know from Sodom and Gomorrah, the Egyptian plagues, the Benjamite, et cetera, how harshly God punishes evil and the innocent. All we can do is ask God to remove the curse during our battle. I do not know, maybe 60/40 or 40/60," PA guessed.

"I just do not have a good feeling about tomorrow," Father Byrne confessed.

"Neither do I," PA agreed. "Maybe it is because we both are emotionally attached to Jeanne," PA added. They both sat in silence, thinking back on memories from their youth. Father Byrne broke the silence when he stood up and headed for the back door. "Where you going?" PA asked.

"Back down the hill to pray," he answered. PA watched the priest walk out of the house. She pulled out her laptop to search for any information that would help her quest for a spell to end the curse. After midnight, she turned off her laptop and let out a sigh, realizing she was on her own. Without any record of anyone ever fighting this beast, she would be in uncharted territory. She finished her night with a prayer to her God, then to her ancestors for guidance.

***

THE BATTLE

First thing in the morning, Momma Jeanne received a phone call from PA to meet at Sharon's office around 4 p.m.

At 11 a.m., the cursed group met at St. Treasea's for confession with Father Cashin. After, they sat down for lunch at the pizzeria across the street, then headed south to prepare for their battle for life.

The cursed group sat in the parking lot of the University. Henry let out a loud sigh as he turned the car off. "Everyone ready?" he asked. No one said a word. "Come on guys, what is the worst that can happen?" Henry chuckled as they climbed out of the car.

They found PA and Father Byrne in the volleyball locker room preparing two large tubs (normally used for icing athletes) of yellow-ish powder and water. The normal smell of dirty socks and sweaty athletes was covered by the nasty smell of PA's concoction. "Hey you all, it is a glorious day today!" PA declared with an enthusiastic voice. "By night's end, you all will be curse free! Did you all sleep well?" She asked with a laugh. "Sharon, Henry, that is one comfortable bed you have, I slept like a baby," PA added to lighten the mood. The couple laughed, not sure if she really slept in their bed or not.

"I bet you are all wondering what we have here," PA said. She went on to explain her yellow concoction. "This here is for you all to sit in and soak. It will protect you from the curse."

"What is in it? It smells horrible!" Henry expressed.

"Well, it is water, a bunch of spices, hyssop, rue, salt, herbs, roots, urine from an African bovine, and ground up dried man's pepper," PA shared.

"What is man's pepper?" asked Henry.

"Oh, I did not say pepper. I said man's pecker, you know, a dead man's dried penis," she said with a laugh. "I would keep my mouth closed while getting into the tub," she chuckled. "This will only keep you safe until we start the ceremony. When the demon appears, do not look into its eyes. Do not say or think its name. It will appear in the middle of the Seal of Solomon. If everything goes well, I will undo the curse. The demon will try to enter one of your souls. Keep praying. Your faith will keep it from entering. Each one of you will need to donate some blood, but we will do that right before we begin the ceremony. Everyone must pray, pray, and pray as we battle this demon."

"So, what happens if the demon enters one of our souls?" Henry asked.

"Honestly, I have no idea," PA paused, "but I am sure it will not be good for any of us," she finished with a laughing smile.

Wilbur called to let PA know the area was cleared and ready. One by one, the cursed gagged as they soaked in the concoction. Once everyone was soaked, then dried, they took a moment for a prayer. After the prayer, the group loaded up and headed to the battlefield. Driving the car to the property, Henry followed the dirt road down to the field next to the cleared off section Wilbur had prepared. Sitting in the car, Henry tried to ease the unknown fear. "Well, I guess we will have to burn the car to get this awful smell out." His two young boys giggled as Momma Jeanne smiled. Looking at his boys, Henry assured them, "God will get us to the other side safely. Make sure you pray like your Catholic school training has taught you." Before PA arrived at the car to get the cursed, Henry looked at his boys and said, "I love you both!"

All the brush and thorns were removed, as well as the top layer of turf, exposing fresh, dark brown dirt. Wilbur had placed cameras in four different locations to record the battle. Large, smooth river rocks were carefully placed to form the 10-foot diameter Seal of Solomon. Circling the area were 12-inch ivory pillar candles evenly spaced apart. Off to the side, next to a foldable table with PA's supplies scattered across the top, a heavy duty propane cooking stand was lit, with an aluminum pot boiling. The clear, still night showed off the beauty of the stars decorating the heavens. The cursed group stayed in the vehicles until darkness covered the field.

One by one, PA escorted the cursed to their spots around the seal. Momma Jeanne was placed across from Henry as Tyler was placed across from Will. Father Byrne performed a final blessing before stepping back. Wilbur and Sharon stayed up the hill to watch from a distance with Sister Elizabeth and Father Cashin, who had arrived for additional prayer support. PA reminded the group to keep their heads down and their eyes closed, and to pray. "DO NOT LET THE DEMON INTO YOUR SOUL," she demanded. With the 8-inch silver dagger, PA sliced each of the cursed's left palm to collect the needed blood into the large boiling pot. After a nod from PA, Father Byrne lead the soft prayer as the cursed joined him. Placing the pot on the fire, PA added graveyard dust, sulfur, snakeskin dust, dried daffodil, and daisy powder. She added half a cup of rust water, a scoop of swamp mud and dirt from under her family crypt, and brought the concoction to a boil.

Beginning the ceremony in her loud, serious voice, PA read Psalm 37, a psalm of David:

"[37] Fret not yourself because of the wicked, be not envious of wrongdoers!

[2] For they will soon fade like the grass, and wither like the green herb.

³ Trust in the LORD, and do good; so you will dwell in the land, and enjoy security.

⁴ Take delight in the LORD, and he will give you the desires of your heart.

⁵ Commit your way to the LORD; trust in him, and he will act.

⁶ He will bring forth your vindication as the light, and your right as the noonday.

⁷ Be still before the LORD, and wait patiently for him; fret not yourself over him who prospers in his way, over the man who carries out evil devices!

⁸ Refrain from anger, and forsake wrath! Fret not yourself; it tends only to evil.

⁹ For the wicked shall be cut off; but those who wait for the LORD shall possess the land."

The group up on the hill watched as the ceremony began, all hoping for good results. Kyle and Roy made their way over to see what was going on. Sharon filled them in on the ceremony being performed down the hill. Kyle looked at Roy with his smartass smile, "I guess you will find out if demons are real." Roy and Kyle joined the onlookers watching for support.

"³⁰ The mouth of the righteous utters wisdom, and his tongue speaks justice.

[31] The law of his God is in his heart; his steps do not slip.

[32] The wicked watches the righteous, and seeks to slay him.

[33] The Lord will not abandon him to his power, or let him be condemned when he is brought to trial.

[34] Wait for the Lord, and keep to his way, and he will exalt you to possess the land; you will look on the destruction of the wicked.

[35] I have seen a wicked man overbearing, and towering like a cedar of Lebanon.

[36] Again I passed by, and lo, he was no more; though I sought him, he could not be found.

[37] Mark the blameless man, and behold the upright, for there is posterity for the man of peace.

[38] But transgressors shall be altogether destroyed; the posterity of the wicked shall be cut off.

[39] The salvation of the righteous is from the Lord; he is their refuge in the time of trouble.

[40] The Lord helps them and delivers them; he delivers them from the wicked, and saves them, because they take refuge in him"

Finishing the Psalm, she poured the boiling mixture around the Seal as she chanted, "SHANKPANA SHANKPANA SHANKPANA," PA called out as she danced around the outer seal with her hands above her head. "SHANKPANA SHANKPANA SHANK-

PANA," she again called out.

A soft drum beat began off in the distance as the temperature dropped and a foul smell settled in from above. Black smoke billowed out from the center of the seal, exposing a dark silhouette that quickly turned to its heavenly form for the first time.

Standing almost eight feet tall with dark brown bulging muscles, long blonde hair covering its midsection like a skirt, and braided blonde hair wrapped around its ankles and wrists. Its chiseled, dark brown face highlighted its soul-cutting, dark blue eyes. The beast's long blonde hair blew in the wind like a Greek God ready to save the world. Its huge, solid white wings were tucked in tight to its back. The group at the top of the hill stared in disbelief, not expecting to see the angel responsible for haunting the cursed group.

"Who be calling Shankpana?" the angel asked with a deep, intimidating African accent, not yet noticing the cursed through the stench protecting them, "Who be calling Shankpana?"

Not acknowledging the angel, PA continued to dance, mumbling words from her beliefs.

"In the name of Jesus Christ, I declare broken and destroyed all spells, hexes, vexes, curses, voodoo practices, witchcraft, occult, masonic and satanic rituals, masonic and satanic blood covenants, masonic and satanic blood sacrifices, demonic activities, evil wishes, coven rituals, all occult, Islamic, and coven fasting prayers and curse-like judgments that have been sent our way, and that have been passed down through my family's generational bloodline. I lose them to where Jesus Christ sends them. I ask forgiveness for, and renounce, all negative inner vows made by myself. I ask you Lord Jesus Christ that you release us from these vows, and from any bondage they may have held us in. Lord, in the name of Jesus Christ, do not remember the iniquities of our forefathers against us. (Psalms 79:8)"

PA kept dancing, chanting the words from her ancestors. The angel, focused on PA, still had not realized the four cursed around it. Shankpana laughed out loud, "You are not welcome here Vudon

Queen, your magic will not hurt me. This is my land, Vudon Queen."

Still not acknowledging the angel, PA continued the dance, mumbling words from her faith. In deep, meditation, the cursed continued repeating Father Byrne's prayer. Looking down, the powerful angel noticed the four cursed souls. "You bring me the souls I search for?" Shankpana laughed as he looked down on the people sitting around the Seal of Solomon. "You bring Shankpana the souls needed for God." The angel tried to overtake Tyler's soul, but was denied. "You got no power over me," the angel yelled as he again tried to overtake Tyler's soul, and was again denied. The angel again laughed out loud, hurting the ears of the group watching from the hill. "You do not stop me. You do not stop my power." Starting his dance, the angel searched for the weakest soul to attack. "Uba uba uba yah yah, uba uba uba yah yah! uba uba, uba yah yah!" Not finding a weak soul, the angel continued to chant, "Uba uba uba yah yah, uba uba uba yah yah! Uba uba uba yah yah!" Thunder rolled in the distance as dry lightning lit up the clear sky. The ground rumbled, causing limbs and leaves to fall from the nearby trees. Powerful wind kicked up dust, making it hard for Father Byrne and PA to see.

One by one, Shankpana attacked each praying soul without success. Unable to find a weak soul, the angel spun fast up into the air and returned down into a yellow glowing ball. Dark storm clouds began to move in rapidly as the wind blew in circular motions all around the point of entry. Lightning flashed up into the sky away from the cursed, lighting up the dark sky. PA started to yell her words from deep within, "Your hostility towards these good, God-fearing people will be powerless as the fire is to water. May God immobilize the power you use completely, blinding your ability to cause harm from this day forth!" The ground shook with such force, it knocked Father Byrne to the ground. PA stumbled around, hanging onto an oak tree's limb for balance.

Realizing the ceremony was working, the group continued to pray harder as the doomed angel spun faster and let loose a loud, ear-burning squeal. The loud, piercing sound caused the group much pain as they continued the prayer, covering their ears. The squeal stopped as smoke rose from the seal and encircled the four cursed. In slow motion, black and white images flashed like a projector in the center of the seal. Unable to turn away, the cursed watched the tragic scene. First, they saw Dred with his eyes open in a blank stare, throat sliced, blood running down his chest, and the tall white man laughing as Dred bled out. Then they saw Banjoe swinging from the tree with the spike stuck through his body, dark red blood bubbling from his mouth, oozing down the spike, still being punched and kicked by the tall white man. Lastly, they saw Tinah crying, with blood running down her legs as she was raped by the tall white man, then thrown to the ground.

Momma Jeanne gasped as she saw her mom and grandmother, realizing by the sharp green eyes that Tinah was her great-grandmother. The four cursed gasped as the images ran through their heads. "Pray," PA yelled, "PRAY!"

Suddenly, everything became clear: the rape, the torture, the murders, down through a history full of pain. Momma Jeanne grabbed her head, crying in emotional outrage and trying to fight off the images as she realized the truth. Her bloodline was created by an evil rape of a child. She tried to pray, but the images kept bouncing around inside her weak human head. Momma Jeanne's body began to shake. Her eyes rolled back into her head as rage, hate, and revenge boiled up through her body. Trying to fight off the negative emotions, she started to pray again, but the need for hateful revenge was too strong for her to overcome. Momma Jeanne let go of her soul and invited Shankpana into her body. Grabbing the dagger, Momma Jeanne stood in the center of the seal, welcoming Shankpana into her soul. A white light flashed in the center of the seal as her soul was overwhelmed. Shankpana let out a loud, painful, victorious laugh, knocking all there to witness onto the ground.

The cursed group became paralyzed in fear as Shankpana sliced Henry across his chest, then stabbing him down between the collarbone and neck into his heart. Henry's dead body fell to the ground.

Spinning around with the grace of a ballerina, Shankpana danced before it grabbed Will by his throat. It lifted him up eye-to-eye and stared at the young, terror-stricken boy before stabbing him through the forehead. Shankpana dropped his lifeless body to the ground.

Sharon started to scream as she ran down the hill in hopes of saving her family. Shak calmly walked over to Tyler and softly rubbed his hair, admiring his old buddy for a moment before slicing his neck and stabbing him in the heart.

Unable to help, Father Byrne and PA stayed frozen on the ground as if time had stopped. Witnessing the horror before them, they could not move. Sharon fell to her knees in shock as she realized her family had all been butchered by the beast.

The group up on the hill cried out in horror as they watched the massacre from a distance.

Shankpana walked back to the center of the seal, standing in its glory. Lifting its head proudly, Shankpana spoke in a loud dark, gargled African voice for everyone to hear, "EVERYTHING I DO, I DO FOR GOD, GOOD OR BAD, THIS BE GOD'S PLAN, IN THE END, YOU GET WHAT YOU GOT COMING! CASSIUS AND HIS ROOTS ALL BE ROTTEN. CASSIUS AND HIS ROOTS ALL BE DEAD!!"

Shankpana shoved the dagger into its stomach, slicing right then left. A bright light exploded up into the sky as Momma Jeanne fell dead to the ground, completing the curse.

THE END